Mastering Soft Skills

With best wishes for all you are
aiming to accomplish!

Mastering Soft Skills

Julian Vyner

Matador
9 Priory Business Park,
Wistow Road, Kibworth Beauchamp,
Leicestershire. LE8 0RX
Tel: 0116 279 2299
Email: books@troubador.co.uk
Web: www.troubador.co.uk/matador
Twitter: @matadorbooks

ISBN 978 1788033 763

British Library Cataloguing in Publication Data.
A catalogue record for this book is available from the British Library.

Printed and bound in the UK by 4edge limited
Typeset in 11pt Gill Sans by Troubador Publishing Ltd, Leicester, UK

Matador is an imprint of Troubador Publishing Ltd

This book is dedicated to my wife Maaike and my daughters Emmelien and Levina. They gave me space and the necessary distractions.

All profits from this book go to Eastside Young Leaders Academy (EYLA), a small group of people in East London doing amazing things with youngsters from disadvantaged backgrounds, training the next generation of influencers and persuaders.

ACKNOWLEDGEMENTS

Dale Carnegie, author of How to Win Friends and Influence People, said, "The ideas I stand for are not mine. I borrowed them from Socrates. I swiped them from Chesterfield. I stole them from Jesus. And I put them in a book. If you don't like their rules, whose do you use?"

While I have not stolen from Jesus, at least not consciously, I have borrowed from many others, including Socrates. To do pretty much anything we have to stand on the shoulders of giants. I am indebted to lots of them. For ease of reading I have referenced all these giants, where I am beholden, within the text or footnotes. If I have neglected to honor someone, dead or alive, I apologize and welcome corrections.

There are quite a lot of others, if not giants then metaphorically very large people with broad shoulders and big hearts, who are happily still alive, without whom I could not have written this. Their ideas, insights, experience and challenges inform every page. Some of these people are former clients, some friends and colleagues, and quite a few attendees on my training courses. Because this list is long and a number asked to remain confidential, I have decided to respect the privacy of everyone. You know who you are: thank you.

There are three things I have not swiped from anyone. First are my thought processes, arguments and conclusions. The intellectual foundations of these are mine; I cannot blame them on Socrates (or anyone else). Second is my writing style which I like to think of as American Business English. Most of my well-educated English (and indeed many American) friends will be dismayed. Sorry. Classical grammar was never my strongest suit. Finally, is my decision to keep with largely male pronouns throughout the book, which is unfashionable to say the least. The reason is simply for ease of writing and reading. For 'him' you can certainly read 'her' if you wish. At least my soft skills star in the final chapter is female.

CONTENTS

Introduction

What it really takes to succeed

"You're late. You've got forty minutes starting from now." With the pleasantries over and our potential client's belligerence accentuated by his Australian twang, we sat down among the unwelcoming stares. My colleague and I were pitching for a very large piece of consulting work, one we knew we had to win if our fledgling business was not to close down. Our competition for the work was weighty: perhaps two of the most successful strategy consultancies in the world, McKinsey and Bain. Things didn't look good.

The idea for this book began as an itch I just had to scratch. It all started back in 1988. I was a just-promoted manager at Bain & Co., when two of my friends persuaded me to join them in starting our own strategy consultancy in London. I was not wholly enthusiastic about it. They had a vision of taking on the big boys in their backyard: in the UK that was the FTSE 100. My own credentials for helping lead this charge were hardly encouraging. I had never done anything like it before. When friendship eventually overcame reason and I agreed to come on board it was with a strong feeling of trepidation, one which fueled an ache to find some edge, somewhere, that would help ensure my personal success as well as that of our modest enterprise.

As it turns out we must have had some something going for us, as the belligerent Australian (and later many others, including the Australian's parent company) took us on. I would have been hard pushed to articulate at the time what that edge was. Nevertheless, our consultancy grew to become quite sizeable in the world of boutique consultancies and we expanded our activities to Chicago and New York (shaking the big boys more than once in the process). In time, we attracted the interest of an IT behemoth, eventually being consumed by it.

What does it take to be successful?

As we grew, the question of what it takes to be successful in our field, the selling and delivery of high-value intangible services to CEOs, and what it was we were doing right, continued to engage me.

We could identify the *must-haves* – a means to get in front of potential CEOs in order to introduce yourself in person; a 'story' which succinctly told them why you were there and what made you different; some evidence of your organization's credibility – that you could do what you were telling them you could do; and, additionally, when pitching for work a well thought through proposal offering a solution at a price ideally in the same ballpark as your main competitors.

Everything lies in the excellence of execution. We found, however, that achieving even very high levels of execution in these areas was insufficient to ensure success. This is because our competition could in general match (or more often better) us in each of them. So, certainly as far as the major international consultancy firms were concerned, our competitors had at least a plausible story (and where they didn't they had a compelling brand name), were able to demonstrate an overwhelming capability based on deep industry expertise and/or client list, had whole teams of people dedicated to best practice in crafting proposals, and could also leverage their expertise to staff projects with fewer people, such that we rarely had much of a cost advantage, if any.

Yet we kept growing. Something else had to be going on to explain our survival against the odds. To some extent our resilience can be explained by an ability to develop clients from one-off transactions to longer-term relationships based on a well-executed mantra of 'do great work, then network'. But the lifeblood of a professional services firm is its new clients and we had a pitch success rate that would be the envy of any firm, then or now. This was despite the lack of any real product or service differentiation, no industry expertise to speak of and an international network notable for its early absence.

So, if the must-haves discussed above are only necessary conditions (that is, if you can't meet them you are not even in the game, but if everyone meets them they are rarely deciding factors), what are the sufficient conditions, the ones where a difference between you and your competitor is enough for the client to decide in your favor? In other words, what is the difference that makes the difference?

Something about 'the people'

The answer had to be something around 'the people'. There is nothing else left to consider. Indeed, when you ask clients about the reason for their choice of service provider, one of the first things they say is "The people", even if they find it hard to be more specific. When you ask service firms what makes them different, likewise one of the first things they say is "Our people".

So, what, specifically, is it about 'the people'? I have been told on more than one occasion that good salesmen are born, not made. It is as if they were sprinkled with pixie dust at birth and as a result they simply had the X factor. Looking at our own partners who did well compared to those who struggled when it came to winning clients, one could certainly draw broad distinctions around differences in style or personality. Unfortunately, these distinctions could never be nailed down beyond frustratingly elusive descriptions like 'confidence', 'presence' or 'chemistry', for example.

How can you teach or train these attributes when you cannot be entirely clear what their components are or even what they mean? If you can't train, then how can you identify who is and who is not born with the pixie dust, other than throwing them all in the pool together and seeing who swims?

Looking for pixie dust

When I became chairman of our business and found myself brooding over how to bring on our young geniuses to partner level, this became a very practical issue for me. Signs of being academically clever and brilliant at delivering work rarely indicated on their own a latent aptitude to win over skeptical corporate buyers.

To help me I had a number of well-known training companies come in and present their wares. It was dispiriting. This was because very few people have actually sat in front of a CEO and sold them a very large slice of intangible promise, time and time again, and those who have are not usually to be found in the training world. As a result, few people in the training community really understood the world we played in.

Where trainers had something interesting to say, the focus was usually on sales systems or processes, or relied on techniques that were designed for low-value products in unsophisticated environments, or delved into the realms of tree-hugging, which offered tantalizing promise until tested in our unforgiving boardroom environment.

I also sought out friends and colleagues in analogous businesses: audit firms and their various consultancies, advertising agencies, marketing services and law firms. Their answers again fell in the broad area of "People skills", but the specifics always remained frustratingly indefinable.

In the end, no-one had the answer to what this X factor was, let alone how you could train it.

Finding the answer

After I left strategy consulting, this question of what makes some individuals successful client-handlers and others not remained with me and I embarked on a study of it.

Eventually I developed a hypothesis, not only about what the X factor was, how it could be dissected into component parts, how it explained my own and others' success, but also how it could be trained. I concluded that while the very best client managers in professional services may indeed be born, not made, with the right training almost anyone with basic aptitude can get pretty close.

I also found that these skills were attributes often shared by people who had reached senior management positions in other fields, unrelated to the marketing of professional services. What these roles had in common was the requirement to work with and through other people, influencing and persuading, in order to achieve success.

Similarly, I discovered that people who were good at winning and managing clients also, on the whole, had the capability to be excellent leaders within their organizations. They were simply good at communicating, motivating and getting things done.

This book is the result of my experience and the study that followed it. The essence of its argument is that beyond the hard must-haves described earlier it is the additional mix of soft skills which determines who succeeds as Influencers, Persuaders and Salespeople, especially in professional services but also in many other fields too. Soft skills, successfully integrated with hard skills – the right brain with the left – are the difference that makes the difference.

In recent years, I have been privileged to stand in front of many seasoned client account managers and teach them these soft skills. The ideas in this book have benefited immensely from the crucible of their scrutiny, and withstood the test.

Understanding what 'soft skills' mean in this book

The Oxford English Dictionary (OED) defines soft skills as *'Personal attributes that enable someone to interact effectively and harmoniously with other people'.* There are two important elements to this definition.

First is the sense of these skills being an attribute, a quality of someone which is an inherent part of their makeup, a way of being, if you like. This contrasts with skills which could be seen as optional add-ons, to be lifted out of the toolbox or left aside as needs dictate.

Second is the sense of them being tied to effectiveness, or a desired result.

These two elements distinguish soft skills from other terms often used interchangeably, such as 'people skills' and 'interpersonal skills'. Persons with people and interpersonal skills are good at getting on with others, the 'harmonious' in the definition above. But the skills may or may not be attributional *and* outcome-driven.

Soft skills can also overlap with 'life skills' and 'social skills'. Life skills are generally defined as those skills that allow us to participate fully, or be successful, in everyday life. They are broader in range than soft skills and so sit above them in the definitional hierarchy. 'Social skills', on the other hand, can mean much the same as interpersonal skills in some quarters, or elsewhere are considered the more narrow range of awareness and abilities we learn through the process of socialization as we grow up. Someone with social skills has an aptitude for interaction with others and, according to some, adapts well to the social grouping in which they find themselves.

So, soft skills are that part of us which helps us achieve what we want, through and with other people, in ways we and they find comfortable.

Connected relationships

In this book, a connected relationship is one where feelings of goodwill exist.

Goodwill means a friendly, helpful or co-operative attitude or feeling. These feelings of goodwill are based on a shared sense of personal regard, as well as a confidence in the professional capability of each other.

This is a subconscious experience which draws two people together emotionally – they simply *feel* comfortable interacting with each other in a work context. It may include feelings of enjoyment in each other's company but these are not a requirement of having it.

Critically, a connected relationship requires a sense of trust, insofar as each has an expectation of the other, alongside high confidence that those expectations will be met in the circumstances of that relationship. So, you might have faith in someone behaving appropriately and always honoring their commitments at work; their behavior outside the office, however, might be another matter.

A connected relationship provides the emotional foundations on which one can build to influence, persuade and sell.

Unsurprisingly, people who are good at building connected relationships have some meaningful level of emotional intelligence. As defined by Daniel Goleman, who popularized the field with his book of the same name, this means the ability to recognize and regulate our own emotions, to identify and empathize with the emotions of others, and to employ these insights to better manage our relationships.

In business, a connected relationship may not require the full suite of emotionally intelligent abilities that a personal relationship might benefit from, or to the same degree, or with the same frequency. But the emotional quality of that connected relationship has to be sufficient to help achieve the mutually desired goal.

The soft skills in this book provide the vehicles through which the most relevant emotionally intelligent abilities are harnessed and deployed to build these connected relationships.

Soft skills versus hard skills

A presupposition of this book is that you have the necessary hard skills already in place.

Hard skills are defined as those skills which are largely knowledge-, content- or process-based. For example, understanding international bribery law, having experience in process improvement, or expertise in copywriting or a particular technical analysis. In other words, whatever your field, you know what you are talking about.

Your effectiveness in influencing, persuading or selling rests heavily on your hard skills. Having these is the reason others will seek out your opinion, or induce someone to hear your arguments, or a potential client to consider your offering of value. These skills grow with application and experience. They are the *necessary* requirements for influencing, persuading and selling.

By contrast, soft skills reside in the realm of how and who we are, the way we talk, act and come across to other people, the impression we give and the feelings we leave behind, sometimes consciously but more often unconsciously. These soft, behavioral skills are not a replacement for the hard skills you need to have. They are additional. In those instances where hard skills offer you no advantage over someone else, your soft skills can become the deciding factor in your effectiveness.

Which soft skills?

What are the particular soft skills we are talking about? Unpacking the term comprehensively into granular components can present an analytic trial. The European Dictionary of Skills and Competencies (DISCO) identifies sixty-three categories under 'Personal skills and competencies', from powers of observation to empathy. Under the separate heading of 'Social communication skills and competencies', DISCO lists a further seventeen categories, including effective questioning, establishing contacts, listening and rhetorical skills. Most of these competencies could be classed as falling within the realm of soft skills.

Although these skills and competencies are no doubt all important in particular circumstances, this book focuses on those soft skills that can be shown to be effective in the context of influence, persuasion and selling in the professional services industry.

These can be broken down into the following five categories:

> ***Rapport***: skills that encourage people to be open to you and what you have to say. These may include skills that help people to like you (if not actually make you more likeable).
>
> ***Trust:*** skills that encourage people to feel that you are trustworthy.

Communication: skills that help you to communicate in ways others find appealing, or add value.

Empathy: skills that assist you in understanding where the other person is coming from, to recognize their feelings if not actually share them, and to leave them feeling understood.

Self-control: skills that help you control your own emotions and feelings, and therefore the impression you make and the unconscious signals you send.

Some of the soft skills in this book encompass two or more of these categories; others are very narrow in scope. What they all have in common is the attribute that, when practiced, they become part of the way you naturally do things.

Faking it

Can you use these soft skills to manipulate, mislead or unfairly gain advantage over someone? Can you achieve a trusted position or be perceived as deeply caring, for example, when in your heart you are self-serving, faithless and callous? Are they merely the neuro-biological equivalent of chessboard tactics, a set of tips and tricks to get you what you want? Simply asked, can you fake it?

Theoretically, that must be possible. Many of us can point to individuals who demonstrate 'the Superman effect', miraculously changing their apparent character to suit the circumstances or dissembling as required to serve their interests. Some of these people can be quite successful in their fields, at least for a while.

For most of us, though, I believe it is difficult if not impossible to fake it. As we shall see later in this book, we can *read* other people subconsciously. We can often sense what they feel and whether they share the same interests as us. A strong divergence of interests leaves a nagging feeling of discomfort. As a result, faking it with soft skills is unlikely to be a successful strategy long term.

The skills in this book work best if you follow two simple moral imperatives. The first is that, as in life, you do as you would be done by. The second is that you genuinely want to help, that the other person's interests are important to you.

A good heart may not actually be a requirement but it probably helps.

Soft skills and the client development process

To underline the specific relevance of these soft skills to life in professional services I have sequenced them to follow the steps in a typical client development process, shown below.

The key process steps in winning and developing clients are simply: i) lead generation; ii) first meeting; iii) receive request for a proposal; iv) present your proposal; v) (if won) do a great job; and vi) use the resulting status you have to find other ways of adding value to that client, in time potentially achieving the position of a Trusted Advisor.

This otherwise self-explanatory process can of course be remarkably complex in practice, with as many variations as there are clients. What is common throughout is the face to face interaction of individuals working together, establishing relationships, influencing, persuading and selling, continuously evaluating and making judgements about each other.

Some of the soft skills we cover relate to multiple steps in this process, some to a few or only one. Using this illustration at the beginning of each chapter will tell you where that soft skill best applies.

The typical client development process in professional services

Referrals
Current clients
Network
Proactivity
LEAD GENERATION
FIRST MEETING
RECEIVE BRIEF
DEVELOP/ PRESENT PROPOSAL
DO GREAT WORK
ACHIEVE ADVISOR STATUS
Cold-calling
Personal networks
Marketing
Invitation

Becoming good at soft skills

For those of us not born with them, developing these soft skills requires some practice. Our behavioral traits are hard-wired into us. It is difficult to uncouple them from what it is that makes us who we are. Attempting to change the way we are is not easy because it involves intellectual buy-in, followed by behavioral adjustment.

Whereas we can usually change our mind quite quickly when presented with irrefutable logic or evidence, changing the way we are is much harder. This is because our way of being, how we think, process information and communicate is embedded into our neurological processes as a result of our DNA and a lifetime's experiences. Changing this requires some application but it is possible. It is a bit like a hardened smoker giving up the habit for something better (although from experience I can tell you that the process in this case is far more fun).

Adopting all the skills in this book is a bit like learning to drive. Many people drive a car without thinking much about it: they think about other things – what's for dinner tonight or where shall I go on vacation. Their unconscious is driving the car for them. Yet when they first learned to drive their conscious mind was overwhelmed with all the things they had to know and do in the correct sequence. They could think about little else at the time.

Learning these soft skills will feel similar to when you first learned to drive. So, pick just one or two and practice them. Play around with them. Experiment in safe environments. When you feel comfortable with the skill and don't have to think too hard about it, move on to another. Gradually you will become unconsciously competent and what was a discrete skill will have become just part of the way you do things, embedded naturally into your personal style.

Different levels of engagement

The idea that your entire academic and professional training is useful only up to a point – that clients don't just buy you for your obvious technical expertise, or colleagues won't listen just based on your hard-won knowledge – can be a hard pill to swallow. But accepting this opens the door to powerful new ways to enhance your effectiveness.

If, like me when I started, you have almost no client-handling experience, you will find within these pages a suite of tools and skills which, if you work to acquire them, will equip you with the unconscious capabilities of the most successful client managers and leaders in your firm.

If you already have client-management experience you can view this book as a smorgasbord: pick from the menu those things that interest you and try them out. If your experience of winning and developing clients is considerable, this book may give you insights into what it is you are doing right.

Finally, if you have yet to reach these Olympian heights in your firm's career structure or you are not even employed in professional services, pick the skills that feel the most relevant to your circumstances and practice them.

Each section of this book is structured to present different kinds of evidence to encourage your engagement, then sufficient ideas to practice so you have the opportunity to experience the effects yourself and so, I hope, feel motivated to refine and improve.

1. Understanding the Hard Facts about Soft Skills

What they are and why they matter

Imagine you are a homeowner and need some major repairs done. The work is likely to be extensive, time-consuming and costly. It is also going to be disruptive since you plan to continue living in the house while the works are going on. But you feel the completion of the building work is necessary to your quality of life. So, you find the names of five building firms and invite them in to take a look and give you their estimate. You meet each of them on site and show them what you want. In due course, you receive their quotes. After the initial shock, you sit down and begin the process of deciding who to appoint.

How do you choose one builder over another?

Collating the evidence that will enable you to evaluate and then decide is, on the face of it, a simple process. When asked, the majority of people will follow a series of steps like the following:

- **Can they do the work in a way you are comfortable with?**
  This is about expertise and capability. Do they have the knowledge, skills and people to do it? We could call these criteria 'Respect'. Do we respect them sufficiently based on their capability? This is largely a rational criterion where analysis of the proposal and a review of previous jobs will give you confidence. Say one firm drops out at this stage because they sound too specialized and another because they rely on using pile-driving machinery that you fear might upset the neighbors.

- **Can you rely on them to do what they say they will?**

This is about commitment and trust. Will they do what they are promising to do in the agreed timeframe? We might call this criterion 'Reliability'. You can probably deduce from their references their likelihood to deliver on their promises, although whether they will do so in your case will always remain something of an act of faith. Say one firm drops out when you take up references suggesting a worrying disregard for deadlines.

The combination of putting the firms through these two criteria, Respect and Reliability, ("Can they? Will they?") means you are left with three very plausible contenders who could do the work in the way you wish on the timescale you want. All three have as a result what we might call 'Credibility'. Without Credibility, it is unlikely you would consider any of them further.

- **Is the cost acceptable?**

This is simply a question of value for money. Are they proposing to do the same as everyone else for less money or perhaps something more for the same amount? We could call this criterion having a 'Solution with value'. To the extent their proposal is specific enough, this is probably the most rational criterion. Two of the firms are very close to each other on price and appear to offer the same deliverables. The third is unaccountably a lot more expensive. They go (you didn't like them anyway). That leaves two.

- **Now what?**

Either firm could do the job to your satisfaction and wallet. How then do you decide? Perhaps at this point it is not surprising that nearly everyone declares their final criterion as feelings-related: "I liked them more" or "I just felt better about them than the others". Between the last two, it just comes down to who you *like* the most.

'Liking' is the most emotional of the criteria, based on feelings and not easily susceptible to analysis. When used in this context, for most people it falls short of actually finding someone necessarily agreeable or enjoyable to be with. Instead it refers to feelings of satisfaction and approval that are hard to pin down beyond the sense that there exists a connected relationship. It may be hard to define beyond the notion of feel-good but the sense of it can be very strong.

Regardless of whether you personally would follow the sequence above exactly (many people would put price, or what I have called a 'Solution with value', first), the process is one of using hard information and analysis, where you can, to narrow down the candidates. If just one firm comes singing through the rational criteria, perhaps because the others all have some major negative, then the decision is easy. Thank goodness. You then just have to check they pass the Liking test. But where more than one passes the rational tests, you need to assess degrees of Liking to decide between them. Who do you feel better about? It may be no harder to do but it is certainly a less rational process.

In this instance we could say we are screening rationally, selecting emotionally.

If this is how we choose builders to work on our homes, what makes us think that our clients, when choosing us as service providers to work with their companies or our colleagues, deciding on an initiative we are proposing that involves our participation, would be any different?

Reasonable faith

In fact, there are lots of reasons to believe our clients or colleagues are entirely rational when evaluating us or our proposals. We are, after all, children forged in educational systems that teach us the primacy of reason. From Plato, through the Enlightenment with its faith in reason, to the utility-maximizing paradigms of Classical Economics and latterly modern cognitive psychology, which sees the brain as just another computer, reason provides us with the rationale to elevate ourselves above animals and gives us the scientific tools to model and monitor human behavior.

As far as corporate selling is concerned, the literature certainly supports this view. The writers Shapiro and Posner concluded that success in corporate sales resulted from a well-executed eight-step process.[1] Put like this it is just a matter of organization. In fact, most books published on the subject of selling to senior corporate buyers offer ideas, actions, processes and models that we can engage with intellectually and rationally, enabling us to examine our strategies for success and helpfully suggesting what we could do differently.

That is reassuring for those of us brought up to believe that success is a matter of good thinking followed by careful organization and excellent execution. If we fail to win we can begin to analyze where in the process we may have slipped up and identify action steps for the next time around. We remain confident that our left-brain skills are continuing to move us forward and while we were not successful this time, on the next occasion our adaptive competence and personal resilience will no doubt combine for success, so we continue to focus on the rational elements of our proposals.

The limits to believing in entirely rational thought

Unfortunately, it is all rather murkier than the Enlightenment might have us think. There is good evidence to suggest that a lot of what we thought of as rational, conscious, data-driven approaches to making choices is merely a cover for something else. In fact, our reasoned evaluations are themselves informed, possibly controlled, by emotional inputs.

The scientist Antonio Damasio has demonstrated that far from the mind and the heart being separate from each other, they are in fact interdependent. He discovered that if key parts of the brain are damaged – the orbitofrontal cortex which sits behind the eyes being the most important – the subject loses all ability to experience emotions. They can think but they can't feel. Even more significant, they can't, *as a result*, make decisions because they are incapable of assigning value to different options. As Damasio writes in his book, *Descartes' Error – Emotion, Reason and the Human Brain*, their "decision-making landscape is hopelessly flat".[2]

From this, Damasio developed the 'somatic marker hypothesis'. He suggested that we attach emotional values to events, people, places and outcomes at the subconscious level. These subconscious emotional tags quickly guide us toward those things that are fulfilling and away from those things that are bad for us, so helping us come to a decision. They do not replace the rational, logical mind; they act as a bias. Using Damasio's analogy, they are like the headlights of a car driving at night: they show us the way. Perhaps Descartes should instead have said something like: "I think *and feel*, therefore I am."[3]

This critical emotional input into decision-making can have far-reaching effects. The authors of the book, *Think Again: Why Good Leaders Make Bad Decisions and How to Keep It From Happening to You*, analyzed a number of decisions from the perspective of neuroscience's more recent insights into how the brain makes decisions. Looking at the delayed reaction to Hurricane Katrina, the demise of Wang Laboratories and the disastrous decision to land paratroops in Holland in 1945, among others, they illustrate the subconscious role of somatic marking (which they term 'emotional tagging') along with pattern recognition in guiding and sometimes overwhelming the decisions of otherwise clever, experienced and supposedly very rational people.[4]

Some go further and say that *all* our rational, conscious decisions are driven by an unconscious, emotional imperative, reflecting Blaise Pascal's observation: "All our reasoning ends in surrender to feeling." In the modern scientific era, the work of Gary Klein demonstrates that experienced decision-makers in stressful situations (such as firefighters, fighter pilots, quarterbacks or missile controllers) make decisions intuitively, successfully relying *entirely* on their unconscious processes.[5]

Others suggest that what we believe is free will is nothing more than an amalgam of these feelings within our subconscious which we confabulate and justify with rational argument. Researchers at the Bernstein Center for Computational Neuroscience in Berlin, for example, found that when they asked volunteers to press one of two buttons at will, the researchers saw part of the prefrontal cortex 'light up' six seconds before the finger moved. "Our decisions are predetermined unconsciously a long time before our consciousness kicks in," the lead researcher John Dylan Haynes said. "There is no such thing as free will," he adds, rather provocatively.[6]

In fact, the world's best-selling author of sales manuals, Jeffrey Gitomer, reflects this when he says: "The sale is emotionally driven and emotionally decided. Then it is justified logically."

Perhaps the balance between our instinctive or emotional and our rational thinking processes is best explained by the father of behavioral economics, Daniel Kahneman. In his book, *Thinking, Fast and Slow,*[7] he describes how we have two modes of thinking, System 1 and System 2. System 1 operates all the time in the background of our unconscious, generating impressions, intuitions and feelings, interpreting what is going on around us in a coherent way. What is the sum of 5+5? When you answered that question, you did not need to think. Your System 1 did it for you.

System 2 by contrast is what you think of as 'you'. It is conscious, deliberate, slow and effortful. System 2 kicks in when a readily available answer from System 1 fails to present itself. So, what is the answer to 126 multiplied by 59? To answer that, most people will need to turn to System 2. But System 2 is also mobilized when you are surprised by something, or an event occurs that violates the model of the world held in System 1.

Learning from System 2, like the answer to 5+5, becomes absorbed over time into System 1's world view. Gary Klein's experts from above, according to this interpretation, rely on System 1 intuition that has been informed and educated over time in System 2.

For the most part, according to Kahneman, this relationship between our two thinking systems works well. It takes care of many of the two to ten thousand decisions we make daily, and easily processes the billions of bytes of data we have to absorb to simply get around. It frees us up to apply our deliberate thought processes only when we need to. We could not operate in any other way.

But System 1 has some glitches. It employs heuristics, which are simplifying shortcuts or rules of thumb, such as 'if X, then Y', that help us to draw quick conclusions about things. Most times, the conclusions generated by these heuristics are right, or at least useful. But particularly under circumstances of uncertainty or risk they can lead to patently illogical and incorrect answers.

The three main heuristics identified by Kahneman (with Amos Tversky in 1974) were: 'Representativeness' (if we see something as similar to something else, we are very likely to conclude that it is the same – pattern recognition); 'Availability' (our judgement about the likelihood of something occurring is weighted by our ease of recalling to mind related instances); and 'Anchoring' (where we end up is influenced by our start position).

These heuristics give rise to specific biases that color our thinking in System 1. Kahneman and Tversky identified some twenty of these biases but further research has so far revealed over fifty. These include Confirmation bias, the Halo effect, Hindsight bias, Attachment bias, Illusion of validity and, from Prospect Theory, where Kahneman demonstrated that people are motivated by the immediate emotional impact of gains and losses, not by prospects of wealth and overall utility, Loss aversion. These cognitive biases are very strong. They happen without us thinking about them. Along with everything else that is going on in System 1, they are, as Kahneman says, the "secret author of many of the choices and judgements you make".[8]

So, when we make what we think are conscious, data-driven choices, the process is far from being an entirely rational one. What we think are sound conclusions based on describable analytic evidence are, it seems, informed by various cognitive biases. These feelings derive in our subconscious from all sorts of experiences and factors. We may think we are being coldly rational but we are in fact not.

Likewise, when we are evaluating our builders against the hard criteria of Respect, Reliability and Solution with value, our conclusions are informed by all sorts of subjective inputs which we would be hard put to identify, let alone explain.

The emotional imperative of Liking

These emotional inputs into the decision-making process are amplified in the case of making a professional services pitch to a corporate client. It all comes down to Liking. This is because, first, people are part of the product and that requires some emotional evaluation, and second, it is often the case that two (or more) firms emerge from the so-called rational screening process, leaving little more than an intuitive judgement to separate them.

i) The importance of Liking in deciding between firms is especially important when it comes to evaluating professional services firms because of the role of people in the delivery process.

When we purchase a consumer product such as a washing machine, a car, a house or an item of clothing, for example, the sales representative does not come home with us. However, for most professional services, to a greater or lesser degree, the sales representative and in some cases their whole team comes home with us. Or if not, they at least visit regularly. Moreover, the quality of the service we receive is bound up with the individuals delivering it, their technical competence, commitment and reliability, their integrity, their personal styles and how we get on with them. It's like hiring builders but worse.

With builders, at least we have some sense of what the product will look like when finished. We might have plans we can look at, for example. If we were buying professional services, however, where advice or creativity are an important component of the product, we may know what we want but we often have no real idea of what it will look or feel like when we get it. It can be quite a leap of faith.

Buying professional services is about people buying people from other people. It is an intensely personal business. Our potential clients are making subjective judgement calls about us as individuals in order to arrive at a conclusion about the likely outputs of the work we are proposing to undertake.

ii) In most pitches for corporate work we will be competing with other firms, and more than one will usually survive the initial screening, leaving the client with Liking as the determining criteria.

Many of our competitors will have similar approaches to us, offered by similar people with similar types of corporate experience, and similar cost structures. As a result, it is rare for one firm to stand out compared to the others based on their written proposal alone.

In any event, it is often very close. A few years ago, one of the largest management consulting firms in the world ran a survey of all their recent client pitches, worldwide. They identified a number of important factual selection criteria from focus groups. They then structured a questionnaire which researchers took to clients where they had won and also to clients where they had lost pitches. Clients were asked to allocate 100 points between this firm and their main consulting competitor (the one who had won if they hadn't, or the one who had come second to them if they had) across the criteria. The average difference in score (out of a possible 100) between the winning firm and the one who came second was only... five. This is buying at the margin.

These surprising results are borne out in my own discussions with clients. As one CEO with great experience of hiring service firms put it to me, "It's increasingly difficult [to choose] these days, especially if you are dealing with the large firms... It usually comes down to a judgement call." Another said, "They have to meet certain basic criteria and then if they are within 10% of each other, which they often are, it's all about my gut."[9]

There are exceptions of course. Sometimes the required expertise is so narrow that only one firm can provide it. Or a firm may field an individual expert of such status that alone is enough to swing it. Sometimes there can be situations where so many firms are conflicted out, there is only one available choice. Or one firm offers to do the work at cost (or less) for capacity utilization or client development reasons. Sometimes one firm in the proposal development process can find an industry insight which revolutionizes the client's thinking. Certainly, achieving a significant advantage in some or all of these rational criteria is a worthwhile goal. It can give you an unassailable advantage. In general, however, it is hard to do and, as we have seen, rarely achieved.

A poorly executed proposal will likely exclude us from selection in a competitive pitch, yet a great one alone is usually not enough either. Even an excellent proposal requires evaluation through the prism of the people planning to deliver it: a subjective evaluation. And even when we pass this stage, as does at least one other, we find ourselves rather worryingly in the position of the two firms of builders described above. We are at the margin. Which of us does our potential client now *choose?* Which of us does our potential client *like* the most?

Helping clients to choose us (or colleagues to agree with our proposals)

Typically, most services firms when selling spend the vast majority of their effort developing a well-crafted proposal that persuasively demonstrates they can and will do what is required to a high standard. This principally covers the rational elements of Respect, Reliability and Solution with value. Very little, if any, time is spent by the services firm thinking about or preparing for the emotional aspect of the evaluation. It is, in general, left entirely to chance.

This is as true when we seek to persuade someone of a course of action within our organizations as it is when we come to win a client.

To avoid falling into this trap in professional services we need to spend more time and effort thinking about our prospective listener from an emotional viewpoint. We need to consider their feelings about us and, indeed, our feelings about them. And in the same way we adapt our rational approach to address their rational concerns, we must manage our emotional projection to create a feeling of goodwill, a connected relationship. We must behave in ways that lead them to feel comfortable with and confident in us.

Creating these feelings to a level where they offer competitive advantage is what makes the difference. Helping our clients, indeed all recipients of our proposals, to this position by developing our soft skills is what this book is about.

Understanding what these soft skills are, how they work with our hard skills, and how the requirements change between influencing, persuading, selling and consolidating a relationship, is the subject of the next chapter.

Chapter 1 Takeaways

- Buyers screen rationally, choose emotionally.
- 'Rational' evaluations are themselves subject to strong, sometimes controlling, emotional inputs.

- In professional services, when choosing to appoint a service provider, Liking is a critical emotional criterion.
- Hard skills alone are not enough; soft skills make the difference:
  - » by promoting feelings which positively inform the rational evaluation;
  - » by encouraging perceptions of your likeability.
- Because soft skills are part of who you are, you are the difference.

Chapter notes

1. Shapiro, Benson P. and Posner, Ronald S. 'Making the Major Sale'. HBR July-August (2006). The eight stages are: i) identify; ii) qualify; iii) develop sales strategy; iv) justify; v) pitch; vi) resource; vii) close; and viii) nurture.
2. Damasio, Antonio. Descartes' Error. London: Random House, 2006.
3. Jonah Lehrer, in his book How We Decide, New York: Houghton Mifflin Harcourt, 2010, describes this complex interplay between our conscious and unconscious, and some of the chemical drivers underlying it.
4. Finkelstein, Sydney and Whitehead, Jo and Campbell, Andrew. Think Again. Boston: Harvard Business School Publishing, 2008.
5. Klein, Gary. Streetlights and Shadows: Searching for the Keys to Adaptive Decision Making. Cambridge, MA.: MIT Press, 2009. A book full of fascinating real-life stories.
6. Smith, Kerri. 'Neuroscience vs Philosophy: Taking aim at free will', Nature. Published online 31 August 2011. For a fuller, very interesting examination of the extent to which free will exists, see: Harari, Yuval Noah, Homo Deus: A Brief History of Tomorrow. London: Penguin Random House, 2015. Chapter 8.
7. Kahneman, Daniel. Thinking, Fast and Slow. London: Allen Lane, 2011.
8. You may feel that you are different, that your rational decision-making process is not encumbered by undefinable emotional imperatives. There is a term for this too: it is called Blind-spot bias.
9. Both these CEOs were quick to say, however, that they would be careful not to articulate their reasons in these terms. Admitting to your colleagues or chairman that you just spent a serious chunk of corporate change based on little more than a 'feeling' is stacked with obvious problems.

2. The Personal Impact Model

How soft skills work with your hard skills to make you more effective

Clients select service providers emotionally, or with at least a very strong emotional component. Soft skills are the catch-all description of our manner and behaviors, our way of being, if you like, which address our potential client's emotional concerns and lead them to feel comfortable with and confident in us. So, what are these soft skills? How do they work with our hard skills? Do they change over time as we progress from a first meeting to a discussion within a long-established relationship?

To help answer these questions it is useful to consider them within the structure of what I call The Personal Impact Model. This cannot be the last

The Personal Impact Model: Skills and Outcomes

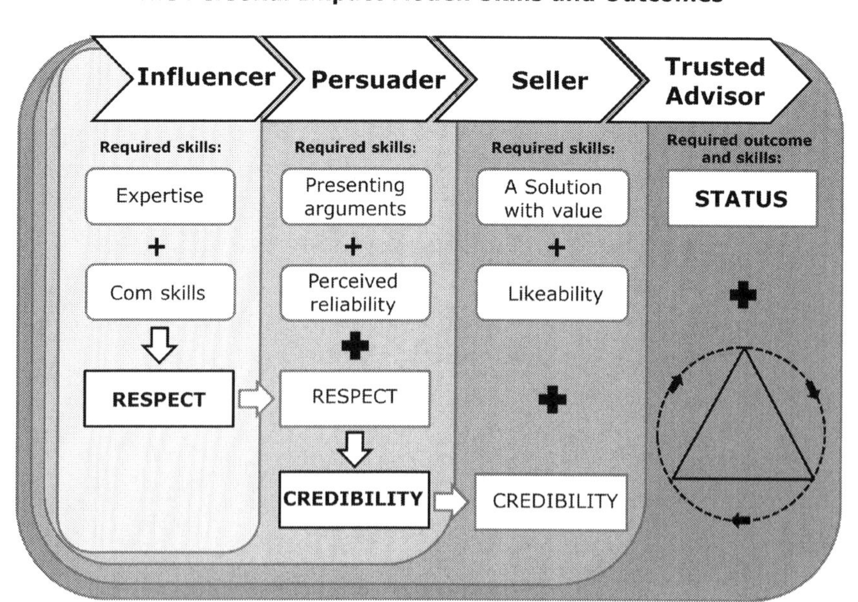

word on the subject but it furthers our understanding and leads to some very practical implications, so I advance it here. At minimum, it provides a framework allowing us to organize hard and soft skills around commonly understood terminology and processes.

The model defines the terms Influencer, Persuader and Seller and specifies the hard and soft skills required to be accomplished at each. It then does the same for a Trusted Advisor. It is summarized below:

I. Influencer

What does it take to be influential?

To define it, influence is simply the capacity to have an effect on the thoughts, beliefs or behavior of someone. It can be reactive – that is, others come to you – or pro-active, where you initiate the interaction. It is also context-specific: you may be influential in some areas but not in others. Finally, there is a passive element to the notion of influence in that exerting it does not always lead to a change. So, you could say, "I influenced them to think about it differently but they decided to go ahead anyway." Think of people you know within your firm. Are there those you believe to be influential but who don't necessarily make things happen? Influence can exist without the attainment of specific goals.

At a personal level we are influenced by people who have the capacity to affect us emotionally, such as our friends and family, and those who have some power over us, such as our boss. We want them to stay happy with us, so they influence our behavior insofar as we believe our behavior affects them.

At a professional level, while emotion can play its part, we are more driven by outcomes that affect our personal success and that of the organization we are a part of. To be influential in a professional environment we need certain capabilities to be effective.

There are two sets of skills we need in order to fulfil the influence requirements: our Expertise – what we know – and our Communication skills – how we say it.

i) Expertise

If we have expertise in a subject that matters to someone else then we have the first base covered. Expertise can include experience as well as value-added ways of thinking about something. The better our expertise in a field the more likely someone else is going to want to avail themselves of it. Ultimately, we could be an authority on the subject and may have unmatched expertise. This expertise is what we spend most of our time in professional services building and offering to clients. The more you have, the more you are potentially influential. But on its own it is not enough.

ii) Communication skills

Successful influence also requires the ability to communicate your expertise. At minimum, it is the ability to convey your knowledge to someone in clear terms. There is a continuum here between those who know but are longwinded and tedious to listen to and those who are crisp and concise. Those who are best at it also demonstrate empathy, the ability to understand the feelings of the person asking them for their knowledge, and impart it in ways the listener finds comfortable to receive, emotionally as well as rationally. Finally, good communicators need to have a degree of affability. Affability means being friendly, good-natured, easy to talk to. It is an agreeableness that encourages approach and rewards attention but may well fall short of actual liking.

Having expertise without communication skills is as bad as having communication skills without expertise. In the first case, people might come to you but probably only reluctantly and then listen through the sieve of their discomfort. In the second case, people are unlikely to come to you at all but will no doubt enjoy bumping into you at the photocopier machine.

Deploying Expertise and Communication skills well can be tested by the extent to which you and the other person *feel* there is a connected relationship – a shared sense of goodwill based on personal regard and confidence in each other's professional abilities.

The combination of Expertise and Communication skills at this minimum standard makes you influential. You know what you are talking about and you communicate it well. In the Personal Impact Model it gives you Respect. According to the OED, Respect means 'a feeling of deep admiration for someone or something elicited by their abilities, qualities or achievements'. It is the base requirement for all that follows.

II. Persuader

What does it take to be persuasive?

Persuasion is significantly more difficult an ability than influence because it presupposes an initial position is overcome to achieve a specific change. The OED defines Persuade as inducing someone 'to do something through reasoning or argument [or] cause someone to believe something'. If influence can affect how someone thinks, the test of persuasion is actually changing what someone believes or does.

To have this ability you need the Respect that comes from knowing what you are talking about and communicating it well. That ensures others will listen. Then you need two other skills: first, skill in Presenting arguments; second, Perceived reliability.

i) Presenting arguments

This is the ability to marshal arguments which elicit agreement and motivation.

Sadly, it is often insufficient to blandly state the facts, no matter how agreeably, and, relying on the other's appreciation of your proven expertise, expect them to change their mind. We hold on to our beliefs like old friends and let them go only painfully. We have an emotional as well as a rational investment in them. We like to believe what we think is right; being right makes us feel good. To accept that we are wrong, that something else is right, involves an unpleasant emotional journey. To get someone to take that journey and feel good about it at the end involves a challenge in direct proportion to how much they have invested in it.

To achieve this, of course, requires fact, evidence and logic. Further, it demands an empathetic understanding of where the listener is coming from, their sensitivities and their wants. Finally, it requires a deft mobilization of statements that in their ordered presentation elicit interest and understanding, overcome potential objections and ultimately secure conviction.

People who have skill in Presenting arguments are seen as people who can add value in very practical ways: they can change what we think and do.

ii) **Perceived reliability**

When you persuade someone, they have to believe what you say. So, 'reliability' here in part means that they can rely on the truth of your words. (At least, they can rely on the fact that you believe what you are saying to be true.) If your act of persuasion is contingent upon some act that you yourself must do, then they also have to believe in your reliability to perform that act.

Maintaining your Perceived reliability requires you to sustain your connected relationship with the other person. If they lose that feeling of being emotionally comfortable with you the discomfort can bleed into doubts about your reliability. This can be hard (but remains vital) to achieve if your proposal is taking them through an uncomfortable personal journey.

Skill in Presenting arguments and Perceived reliability, added to Respect, enables you to be persuasive. In the Personal Impact Model it gives you Credibility. The OED defines credible as 'able to be believed; convincing... capable of persuading people that something will happen or be successful'. Credibility means you are capable of leading your audience to believe or behave differently.

III. Seller

What does it take to be a Seller?

Selling is a transaction of value, one thing exchanged for another. What makes it tougher than persuasion is that one party has to be convinced to part with something of value (usually money) for something else. If you are competing with several others trying to do the same, then the challenge is less persuading the buyer to part with their money, because they may already have decided in principle to do that, but to part with their money for *your* service rather than someone else's.

Being able to sell has career-long benefits, even if you never get to face a client. Often when you try and persuade someone to do something for you they will incur a cost, or a potential cost. This may be time, effort or potential risk of reputation loss for them if it all goes horribly wrong. These are all instances of selling, since a transaction takes place. Selling and persuasion can feel pretty similar in execution and the terms are indeed often used interchangeably – "I sold them on the idea", for example. Yet it is the exchange of value, even if that has nothing to do with money directly, which distinguishes selling from mere persuasion and which represents the much higher hurdle.[1]

To even be in a position where you have the opportunity to sell, you need Credibility. It is most unlikely you will be taken seriously, or be invited to the table, without a strong brand if you don't have Credibility in the eyes of the other person.

In addition to having Credibility there are two things you need to have to be a successful seller.

i) A Solution with value

A Solution with value is a proposed plan or process which offers the prospect of creating benefit.

This is at the heart of what most of us do when pitching for work to corporate clients. We lay out our analysis of the situation, the key issues that need to be resolved and our process for doing so. We then aim to provide comfort to our potential client that we can be entrusted with the task by referring to the many times we have successfully done so in the past, and inviting them to chat with our extensive client list. From the perspective of the client, it is a question of evaluating our understanding, assessing our process and its likely success, estimating the value that might accrue and setting that off against the cost. And then comparing all this against the Solution with value offered by our competitor(s).

If our proposal is centered within our own organization, to get people on board still requires a Solution with value. In this case the value must be targeted toward them and their needs.

ii) Likeability

Being Likeable means having sufficient affinity with someone to feel comfortable at the prospect of working together to achieve a desired goal.

Liking is a higher hurdle than having a connected relationship, although the latter is a required first step. A connected relationship ensures, at minimum, a mutual regard and confidence in each other's professional abilities. It guarantees that someone will listen to you. Liking, however, requires a sense of *comfort at the prospect of actually working together.*

The other person does not need to feel that you are the most wonderful, personable individual or team he or she has ever met. The key here is liking you enough to feel they could comfortably and productively work with you and in doing so have reasonable confidence of achieving the goal.

Because in professional services the role of people in the selling and delivery of work is so critical, Likeability is essential to successful selling.

To win a competitive pitch one needs either to have an acceptable threshold of Liking and a superior Solution with value, or an equivalent Solution with value but a higher level of Liking. Of course, being better against both criteria leads to the surest outcome.

IV. Trusted Advisor

What is a Trusted Advisor?

When you ask clients this question you get a range of answers, yet constant themes. These themes are illustrated in the following answers:

- "He is someone I can talk to about anything."
- "I have the sense they won't do anything against my interests."
- "They are consistently reliable and they always get back to me quickly."
- "He makes me think."
- "They nearly always talk sense, even if I don't always agree with them."
- "She thinks about everything that affects me, not just those things in her area of expertise."

The Trusted Advisor is that person whose track record of work, personal qualities and strong relationship with the client leads to them frequently being the first person the client calls, on a range of subjects. It is this demanding combination that elevates the role of Trusted Advisor beyond that of a preferred contractor into something more personal, more influential and wide-reaching. It can lead to non-competitive work opportunities which over time may be very significant. It can also be personally rewarding. For these reasons it is a position many client handlers aspire to.

What does it take to be a Trusted Advisor?

There are five components. Importantly, it requires the Status that comes from a successful track record of doing great work for, and as a result adding value to, that client and, additionally, the development of three existing skill areas and one new critical orientation, putting the client's interests first.

i) **Status**

Winning the initial work and then delivering the Solution with value at or above the expected level gives you Status for that client. Status is your personal and professional standing with that client. The better the delivery, the better your Status.

Status can confer a hall pass which allows you unlimited access to the client. It can also be the basis for further introductions to other parts of their organization. It can put you in prime position for any other workflows that may be forthcoming. Finally, it can enable you, based on your inside knowledge and network of personal relationships, to identify opportunities for both you and your client to collaborate further.

The requirements of a Trusted Advisor, having achieved Status

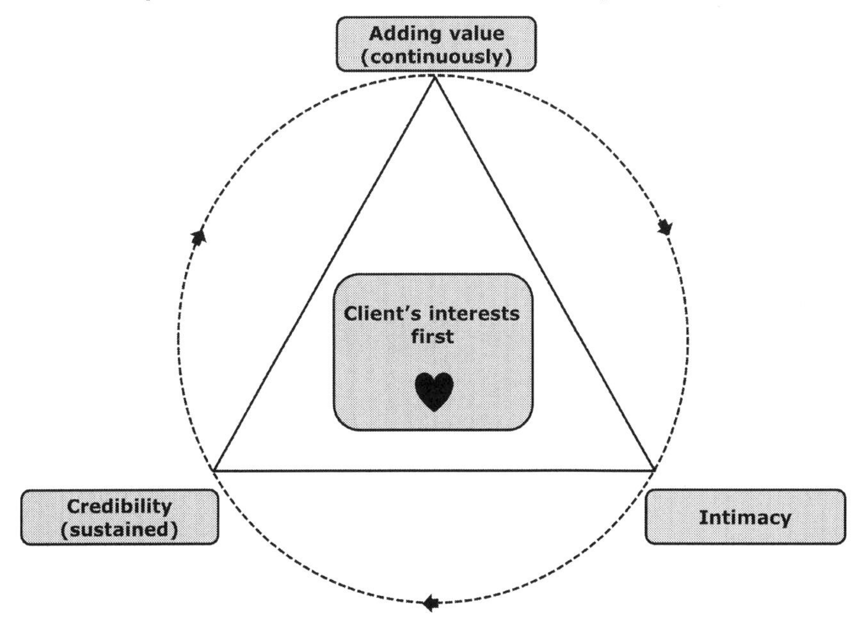

Many client handlers reach this level of having Status and many stay at it. It can be productive for all parties. You are in the position of a preferred supplier and likely to be considered for all future tenders.

The four additional elements to become, and remain, a Trusted Advisor, once Status has been achieved, are summarized in the illustration above:

The three elements of sustained Credibility, being a continuous source of Added value and some degree of Intimacy work together and help reinforce each other. Remaining a Trusted Advisor entails unremitting discharge of each element's requirements. Hence, maintaining such a position over time can be very demanding.

ii) **Sustained Credibility**

The skills that secured your position at the table, which gave you Credibility in the first place, must be maintained. Some may need to be enhanced. These skills are, you will recall, Expertise and Communication (maintaining Respect), plus skill in Presenting arguments and Perceived reliability.

These skills have to be adapted to suit the new relationship: what you had to demonstrate with a new client to win a first piece of work will be qualitatively different to what is necessary to maintain if not build a relationship now established.

For example, a key skill component of your Credibility requiring constant demonstration is Perceived reliability. This now has to be done via a myriad of large and small actions over time, such as returning all calls within (say) a couple of hours, and making commitments all of which are delivered on time and in full. Doing this once or twice to establish your Reliability in the first place is one thing, doing it consistently, over possibly years, is quite another.

Similarly, your Expertise may be stretched, and your Communication skills and skill in Presenting arguments called upon in unfamiliar and testing circumstances. Successfully doing this over time in formal and informal situations, with and without preparation, will all be necessary to sustain your Credibility.

iii) **Adding value continuously**

By having Status you will already have demonstrated that you can add value, probably within the confines of a specific brief. The Trusted Advisor continues to add value in their area of expertise, formally and informally. Additionally, their judgement, insights, questions and ideas are increasingly sought on issues outside of their area of expertise.

The first time a client handler is approached for their opinion on a subject about which they may know very little is often a sign of the changing nature of the relationship. It can be challenging if not scary to offer thinking outside one's area of expertise, especially when the downside of being found to be 'wrong' may be significant in terms of the ongoing relationship. Yet the most effective Trusted Advisors get called to help their clients on a range of matters, professional and sometimes personal too.

To achieve this requires moving away from the traditional model of value-adding, based solely on what you (or your firm) know or can find out. Instead it becomes a question of how you can help your client think through an issue based on the questions you ask and the ideas or insights you can bring. It is a different skill set, one closer to that of a coach than a knowledge provider.

iv) Intimacy

To be initially hired by your client you had to have won their Liking. This means, at minimum, you built a connected relationship which was sufficiently comfortable for them to believe they could work effectively with you. Having Status means that during the course of delivering the project you did nothing to worsen their opinion of you; hopefully they came to like you more.

To be a Trusted Advisor, this state of personal relationship needs developing to what is best described by David Maister, Charles Green and Robert Galford in their book *The Trusted Advisor*, as 'Intimacy'. Intimacy is not liking, although it is hard to imagine in practice Intimacy existing without it. Intimacy, as the authors put it, 'make[s] a connection to the interior, emotional state of the client'.[2] It enables difficult subjects to be discussed with mutual respect and complete confidentiality. It presupposes empathy and emotional honesty. It means the client feels completely *safe* with you emotionally, and possibly you with him. It is a step change in the nature of the personal relationship.

v) **Putting the client's interests first**

This is at the heart of what being a Trusted Advisor means.

All clients know that their service providers are there to make money. They are aware that the account handler is looking for further opportunities to generate revenue for their firm (and hopefully to add further value to the client). This inevitably sets up a tension which can vary in significance depending on the circumstances. It is, however, one most clients are familiar with and practice allows them to live with it comfortably enough. But it does set up a question in the client's mind each and every time the client handler goes to his client with a suggestion involving further work – "Is this something he is doing because he thinks we really need it or because he is under revenue pressure this quarter?".

Likewise, if and when a client approaches their account manager to discuss a business-related issue or idea, how sure can they be that the manager's response will be unbiased? In an environment where, as one CEO put it to me, "Everybody wants something from me", it can be hard to know who you can talk to with complete openness and honesty.

A Trusted Advisor breaks down these barriers by simply putting their client's interests first. At all times. Only by doing so will a client feel that they genuinely share the same agenda and all advice will be directed toward that end.

There are many ways to demonstrate that an account manager and his firm put the client's interests first, although the ultimate test is probably their willingness to recommend another firm for something, instead of their own. There are also times when the situation may not be black and white. At the end of the day, the only thing that matters is how the client feels.[3]

Where is 'Trust' in all this?

Trust is actually everywhere. It is defined in the OED as a 'firm belief in the reliability, truth, or ability of someone or something'. Trust is context-specific. I may trust you to do what you say you will do in a particular circumstance; I may not trust you to show up on time. Trust needs to be specific to have meaning.

So, trust is present in each skill area. To be an Influencer someone needs to trust what you are telling them is true and that, through your communication, you are believable. To be a Persuader someone needs to trust that what you say and promise is reliable. To be a Seller your prospective buyer has to trust that you will do what you say you will and they have to trust their own feelings about you. To be a Trusted Advisor your client needs to trust that you will always act in his best interests.

Hard versus soft skills

There are six capabilities that together make up the requirements for someone to successfully Influence, Persuade and Sell in professional services. Three of these depend largely on hard skills, three soft. Both types are present at each stage of the Personal Impact Model, from Influencer to Seller.

- To be an Influencer requires Expertise (hard) and Communication skills (soft).
- To be a Persuader requires, additionally, Skill in presenting arguments (hard) and Perceived reliability (soft).
- To be a Seller requires, additionally, a Solution with value (hard) and Likeability (soft).

Hard versus Soft skills in the Personal Impact Model

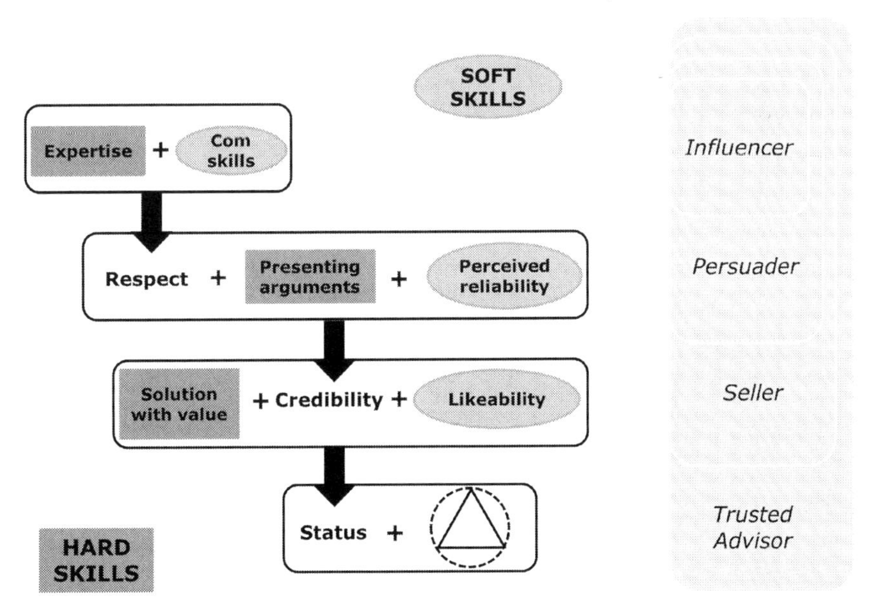

One could argue that some if not all the capabilities have a component of hard and soft skills in them. This is especially true for two of them:

i) The first is skill in Presenting arguments. Here the knowledge required can be identified and the process to acquire it learned. However, applying the knowledge well requires an appreciation of the psychological and emotional dimensions of persuasion. For that reason this skill is included in this book among the other, more clearly soft, skills.

ii) The second is Solution with value. While this capability requires largely hard skills at the level of Seller, for the Trusted Advisor it depends much more on soft skills. In particular, the soft skills discussed in 'Engaging Conversations', Chapter 11. While useful for managers at various levels, for the Trusted Advisor these skills become the main route through which he is able to continuously provide Solutions with value.

Using the Personal Impact Model to think about meeting goals

The Personal Impact Model can act as a guide to what we need to establish when we meet a potential client for the first time, and in what sequence. Subconsciously, the skills progression from Influencer to Seller seems to track how a prospective client might evaluate us in first and subsequent meetings. It can also closely mirror our own thought processes when we are in a position of evaluating someone in a professional context (although, depending on the situation, a number of other factors might also come into play).

Going back to our builders, the first thing we wanted to know was whether they had the right capability to do the job (Expertise) and the ability to explain it well enough for us to understand (Communication skills). That earned them our Respect. Without that we wouldn't have taken things further. We only then were willing to listen to their ideas and suggestions (skill in Presenting arguments) and their ability to deliver on their suggestions (Reliability). At this point we thought them Credible enough to entertain a specific proposal (Solution with value) and give time to our consideration of how we felt about working with them (Liking).

So, our builders (or at least two of them) did a good job of going for

Respect first, then Credibility, then Liking. If they had attempted to go for Credibility before first establishing Respect we would have been unlikely to listen seriously to them. That is because they had yet to establish their Expertise in our eyes. Why would we be willing to listen to their ideas if we were unconvinced at that point that they knew what they were talking about?

Similarly, they avoided the common pitfall of going for Liking first. People tend to buy from people they like and knowing this, either of our two remaining builders could have walked in smiling broadly as if they had just rediscovered a long-lost best friend. Anyone with extensive experience of buying will confirm how they react negatively to a potential provider seeking to influence their level of Liking before first establishing Respect, and possibly Credibility too. Going for Liking before Respect can actually backfire: you can lose any chance to gain Respect.

For those of us in professional services lucky enough to get a first meeting with a prospective client buyer the goal of that first meeting must be to achieve Credibility. At minimum, if we achieve nothing else in that meeting, we leave our potential client feeling that we know what we are talking about, can communicate well and are capable of persuading him to think about something differently. Credibility means you could potentially add value. It therefore increases the chance of you being invited to the table if a suitable issue arises.

The road to achieving Credibility has, however, to pass through Respect first. It is the first base. It is unconvincing to try and persuade someone of something (a Credibility skill) until they are persuaded that you have Expertise in it (a requirement of Respect).

So, in first meetings go for Respect first, then Credibility, then Liking. Although of course the client's assessment of Liking begins as you walk in the door, this does mean that if you plan on saying something specific designed to build the personal relationship, save it for the end and only if you feel you have Credibility already established.

A Trusted Advisor, or even a client account manager with Status, can find themselves employing the skills in different ways at different times as they walk the halls within their client. Sometimes they will be merely acting as Influencers (using their Expertise and Communication skills); sometimes as Persuaders (using in addition their skill in Presenting arguments while being seen as Reliable); and other times as Sellers (bringing additionally a Solution with value to the table).

As a Trusted Advisor seeks to make an increasing personal impact from Influencer, through Persuader to Seller, they need to maintain the nested skills that gave them Respect and Credibility in the first place.

Soft skills and the Personal Impact Model

We can summarize the most important components of the Personal Impact Model below.

Capability	What it is	What you need	Outcomes
Influence	A capacity based on what you have -organisationally -personally	1) Expertise 2) Communication skills	Respect
Persuasion	An action that changes an idea or behavior, against resistance	1) **Respect** 2) Reliability 3) Skill presenting arguments	Credibility
Selling	A transaction with an exchange of value	**1) Credibility** 2) Solution with value 3) Likeability	Status (with delivered performance)
Trusted Advisor	A standing where you are the first call		Basis to build partnership

The model helps us disentangle the overlapping threads when we come to think about what influence, persuasion and selling mean, and what skills are required for each. It emphasizes the importance of earning Respect before even attempting to persuade or sell. The model also shows how the respective skills that make up an effective professional services salesman feed into the crucially reshaped skill set of a Trusted Advisor.

Finally, the model helps us to identify and appreciate the importance of soft skills at each stage. Without them we could not be effective Influencers, Persuaders or Salesmen.

In the following pages we cover ten core soft skill groups. A few are relevant to just one of the categories above. Many are applicable to more than one. But because these soft skills help determine our overall behavior and, in some cases, our thinking, they all have some positive effect on our ability to be a better Influencer, Persuader and Seller in whatever situation we find ourselves. Individually and collectively they affect our way of being: who we are.

Chapter 2 Takeaways

- To Influence, Persuade or Sell, soft skills are as important as hard skills.
- The skills are nested:
  - To be a Seller requires a Solution with value and Likeability, as well as the Credibility that comes from having the skills of a Persuader and an Influencer.
  - To be a Persuader requires skill Presenting arguments and Perceived reliability as well as the Respect that comes from having the skills of an Influencer.
  - To be an Influencer requires Expertise and Communication skills.
- Sequentially, you need to demonstrate you have the earlier skills before the latter ones, hence always go for Respect before Liking in early meetings.
- To win a competitive tender in professional services requires you to have demonstrated sufficient Credibility as well as superior performance in one or both of:
  - a Solution with value;
  - Likeability.
- The requirements of a successful Trusted Advisor are an evolution of the skills required to be a successful Seller, as well as, critically, a perceived commitment to always put the client's interests first.

Chapter notes

1 If you struggle with the idea of thinking of yourself as a Salesman, you are not alone, certainly in professional services and in some other fields too. Don't let it become a psychological or emotional barrier. Just think of yourself as a Persuader or an account manager or whatever works for you. Remember, though, that if your act of persuasion involves a transaction of value you will still require the additional skills necessary to sell, however you describe yourself.

2 Maister, David H. and Green, Charles H. and Galford, Robert M. *The Trusted*

Advisor. New York: The Free Press, 2000, p77.

3 Readers interested in exploring this area of Trusted Advisor further may want to get familiar with the excellent work and writings of Charles Green, in his books and his website (Trusted Advisor Associates). Much of my own thinking is influenced by his writings over the years and the Personal Impact Model shares much with his categorization. Many individual actions are available to the client handler if they wish to develop their path to Trusted Advisor; Charles Green's work is stimulating and comprehensive in this regard.

3. Connecting Emotionally

Learn the gentle dance of body matching

Jill walked into the office of a potential client and they just hit it off. She felt relaxed and comfortable with them and the conversation flowed freely. The smiles on both sides were genuine and her new friend listened attentively to her pitch which, because she was at ease, she delivered well. The discussion moved smoothly to an agreeable discourse about their business. A few days later Jill had a first meeting with another potential client. This time, however, they appeared to be on different wavelengths from the outset. Nothing she did seemed to engender any positive response. Jill felt uncomfortable throughout and as she left the meeting she felt both a sense of failure and relief that the meeting was over.

Most of us in professional services have experience of both kinds of meetings. There seem to be some people we just connect with and some we don't. This connection is often called 'rapport' or 'chemistry'. We usually know in the first minute or two of meeting someone whether we have it or not.

There's a lot going on when you have rapport with someone. Defined as 'a close and harmonious relationship in which the people or groups concerned understand each other's feelings or ideas and communicate well', it is that feeling of being on the same wavelength as the other person (or people). It is easier to describe in terms of how it feels rather than what is actually going on below the surface. At minimum, it is a feeling of connectedness at a subconscious level in which you both feel comfortable with each other. Having this emotional connection makes everything else that follows in the relationship easier.

Traditionally, salesmen everywhere have sought to find common ground with a new prospect. This has usually been attempted at the conscious level through our dress, the language we use, our behaviors, values and our attempts to find common interests and friends. These are all obvious attempts to find commonality, acceptance and even favor. Essentially, we are trying to be more like the other person or to persuade them we are like them. And the reason, very simply, is that we are most comfortable with people who we feel are like us.

Sometimes it works and sometimes it doesn't. With experienced buyers of services it rarely does. Often an experienced buyer will see very quickly what is going on, know that their feelings are being managed and their defenses, like a castle drawbridge, are quickly raised.

Rapport, on the other hand, works at an unconscious level. It is a feeling of comfort with and even enjoyment of another's company. You may indeed have some commonality with the other person and some of it may even be significant but it is not necessary to having rapport. At its best, having rapport with someone incorporates strong feelings of respect, understanding and empathy, and nothing to do with whether you share an interest in stamp collecting.

When you do have rapport with someone it is like being in a state of fellowship with them: each of you is open to the other's influence. Respect is held for the other's opinion. It is not necessarily friendship – you can have rapport but actually not get on personally. Nor is it agreement – you can disagree while still having rapport. In a meeting with someone new, where you have such rapport, everything feels easy, flowing and relaxed. The other person will listen to you with interest and an open mind regardless of what he may conclude at the end of the meeting (because having rapport doesn't mean either of you check in your brains or free will at the door). Most importantly, he will, at a deep subconscious level, feel profoundly comfortable with you. Rapport operates entirely at the unconscious level: you just 'know' whether you have it with someone or not.

Rapport is a little different from having good personal chemistry with someone, although it is probably a prerequisite. Personal chemistry is defined by the OED as '[the] complex emotional or psychological interaction between people'. There is no generally accepted definition of what 'good' personal chemistry is. For my part, however, when I think of those people with whom I have what I would call good chemistry, it feels a lot like rapport except additionally we like each other, usually a lot. This is the key definitional distinction between the two in my view: good personal chemistry requires genuine liking of the other person, rapport does not.

Unlike personal chemistry, rapport is controllable: we can take specific, tangible actions that will allow us to quickly achieve it with almost anyone. Building rapport is the single most important skill you can learn because it is a necessary condition for all that follows.

Where does Rapport sit in the client development process?

Rapport is most critical in first meetings with clients. In the absence of any other substantial information about you it becomes the critical component determining whether that meeting will go anywhere. This is also true of *all* first meetings with someone important to you.

Thereafter, subsequent meetings will increasingly be informed by evidence of your hard skills, and where initial rapport was established, by an acknowledgement that it is there. Maintaining sufficient rapport in those meetings remains essential, however. The longer the relationship, the less you have to consciously think about rapport, until it eventually becomes a question of simply ensuring there are no negatives.

Getting rapport

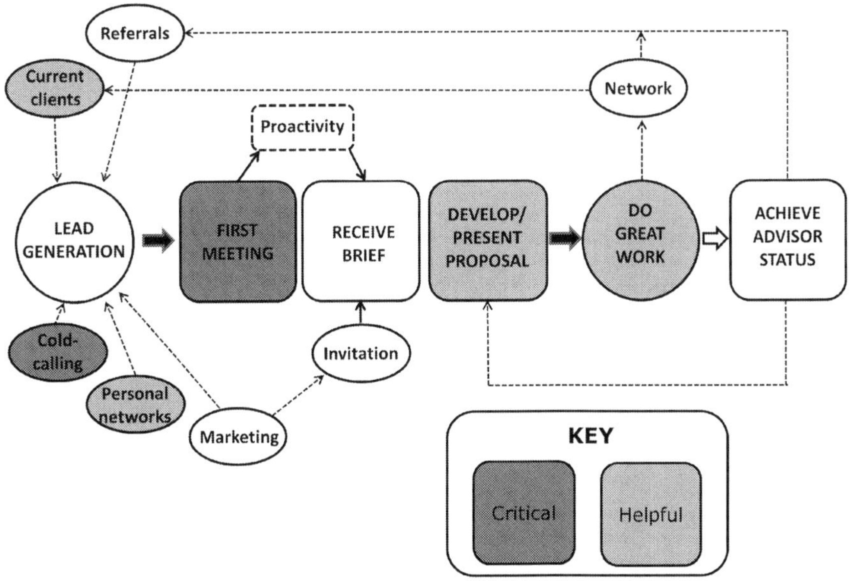

Referrals
Current clients
Network
Proactivity
LEAD GENERATION
FIRST MEETING
RECEIVE BRIEF
DEVELOP/ PRESENT PROPOSAL
DO GREAT WORK
ACHIEVE ADVISOR STATUS
Cold-calling
Personal networks
Marketing
Invitation
KEY
Critical
Helpful

What Rapport looks, sounds and feels like

You can achieve a good level of rapport quite quickly with almost anyone by learning the physiological dance of body and voice matching. Like all good dances it takes some training but with practice it can enhance your personal effectiveness enormously.

When we have good rapport with someone we tend to copy or get close to some significant part of their body posture and body movements, the volume and pitch of their voice, and sometimes their rate of breathing. In the language of such things, this is called *matching*. When we are with someone we feel uncomfortable with, we do the opposite: we mismatch.

Sometimes this replication of physiology is called mirroring. Here the replication is *exact*, as if you were looking at the other person in a mirror. By contrast I use the term 'matching' to denote the process of *broadly approximating* the other person's physiology. Matching may incorporate elements of exact copying, or mirroring, or it may not.

This happens naturally. When you see two people who like or love each other (and who as a result have rapport) you will notice that often their postures tend to match each other. Sometimes they match the position of their arms or legs. Often they will speak at the same pace, sometimes with the same tone of voice. Occasionally they will match each other's rate of breathing.

You will likely have experienced this yourself. When you meet a colleague in the corridor whom you like, how closely does your posture match theirs? Sometimes this is hard to control. I remember the first time I went to Starbucks with my soon-to-be wife (I asked her to marry me two weeks later). I quickly noticed that we matched our postures, arms and feet positions and pace of speech exactly (in fact we were almost mirroring each other). When I tried to break out of this, say by switching my weight from one foot to the other and moving my arm position, I felt distinctly uncomfortable, so I quickly moved back to the exact position I had been in. You can see something similar in a restaurant where couples are eating across from each other: if they are getting on, when one raises a glass to their lips the other usually follows.

The reverse is true. When we are with people we don't have rapport with we tend to have different body postures, different voice patterns and different rates of breathing. This mismatching is usually because we don't like or respect that person. When you meet a colleague in the corridor whom you have no rapport with, how does your body posture and movements compare with theirs? Most of the time you will find they are very different. The anthropologist Desmond Morris in his book *Manwatching* was one of the first to point out this tendency to match another's physical actions among humans, something he called 'Postural Echo'. He described it at the time as something which "friends do... unconsciously as part of a natural body display of companionship... There is a good reason for this. A true bond of friendship is usually only possible between people of roughly equal status. This equality is demonstrated in many indirect ways but it is reinforced in face-to-face encounters by a matching of the postures of relaxation and alertness. In this way the body transmits a silent message saying: 'See, I am just like you'; and this message is not only sent unconsciously but also understood in the same manner. The friends simply 'feel right' when they are together".[1]

The researchers Chartrand and Bargh described this as the 'chameleon effect'[2]: that one's behavior passively and unintentionally alters to match that of another's in a social interaction. They put this down to the *perception-behavior link*, where just the perception of another's behavior automatically increases the chances of doing that same behavior yourself. They found in their experiments that people engaging in a task together unconsciously match the *motor behavior* of those they work with. Significantly, they further discovered that where one party consciously mimics the postures, mannerisms or movements of the person they are working with, the work went more smoothly and the participants liked each other more.

When you are in rapport with someone you tend to physiologically match each other, even if you are not consciously aware of it. The reverse is also true: when you physiologically match another person consciously, you tend to get into a rapport with them.

There are people gifted in their natural ability to do this, to attune themselves with others at a non-verbal level, achieving a very high level of rapport entirely unconsciously: super-empathics, if you like. In his book *The Tipping Point*, Malcolm Gladwell describes his conversation with the financial products super-salesman Tom Gau: "... we almost immediately fell into physical and conversational harmony. We were dancing. Even before he attempted to persuade me with his words, he had forged a bond with me with his movements and his speech... It isn't that Gau was deliberately trying to harmonize himself with me... What we are talking about is a kind of super-reflex, a fundamental physiological ability of which we are barely aware. And like all specialized human traits, some people have much more mastery over this reflex than others.'[3]

The key elements of matching

So, how can those of us who lack the extraordinary natural empathy of a Tom Gau get close to achieving the benefits of being in physiological rapport with someone? In theory it is quite simple. With practice, and some care, it becomes entirely natural. Eventually it becomes unconscious. From more years of experimentation than I care to think about I have found the following elements to be most useful.

Posture

You and the other person should be standing or sitting together. Then you should aim to hold your posture as closely as possible to theirs. A good way to think about this is to imagine the shape of the other person's spine and to hold yours in a similar position. It doesn't have to be any more exact than that.

Arm and leg position

Aim to match or even copy the position of their arms and legs. Are they open or crossed? Are the legs crossed at the ankle or the knee? How are the hands held? One can match (same arm, same position), mirror (opposite arm, same position, if facing each other) or approximate some or all of these parts. In fact, I have noticed little difference in achieving a rapport whether one matches or exactly mirrors arm and leg positions, providing these are natural postures.

Head angulation

Is the head upright or tilted? Broadly aim to match the angulation of the head with reference to the body. If there is some movement, say nodding, aim to match that too.

Pace, pitch and volume of voice

If you can match someone's pace, volume and pitch of conversation, they will feel much more comfortable with you. If their voice speed and pitch is very different from your natural voice then make a move towards theirs without attempting to match them exactly as it will feel too unnatural for you (though I have seen lots of evidence that the other person doesn't in fact notice, although if there are other people around who know you well, they will). This is obviously especially useful on the telephone.

Energy level

Are they upbeat, calm, relaxed, reflective? Or are they simply high, medium or low energy? Aim to approximate their level of energy if you can, or at least make a move toward it. Sometimes energy level can also be a proxy for mood – if you can identify their mood and then match that yourself, at least initially, the effect can be instantaneous.

There are other areas of matching which some hold to be useful. These include 'cross-matching'. This is where the position or movement of someone else is matched by another part of your body: tapping your finger in synch with their footfall as they walk around the room or crossing your arms if they cross their legs, for example. I have never found this to be especially effective; sometimes I have found myself actually feeling uncomfortable trying to do it.

On the other hand, I have found that matching the other person's rate of breathing can be very powerful, especially in helping to develop surprisingly quick levels of empathy. It is very hard to do in the course of a normal conversation but if you are in listening mode just breathe out slowly as they talk and breathe in when they do.

Most effective, and easiest to do in my experience, is simply to match body posture (the way they hold their head, torso, arms and legs) and their energy level (reflected usually in their pace of speech). On the telephone, pace, pitch and volume of voice are all relatively easy to match.

In general, after a few moments of matching someone you should start to notice a difference in your feelings with regard to them. You become more relaxed, more comfortable and everything starts to feel a little easier. 'Harmony' might be too strong a word to describe it but it can start to feel something like that. Sometimes it can happen within a few seconds of starting to match; at other times it might take a minute or longer. You (and they) will feel it when it happens.

Matching in practice

When matching someone physiologically in a professional environment there are three very important guidelines to bear in mind.

i) **Never aim to match exactly.**

This is mimicry. Despite research evidence from studies conducted at INSEAD Business School and Duke University (and elsewhere) that mimicry results in a greater number of positive outcomes, these are experiments, and controlled mimicry is necessary in order to accurately measure the inputs and effects in these studies.

In the real world, if you adopt mimicry, the *exact* copying of the other's posture and movements, it will become obvious quite soon that you are copying them and they will feel uncomfortable. They may even be annoyed. You would lose the rapport, and any further chance of it, instantly.

It is also unnecessary. You can often get quite an acceptable rapport just by *not* mismatching!

If you get, or have, an excellent rapport, you might well notice that you have come to mimic each other in perfect harmony. In this case it has become a natural by-product of your rapport. That's fine. It is the intentional mimicry at the beginning of an interaction, where rapport has not yet been established, that is to be avoided.

ii) **Wait before following a change in posture.**

When the other person makes a move, say unfolding their arms, and you want to continue matching them, wait a few seconds before following them with a similar move. Wait at least three seconds. If you move too soon after them you will appear again to be mimicking. This may matter less in a social situation where the stakes are not so high but in a professional environment it is not worth the risk of endangering the rapport you have been so carefully building.

The exception to this is where you have already achieved a rapport and not to follow immediately would leave you in an uncomfortable position of mismatching, hence breaking the rapport. There can be no hard and fast rules in such a situation – you just have to go with your feelings.

iii) **Only do what you feel comfortable doing.**
Never be uncomfortable. If you are, the other person *will* sense it.

Done properly this should be an entirely natural dance, an elegant synchronization of two peoples' physiology. After a while it will become unconscious. That is what you are aiming for. Until then, as you practice, use your sense of comfort as your guide to what is or is not appropriate. If the content of the meeting runs away with you and you find yourself struggling to both follow the conversation and think about matching, concentrate on the conversation; come back to matching if you can when you are more comfortable.

Exercises

There are some easy things you can do to experience the effects of matching and to practice.

i) **The argument**
An easy way to demonstrate how well matching works is to have an argument with someone. The next time you are with a colleague having an argument, firstly match their posture as closely as you can – sitting versus standing, arms and legs crossed or not, erect or slumped, head straight or angled, talking quickly or slowly.

Get as close to matching them physiologically as you comfortably can.

Feelings about the discussion:

When...	MATCHED	MISMATCHED
AGREE	Easy Pleasurable	Uncomfortable Desire to wrap up
DISAGREE	Constructive Open-minded	Positions hardened Difficult Unpleasant

Notice how you feel. Then, start to mismatch them. Again, notice how it makes you feel. Later, find the opportunity to do the same when next you are having a discussion on something you agree about – match then mismatch and notice how the two states make you feel. The different feelings usually aroused in each case are summarized in the two-by-two above.

The effects of this can be little short of astounding when you first encounter it. The realization that you can have a heated argument with someone AND both of you feel the debate is civilized and constructive is revelatory. Incidentally, the exercise works just as well even if both parties are aware of it, so you can be quite open about what you are doing.

ii) Making a new friend

At a social dinner, pick someone unknown to you on the other side of the table and a couple of places down. Don't look at them but body match out of the corner of your eye: eat and stop eating as they do, pick up your wine glass when they do, match how they hold their arms when not eating – after a while they will feel drawn to you, probably look over at you during the evening and almost certainly come over to talk with you at the end. You will have made a positive, comfortable connection. It is up to you then to use it with respect.

Similarly, if you are with a group of people standing around talking together (say at a drinks party), pick the one you would most like to chat with on your own and match them closely. After a while they will be drawn to want to talk with you. Of course, whether they will continue to want to do so after the initial pleasantries will depend on how well you maintain the rapport and what you have to say. But matching has helped get your relationship off to a good start.

iii) Instant connections

You can do this with people you expect to have only a very short interaction with, such as shop attendants and hotel check-in clerks. If you are expecting a difficult interaction for whatever reason, it can be even more revealing. Start with a smile and then quickly match their whole posture – body, head angle and arms. Then have your conversation. In these often very short interactions you can even mimic to test the benefits quickly. Notice how you feel when you do so. Do you feel better? Do they respond positively? Even if the outcome is not what you desired do you feel the process to be an agreeable one?

Physiological matching is an art and it requires practice. Until you feel confident and competent, practice it in very low-risk situations – at the shops, a social dinner, with a subordinate, a nice boss or junior clients you have a good relationship with. Practice getting into a rapport with people as quickly as you can and notice the feelings you have when you do.

The limits of matching

Interestingly, the rapport effects of physiological matching in my experience are less noticeable if you employ it with people you are already close to, such as your partner or a very good friend. That is because you already have a good level of rapport based on a history of shared positive experiences and in these cases consciously matching them is unlikely to change much how you both feel. What you should notice, however, is that because of this level of existing rapport, your bodies naturally fall into physiological matching. Hence, using close friends or partners as subjects for low-risk practice is less helpful than with people you don't know so well.

The test of rapport

There is a very simple way to discover if you have a rapport with someone: make a move and see if they follow you. So, you move your arm into another comfortable position or cross your legs or shift your seating position, for example. In the jargon of body matching this is known as *leading*. If they follow you with a similar move, you are likely to have rapport with them. If not, you probably don't.

In theory, you should wait until you *know* you have rapport before making an important suggestion or proposal. Simply having physiological rapport does not guarantee that people will agree with you or behave the way you wish but it probably does help ensure they will consider your suggestion openly if not in a positive spirit. So, ideally, one would pitch an idea only when rapport had been confirmed: you make a move and they follow you.

In practice, matching followed by leading to test rapport is hard to do. Imagine being in conversation with a new client prospect and after a while, as you come close to the point you wish to lead the conversation in a different direction, you make a physical move to check if you have a rapport but he doesn't follow, so you carry on matching and a few moments later you check again with similarly no matching response. This might go on for a while. Assuming you can keep the conversation going that long and he is not distracted by your fidgety moves and possibly aimless twittering, how long do you carry on for?

So, I always ignore the test. Rapport is something you just feel. After a while you know if you have it or not – so stick with your gut. And if you don't get it, for whatever reason, you probably have to carry on with your conversational agenda regardless. However, sometimes you will be in conversation with a client and you make a move – probably unconsciously – and you notice something... he follows you! What does that tell you? If fortuitously you have something really important you have been waiting to say, now is the time to say it!

Rapport and Respect

Rapport can be very difficult to establish if the other party has no Respect for you or you have yet to establish it. Respect is the combination of your Expertise and your Communication skills, your basic competence. Of course, this may not matter in a social context. In a professional context, it can be critical.

People seem reluctant to engage in a rapport with someone until they feel that, professionally, they have something worthwhile to offer them. I offer this as an assertion but you can try it out for yourself. Where Respect does not exist, you will often find that the other party mismatches you as you attempt to match them. It can become fidgety and feel very uncomfortable. It also makes sense. If I am being sold to, my subconscious defenses are immediately raised until I know they have something to say that I want to hear; I am reluctant to feel emotionally comfortable with them until then.

How does this affect our attempts to build rapport with someone we first meet, say at an introductory meeting? How can we gain Respect, in order to build rapport, if we need rapport to aid our Communication skills, a component of that Respect? Isn't that a Catch 22?

Even in a first meeting we are likely to have some Respect before we walk in. This might either be borrowed or organizational Respect – in the first instance, perhaps because we secured an introduction from someone our prospective client holds in high regard; in the second, perhaps because of our firm's reputation or our job title. In either event we can probably then move quite quickly into the gentle dance of matching.

If neither of these is the case, then we have to act in ways to get Respect very early into the meeting, if not immediately: this in covered in Chapter 5, Making a Great Impression. Where we have achieved some initial Respect, from the halo effect of others, from our organization's presence in the market or from our own actions early in the meeting, we then have to maintain it by demonstrating our personal Expertise and our Communication skills.

If you find yourself struggling to build a feeling of rapport (or worse, notice the other person consistently mismatching you), then you would have to conclude they are unwilling to give you Respect, for whatever reason.

Breaking rapport

If you are in rapport with someone and finding it hard to end the discussion, mismatch them. The mild emotional jarring you and they will feel can act as a natural full stop, making it easier for you to end the meeting. You may have done this unconsciously in meetings where you (or the other person) suddenly stand up as they communicate their desire to bring the meeting to a close. Standing up when the other person is sitting is an obvious mismatch. It makes it easier to finish things.

On occasion, I have found this useful, though the mood shifts slightly from one of harmony to a feeling of being slightly unsettled at the end. That may be an outcome you are happy with. If not I would aim to remain in a rapport and talk the meeting to a comfortable close, if I could.

Rapport and the Personal Impact Model

Rapport is the bedrock of your ability to be an effective Influencer, Persuader or Salesperson. It is the most effective tool you have to quickly build a connected relationship.

As an Influencer, having a degree of rapport will allow your listener to feel comfortable hearing what you have to say – its contribution to your affability is a very helpful component of your Communication skills.

As a Persuader, rapport contributes to the belief that you are or will be Reliable. It does this by promoting the feeling of an expectation that is likely to be fulfilled: "I feel comfortable with this person now; regardless of what happens I see no reason why I shouldn't feel the same way with them in the future." Rapport also encourages someone to be open to your proposal, listen to it and weigh your points thoughtfully; as a result, it promotes your skill in Presenting arguments.

As a Salesperson, rapport opens up the possibility of achieving Liking. If Liking is defined, as it is in the Personal Impact Model, by the sense that we can comfortably and productively work with someone, having rapport is clearly a precondition.

Summary

One could argue that being in rapport with others is so important we should aim to get it with everyone we meet. It would raise the quality of all our relationships, like boats on a rising tide.

A friend of mine has an extraordinary record in the field of professional services: he has built from scratch two very significant services businesses. When I interviewed him for this book I asked him what the secret was that allowed him to turn so many first meetings into productive client relationships. He mentioned a number of things but the first thing he said was, "I always want to get into rapport with the client. It's my priority. If I can't, for whatever reason, I am already thinking about how best to end the meeting so I can put my efforts elsewhere. I know if I don't [achieve a rapport] we will really struggle to get anywhere."

Rapport is the first thing to aim for in all client interactions. Arguably, in all interactions, period. It's a bit like money: you can probably survive without it but having enough makes everything else much easier. Its absence in important meetings can make those meetings feel like you are walking through mud.

Where a good relationship already exists, rapport is easy to slip into. And in those meetings where you just hit it off, where you find actual good personal chemistry between you at the outset, it requires no effort at all. In a first meeting with someone where you don't just hit it off, however, it just takes some care, effort and a little skill.

The benefits of achieving a rapport are profound because you will have created a situation where the other person feels more comfortable with you and as a result happier to listen and engage. You will be well on your way to having a connected relationship. The other person won't, as a result, necessarily agree with you on everything you say, unfortunately, but they will listen in a receptive frame of mind. This shared rapport will also help *you* to feel comfortable and as a result better able to be at your best.

If you can achieve just this you have every chance of doing well in that meeting; if you are in a competitive situation, all other things being equal, you have just given yourself a big advantage.

Chapter 3 Takeaways

- Rapport is essential to quickly building connected relationships.
- Having rapport opens up the possibility of influencing, persuading or selling.
- You achieve rapport by gently engaging in the artful dance of body matching.
- With practice, the process of getting rapport becomes unconscious.

Chapter notes

1 Morris, Desmond. *Manwatching: A Field Guide to Human Behavior.* New York: Abrams, 1977. p43.

2 Chartrand, T.L. & Bargh, J.A. 'The Chameleon Effect: The Perception-Behavior Link and Social Interaction'. *Journal of Personality and Social Psychology,* 1999, Vol.76, No.6, pp893-910. Available online at: www.yale.edu/acmelab/articles/chartrand_bargh_1999.

3 Gladwell, Malcolm. *The Tipping Point: How Little Things Can Make a Big Difference.* New York: Little, Brown and Company, 2002. p83.

4: Talking with Your Senses

Make your communication more appealing, enriching and believable

I was once asked to present the findings of our work to an incoming chairman. The work had been instrumental in changing the company's strategy and the CEO felt it best if I was the one to brief the new chairman on the detail. I was very proud of the work and keen to share it in all its glorious detail. To that end, I pulled together a concise 200+ pack of slides charting the analysis.

The meeting started well but after a few minutes I noticed something odd: the chairman was not looking at any of the slides as I revealed them. Instead he just looked at my face. He was attentive but I felt distinctly uncomfortable as he appeared to be ignoring my slides. It felt like he was staring at me. I realized that continuing like this for the remaining 190 slides, assuming I was allowed to get that far, was probably not the best idea.

So, after a moment, I put the slides down and to one side and did something I had never done before: I just told him the story of the project. The story had a beginning, a middle and an end. We only looked at one slide toward the end, a summary of the financials. It turned out to be a good meeting, even though it took me quite a while before I understood what had happened and why it turned out I had luckily done exactly the right thing.

There is evidence to suggest that people fall into definable groupings in terms of how they experience the world around them. This affects how they process that information internally and how they communicate their feelings and desires to the rest of us. These are known as Representation systems. There is little supporting scientific research behind this evidence. On the other hand, many very smart, well-educated and cynical people buy into it from the evidence of their own eyes, ears and feelings, as I do. And that is because the real-world practical implications of using sensory language to develop connected relationships are very significant.

First, the theory. We can only experience the world through our five senses of sight (Visual), sound (Auditory), touch and feelings about things (Kinesthetic), smell (Olfactory) and taste (Gustatory). Passing through whatever other value filters we have, these experiences are stored in our brains and together contribute to our own personal map of what is reality. We *represent* these experiences to ourselves in a mixture of sights, sounds, feelings, tastes and smells (so I remember the first time I met my wife with a mixture of pictures, sounds and feelings, for example). We can also create or imagine experiences using these representations (I can for example create a vivid picture of what a parachute jump would be like for me, an experience I will do what I can to avoid).

In order to think, we access these representations of sight, sound, feelings (and emotions) and to a lesser extent smells and tastes, all the time.

Experience, our senses and the words we use

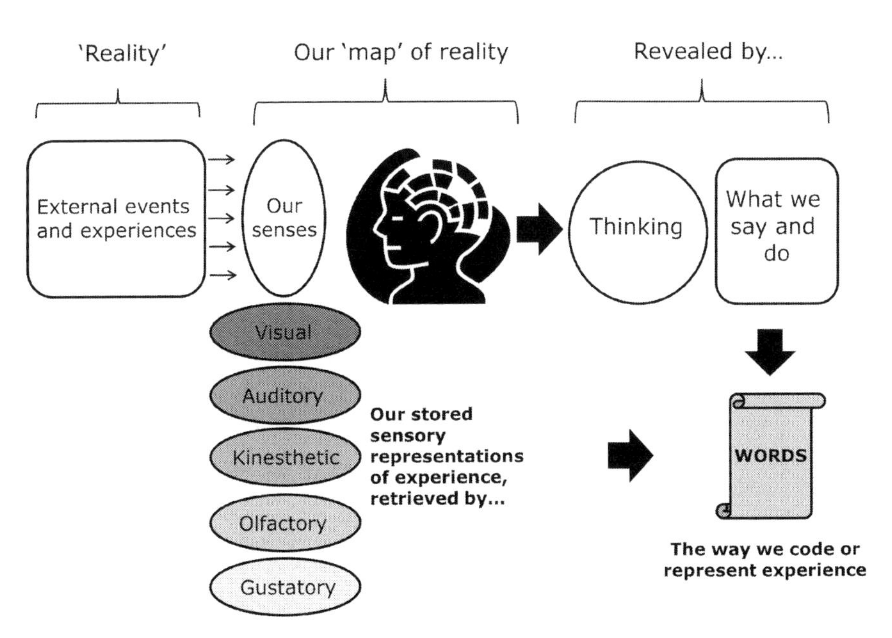

- We use our visual system to recall pictures of places, people or events. We also use it to fantasize, daydream or imagine.
- We use our auditory system to recall sounds and also to hear our own voices or to listen to music internally or to hear other people saying things in our heads or to have a conversation with ourselves.
- Our kinesthetic system combines our sense of touch as well as our internal feelings and our emotions which have an effect on our body, on how we feel.
- Our gustatory and olfactory systems are less important for our purposes so I will ignore them going forward but when you recall a good dinner you had or imagine one you are planning, you are using these systems.

There is another system, called Digital. Since Richard Bandler and John Grinder first introduced the concept of Representation systems to the world in 1975, the Digital system has come to mean non-sensory thinking in general: analytic, factual, logical, the use of abstract concepts and statistics.[1] One could say that the Digital system is another way of describing the left brain's rational mode of information processing. By contrast, the sensory Representation systems fall within our experiential mode of processing information, the right brain, with its more unconscious, emotionally engaging and perceptual characteristics.

All of us use these Representation systems to think at various times. In fact, most of us also have a preferred or *lead* system which we tend to favor, especially when under stress. In my case it is Visual. Other people are strongly Auditory or Kinesthetic, favoring those when under stress. Many people are a mix and some are an equal balance of all three.

If you go to the end of this section and complete the short questionnaire you can quickly discover where your own representation preferences lie.

Having completed the questionnaire, you will fall into one of three camps: you have a strong bias to one system; you have two broadly equal preferences with a weaker third; or you are evenly balanced across them all.

Where does sensory language sit in the client? development process?

Using sensory language is most critical in those situations where you are establishing a connected relationship for the first time, in first meetings. It reinforces rapport and underpins your Communication skills. Because sensory language can also promote feelings of trust, it is important when you come to present proposals or to persuade someone in general.

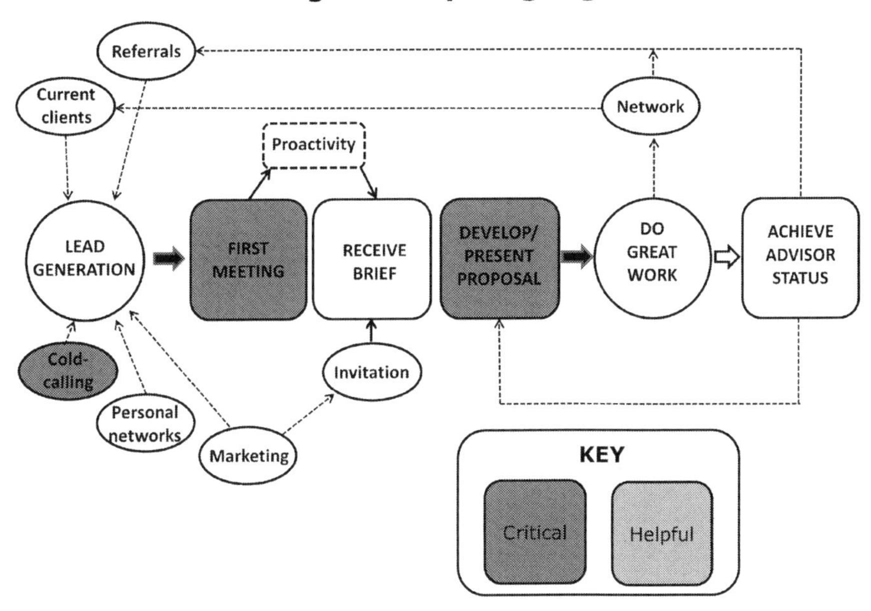

Revealing language and behavior

Our Representation system preferences affect how we think, how we like to receive information and some of our behavior. They are also revealed by the words we most commonly use. As you read the following, think about where this might apply to you.

Visuals: People who are strongly Visual tend to use predominantly visual words and phrases. Words like see, clear, imagine, reveal, focus, look, dim, picture, bright. And phrases like, "I get the picture", "Look forward to seeing you", "It's clear now", "I see what you mean".

Visuals think in pictures and talk and write using visual words. When thinking in pictures they often raise their eyes upwards as if seeking inspiration from the skies or sometimes they stare ahead with an apparently glazed expression. They can find the words of other people an unwelcome intrusion when they are thinking. They are most comfortable receiving or processing information in graphic form, such as on a slide. They find it easier to remember faces than names. They think fast because pictures are easy to bring up in their processing, and can sometimes struggle to express their thoughts adequately in words. They much prefer meeting face to face and some (like me) will do whatever they can to avoid using the telephone.

Auditory: People who are strongly Auditory tend to use predominantly auditory words like sound, hear, tell, resonates, say, click, loud. Phrases like, "Tell me how it is", "Talk soon", "This rings a bell" and "Sounds good" are very common phrases for an Auditory.

Auditories think by talking to themselves. Some actually need to talk out loud in order to do this. They listen very carefully to the word choice of others and also the tone of voice being used. They pay particular attention to their own word choice. Often, they will listen with a slight tilt of the head (as if they are holding a phone in the crook of their neck) and they like taking notes which helps them to think. They sometimes move their eyes down to the left when listening to themselves talk or think. They like using the telephone. Unsurprisingly they find it easier to remember names than faces. They don't much like graphic representations and would prefer to talk things through.

Kinesthetic: People who are strongly Kinesthetic tend to use words like feel, grasp, firm, tackle, weigh, sense, pressure. They use phrases like, "In touch with reality", "Hold on", "Warm regards", "I got a handle on it" and "That doesn't feel right"; these all feel very comfortable expressions for a Kinesthetic.

Kinesthetics think by checking in with their feelings. They often move their eyes down to the right when thinking. They take longer to decide and once decided tend to stay firm in their decision. In a meeting, they like to hold or play with something such as a pen. They tend to sit in a way that makes them feel most comfortable, possibly slouched or leaning back; they are often tactile. If they don't like what they are seeing or hearing, they can find it hard to sit still.

Digital: People thinking in the Digital system tend to use non-sensory words like accommodate, comprehend, capability, qualify and most words of greater than three syllables. Phrases like, "analyze the potential", "considering possibilities", "a viable solution", "promoting a philosophy" are all expressions using non-sensory words. All of us have to think digitally some of the time, otherwise we would be unable to think analytically, theoretically, conceptually or abstractedly. Most of us brought up in the social sciences tradition or trained in the largely American school of business empiricism are very good at this. Some of us even sound as if we think like this all the time.

Digital language reflects the fact that we all have to think in non-sensory terms on occasion. Therefore it is a component of the thinking and language of each of the three sensory types and each will use it to varying degrees, as required. In the business world, replete as it is with data-driven analysis and jargon, such language can be prevalent. It is therefore misleading to suggest that someone is primarily a digital because that would be to deny their ability to experience and process experience via their senses. However, in some discussions it can appear as if the person is indeed digital because there is an absence of any sensory words in their language and they hold your eyes with a fixed intensity.

Representation systems in action

Let's imagine you need a nice new armchair and you visit a good furniture store with your partner. If you are a Visual you will predominantly assess the armchairs based on their looks. You will create a picture in your mind of what the armchair looks like set in the room at home and you will decide based on what looks best. As you talk about the options (if you do at all, because you probably have a clear picture quite quickly of what you like – Visuals, because they think in pictures, can think quickly) you will use Visual language ("I like the color and shape of this one."). You will find any words being spoken by others as an intrusion in your thinking process.

If you are an Auditory you will probably tilt your head and be keen to hear what the salesman has to say about the relative merits of the armchairs. You will pay close attention to his choice of words and his tone of voice. You will want to discuss it with your partner and even talk to yourself about the pros and cons and you will use Auditory language as you do so ("It sounds to me that the best choice is this one."). You might give the armchair itself only a cursory glance.

If you are Kinesthetic you will want to sit in the chair, move around on it and imagine how it would feel to sit in it at home surrounded by your other furnishings. You might take a while to decide (emotions and feelings take a bit longer to access and confirm) but you will be pretty certain on the choice you eventually make. As you discuss the options with your partner you will use predominantly Kinesthetic language ("This one is the most comfortable but I feel I will be happier with that one in the room."). It will help you if the whole experience in the shop is agreeable.

If you are being Digital you will have probably constructed a spreadsheet, with criteria along one axis and options along the other, and you will perform a box-checking exercise. You will probably use a lot of digital language ("Evaluate... analyze... consider the options... meets most criteria"). And then, if you don't like the outcome based on your subconscious Visual/Auditory/Kinesthetic (V/A/K) preference, you will in all likelihood change the criteria or the relative weightings to get the 'right' result (incidentally, most men appear to buy cars like this). At least this way you have a demonstrable rationale.

If I was the furniture salesman in this example and I was able to identify that you were predominantly one of the above types I would adjust my approach accordingly. Most importantly, I would use the language that best fits with your Representation system. So, if you were a Visual, I would use mainly visual language, and so on. Essentially, I would be communicating to you in the same way that you process information: Visual or Auditory or Kinesthetic. My words would slide more easily into your internal processes without having to be translated first. I would literally be speaking your language.

The result is that, whether you like it or not, you would feel a greater degree of trust in what I was saying and in me.

Most common Representation system combinations

As is often the case, things are rarely so straightforward in real life. It is unusual in my experience to come across someone who displays the characteristics of one Representation system exclusively. I have, pseudo-scientifically from the hundreds of senior executives attending training courses, and completely unscientifically from meetings with and observations of others over many years, found the following to be the most common combinations:

Visual/Kinesthetic (V/K)

These people think in pictures and then check in with their feelings. Their language is predominantly Visual and the extent to which they are comfortable with Kinesthetic words is usually a function of how in touch they are with their feelings, and the circumstances. They definitely process information best when it is presented in graphic form.

Auditory/Kinesthetic (A/K)

These people think in words, spoken or unspoken (self-talk), and then check in with their feelings. Their language is predominantly Auditory and, as with Visuals, the extent to which they are comfortable with Kinesthetic words is again usually a function of how in touch they are with their feelings, and the circumstances.

Visual/Auditory/Kinesthetic (V/A/K) mix

These people think in pictures, words and feelings and their language is a rich and engaging mix of sensory words from each of the three Representation systems. They make decisions based on a particular sequence of pictures, words and then feelings (so, for example, they decide to buy something based on how it looks, then on what others say about it or after talking to themselves, then they check how they feel about it), or feelings, pictures and then words, or whatever their preferred sequence is for that action. Some people are a complete balance of the three systems all the time while others attach a slightly greater importance to one or two systems at different times but are still, for all practical purposes, a mix. They are often good with both names and faces. They are happy to receive information both Visually and Auditorilly but can comfortably deal with either alone.

It is my experience that, in general, women make up the larger proportion of the V/A/K mix population and even for those where one of the three sensory systems is dominant, the other Representation systems are always present to a significant degree. This is likely explainable by differences between the male and female brain; Anne Moir and David Jessel in *Brain Sex: The real difference between men and women*, were among the first to describe how the female brain is structured with a larger corpus callosum – the bundle of fibers that link the right and left sides of the brain – relative to brain size, giving women 'a greater capacity to integrate and cross-relate verbal and visual information'. Moreover, the female brain has emotional capacities on both sides whereas in the male they reside on the right side only.[2]

Kinesthetic (K)

These people decide based mainly on their feelings. That is not to say that they don't analyze or think conceptually – they do. It is just that any decision they make has to pass the feelings/emotions test and if it doesn't they revisit their analytical thinking.

Strongly Kinesthetic people can sometimes be hard to identify in the business environment because circumstances rarely lend themselves to unrestrained use of kinesthetic language. Where the individual is comfortable expressing themselves in largely kinesthetic language then their type is obvious. This can be unusual, however, since few, at least outside the creative industries, will comfortably reveal in public that a position they support or decision they make is largely driven by how they feel!

In many cases these Kinesthetics can come across as quite Digital because that remains the principle language they can safely and comfortably express themselves in. The expression of their thinking is entirely analytic and conceptual. When listening to them your intellect is engaged but not your senses. In a first meeting you may struggle to discern their Representation system but it will be there, hidden under the blanket of their caution, and it is likely Kinesthetic.

The value of Representation systems

Bandler and Grinder describe the usual reaction of students to the concept of Representation systems in a way that mirrors my own and my experience sharing it with senior executives in the business world: "Our students first go through a stage of not believing this; secondly they begin to listen to people in this new way and become amazed at what they can learn about themselves and those around them; thirdly, they learn the value of this knowledge."[3]

For many people it is a surprise when they first learn that others process information so differently from themselves. For someone with a strong Auditory lead system, for example, it can come as a shock to hear that there are people with a different lead system who make pictures in their head.

Or that there are others who rely on their feelings almost exclusively to decide something. And some of these people never have conversations with themselves! Visuals, likewise, can be dumbfounded to hear that some people simply cannot make pictures in their head.

Knowing this information about you and about someone else can explain many things about our feelings in that relationship, personal or professional. People with the same language system preference tend to naturally get on with each other – they 'speak the same language', literally. Each person's words naturally slide into the other person's preferred way of processing information. Speaking in the same language system as another, or including a proportion of their language in yours, promotes a feeling of goodwill. It makes rapport building easier. It creates a sense of trust between you because you feel instinctively that you understand each other, how the other thinks.

If the person you speak to also includes a variety of words, phrases or metaphors from the language systems you are less comfortable with, you additionally feel drawn in as your senses are enlivened, processing the sounds, pictures and feelings in their language. It is a feeling similar to that which we feel when we read good poetry; it is not only the message or content we are reacting to, but the mix of sensory language causing our neurons to fire off as they access in our brain the mélange of sounds, feelings and pictures stimulated by the verse. We feel bonded (because they share enough of our language system) *and subconsciously enriched by them.*

Exercises

1) Tell a story

A revealing exercise is to tell a story, any story you want to make up ('Jack and Jill' works well). For the first two sentences use only Visual words (along with any necessary Digital, non-sensory words that link them); then for the next two sentences use only Auditory words, then have two sentences in Kinesthetic and finally two sentences in Digital. If you have a strongly preferred Representation system you will astonish yourself at how difficult it is to string only two sentences together in the other systems. If your background is creative rather than analytical, you will find the Digital system almost impossible to talk in.

2) **Interact with those close to you**
   As an exercise, identify the preferred Representation systems of your family and a few close friends. Listen closely to the language they use. Or have them fill out the questionnaire at the end of this chapter. Where their system is different from yours, start using words that fit their Representation system rather than yours. Notice the difference in your interactions. You should find the conversation flows more fluently and they are willing to open up more. You may even notice they feel better disposed to you.

I have twin daughters. One is strongly Visual, the other Auditory. Because I am strongly Visual I more naturally get on with the first, which means I have to think less about my communication with her. With the second, I need to use a lot of Auditory language if I want her to respond fully, or to feel connected with me, especially if she is upset.

Being a strong Visual I have noticed over the years that a dominant proportion of my friends are strongly Visual too. My weakest sense is Auditory and I have noticed that those who are strongly Auditory are those I find it hardest to get on with, unless I consciously use more of their language. I have become much, much better at this. I have discovered that applying these lessons can make a big difference in the quality of my interactions with people, both professionally and personally.

How do we use this knowledge to build a connected relationship in a business meeting?

There are two main ways.

i) If we can discern a preferred Representation system we should aim to match the other person's representational language

When we do, they will feel a positive unconscious connection with us, a feeling that we truly understand them, and our words will be received without first having to be translated. It promotes, above all things, a sense of trust. So, in the opening story of this chapter, the incoming chairman was strongly Auditory. He wanted to listen carefully to what I said. He was uninterested in pictures. Putting aside the slides and telling him the story worked better for him.

If you have two people with different Representation systems, one strongly Kinesthetic and the other strongly Visual, say, things can start to feel uncomfortable and unproductive quite quickly. Take the following made-up example:

Jack: "I can't grasp your point about the accounts department!"
Jill: "Look, it's perfectly clear. We need to see what's happening with a report before we decide."
Jack: "Well, I'm uncomfortable with that approach. Let's sit down with John and thrash it out person to person."
Jill: "I think we lose the big picture that way. With so many changes on the horizon we need to have the options laid out in black and white."
Jack: "Hold on, that's a bit hasty…"

These two people agree that something needs to be done about the accounts department. But Jack is Kinesthetic and Jill is Visual. As a result, their discussion about the right process is painful and unconstructive.

To be most effective in communication you need to be able to translate your own language system preference into that of the other person's. Some examples of possible translations are shown below:

VISUAL	AUDITORY	KINESTHETIC	DIGITAL
I can't see it	Double Dutch to me	Can't make head or tail	I don't understand
It's not clear yet	Can't say that's right	No grip on this	I don't know
I get the picture	That rings a bell	I get your drift	I understand
My view is…	Something tells me	I feel that…	I think
It's all unclear	Sounds confusing	None of this fits	This isn't right
Look over	Discuss	Go over	Consider
I see	I hear you	I get it	I understand

To do this well, requires good listening and, unless you are one of the blessed who uses a natural mix of Representation systems, some practice. It is worth it. In one-on-one meetings with someone who has a very strong Representation system preference it can make all the difference between a good meeting and an average one.

ii) Where the other person's Representation system is unknown, or where you are dealing with a group, use a V/A/K mix of sensory language at the beginning and at the end of the conversation or presentation.

With someone you don't know, you can't expect to know their Representation system at the outset, so to ensure that some of your initial communication is expressed in their preferred system you need to cover all the bases. The way to do this is to couch your introductory words in a V/A/K mix. For example, one could say something like:

"It's good (K) to finally shake (K) your hand, Jack. Thank you for finding time for us to talk (A). We've been looking forward to seeing (V) you."

Or: "These look (V) like very comfortable (K) offices. I've heard (A) this is a good part of town to be in and I can see (V) why. Do you feel (K) at home here?"

Where that part of our communication matches their preferred system, they will feel a positive connection with you. Because this sensory connection has been established they will also feel a slight sense of emotional enrichment as they then process the less familiar sensory words. This also works well with a group of people where there is likely to be a mix of Representation systems.

If you further structure your introductory V/A/K mix of language in the K/A/V sequence, you will be using what has come to be described as the 'Charisma Pattern'. Take, for example, President Obama's inauguration speech on January 20th 2009:

"My fellow citizens,
I stand here today humbled (K) by the task before us, grateful (K) for

the trust you have bestowed, mindful of the sacrifices (K) borne by our ancestors. I thank (A) President Bush for his service to our nation, as well as the generosity and cooperation he has shown throughout this transition.

Forty-four Americans have now taken the presidential oath (A). The words (A) have been spoken (A) during rising tides of prosperity and the still waters of peace (V). Yet, every so often, the oath (A) is taken amidst gathering clouds and raging storms (V/A/K). At these moments, America has carried on, not simply because of the skill or vision (V) of those in high office but because We the People have remained faithful to the ideals of our forbearers and true to our founding documents.

So it has been. So it must be with this generation of Americans."

These introductory remarks broadly follow a sequence of Kinesthetic words first (the theory being that Kinesthetics take longer to get up to speed), Auditory words next (Auditories being quicker than Kinesthetics but not as quick as Visuals) and Visual words (or where underlined, visual metaphors) last. The theory is that by the time you have connected with the Visuals, the Kinesthetics and Auditories will also be with you and, providing you maintain a mix of sensory language thereafter, the whole audience is more likely to follow you, emotionally if not intellectually.

This particular V/A/K sequence arose from investigation into the compelling linguistic power of the speeches of Martin Luther King and John F. Kennedy. Having read many of these speeches myself I can confirm that they do indeed reveal this sequence, especially in some of the more memorable passages. But they also reveal other V/A/K combinations.

What appears to matter most here, it seems to me, is the naturalistic and fluent mix of sensory language, rather than the specific V/A/K delivery sequence. Such a language mix ensures everyone's processing preferences are met, drawing them in and then engaging them on an emotional level. For those with one strong preference, say Kinesthetic, they are enriched by exposure to the other sensory systems they may themselves employ less often. People who are a mix of all three Representation systems do this naturally all the time; they are as a result often inexplicably attractive to us. If you are one of these people, in the world of communication you are blessed.[4]

In an ideal world we would continue the whole conversation using a

V/A/K mix, endowing everything we say with the engaging seduction of a JFK speech. In practice, unless you are already a mix of all three Representation systems and your conversation is naturally strewn with V/A/K words, it can be hard to do.

So, in a meeting where we are dealing with a person or group of mixed or unknown Representation preferences, or even one strong preference that is different from ours, concentrate on using a mix of sensory language in the introduction and at the end. If you are unsure of yourself, you can even mentally prepare (or write down) your opening and closing remarks ahead of the meeting.

For the balance of the meeting be yourself. Use the language you are most comfortable with.

If the subject matter warranted, you could even be entirely Digital. This actually has advantages. Digital language does not promote rapport but good digital thinking and the associated language can be an important part of gaining Respect because it can help to demonstrate that you know what you are talking about.

At the end of the meeting close again with a mix of sensory language to help re-establish that positive sensory connection. This strategy allows you to engage emotionally at the most important moments – the beginning and the end – promoting feelings of rapport and helping to establish trust, while freeing you up to concentrate on your material for the rest of the discussion.

Sensory language and the Personal Impact Model

Matching someone's Representation system promotes Respect because it enhances your Communication skills, making it easier for them to hear what you have to say. It makes you a better Influencer.

It also enhances Credibility because when you speak to someone in their language system, requiring no translation from them, it is easier for them to process and accept what you say. It promotes the sense that they can trust what you say, making you more Reliable in their eyes. It makes you a better Persuader.

Finally, because we are simply happier talking with those people who process information the way we do, it promotes Liking, making you a better Seller.

Summary

Becoming aware of Representation systems and starting to listen out (and look) for them can open up a whole new world for you. You become much more aware of your own preferences. As you work to match others' processing preferences you will find your own senses developing and your comfort in expressing them.

Compared to personality models like Myers Briggs, the Enneagram or DISC, for example, each of which have their strengths, working with Representation systems requires very little information, which is easily acquired. And, where it is clear, the information is immediately actionable.

The key benefit is that you will find interactions with people becoming smoother. That sense you can have of mild grating discomfort with some people is usually no more than a sign that their processing system is different from yours. With practice you can discover quite quickly what it is and adjust some of your sensory language to match theirs. It can be as simple as using only a few words or phrases such as, "I hear that" for an Auditory, "I feel that too" for a Kinesthetic or "I see that" for a Visual. They will feel much more comfortable with you and, as a result, you will feel more comfortable too.

Chapter 4 Takeaways

- Using the right sensory language makes you more appealing to the other person – the listener finds it easier to talk with you, senses you get what they are saying and is much less likely to mistrust what you say.
- Where you can use an engaging mix of sensory language the listener will feel enriched and drawn in to you.
- Where you can, match the other person's Representation system in your language; where you cannot, ensure you employ a mix of all three language systems at the beginning and end of the conversation.

Chapter notes

1 Bandler and Grinder were the co-founders of Neuro-Linguistic Programming (NLP), variously defined but perhaps best described as 'the study of the structure of subjective experience'. That means how our minds and bodies work together,

the language we use to make sense of our world and the behaviors we develop as a result which help or hinder us.

2 Moir, Anne and Jessel, David. *Brain Sex*. London. Michael Joseph, 1989. p48.

3 Grinder, John and Bandler, Richard. *The Structure of Magic II*. Palo Alto, CA.: Science and Behavior Books, Inc., 1976. p17.

4 For this reason it is a good idea to ensure that your written communication is always peppered with a good mix of V/A/K language. While you may know the preferred Representation system of the recipient, you rarely know who else will be copied in on it.

Representation system (language preferences) self-assessment

Mark the answer that represents your choice. If more than one, mark both. Answer quickly.

1. I find it easiest to remember:
   A faces
   B. names
   C. doing things with particular people

2. I usually find you can tell if someone is lying by:
   C. how they make me feel
   B. how their voice changes
   A. what their eyes do

3. When I am choosing food in a restaurant, I tend to:
   A. imagine what the food will look like
   C. imagine what the different choices will taste like
   B. discuss the options with my friend

4. I feel especially drawn to other people by:
   B. what they say
   A. how they look
   C. how they make me feel

5. When I worry about something, I:
   C. am physically unsettled

A. visualize what could happen
B. talk it through with myself in my head

6. My earliest memory is:
   B. someone speaking to me
   C. doing something
   A. looking at or seeing something

7. If I have to concentrate, I find what helps me best is:
   A. focusing on the words and pictures
   B. talking it through in my head
   C. playing with something tangible or moving around

8. When I learn something new I find it easiest at first to:
   C. figure it out by doing it
   A. watch how it is done
   B. talk it through with my instructor

9. I decide on what to furnish my home with mainly because I like:
   C. what it feels like or how I will feel with it
   B. what the salesman tells me
   A. how it will look

10. When I go to a concert I tend to:
   A. watch closely
   C. move in time to the music
   B. listen carefully to the words

11. When I buy a car I am most likely to:
   B. discuss what we need with my partner
   A. read all the road tests
   C. test drive as many as I can

12. If I am going somewhere unfamiliar I like to:
   C. use my good sense
   A. look at a map
   B. ask for directions

13. When I take time off I most like to:
    - A. watch television or movies
    - B. chat to friends and family
    - C. do some activity

14. If I have to assemble flat-pack furniture I:
    - C. start by handling the various pieces
    - B. read the written instructions carefully
    - A. first look at the drawings

15. When I buy clothes for myself I first:
    - A. look for myself and imagine what they would look like on me
    - C. go and touch what takes my fancy
    - B. tell the shop assistant what I want

16. When planning where to go on vacation I tend to:
    - A. look at brochures and read the guides
    - B. listen to recommendations from people I know
    - C. imagine how I would feel at the various destinations

Add up the number of times you marked A, B or C.

If you have mainly As you are predominantly Visual

If you have mainly Bs you are predominantly Auditory

If you have mainly Cs you are predominantly Kinesthetic

Most people will be a mix of two Representation systems; sometimes equally, sometimes with one dominant. Others will be an equal mix of all three.

Remember that labels such as these can sometimes be a prison. Where you are today is not necessarily where you will be tomorrow. What we are is to a large extent in our own hands.

5. Making a Great Impression

Take control of the first few seconds

The CEO was not in the best of moods. His day was crammed full of meetings and there was a bunch of things he needed to get done before it was over. And here was this meeting with some firm his PA had put in the diary, for a full hour. Well, they were here now and it was too late for him to postpone so he had better get it over with. They wanted him to use their services, obviously. Otherwise they wouldn't be paying him a visit. He'd agreed in principle to the meeting some time ago because they sounded interesting or everyone had heard of them, he couldn't remember which. So, he steeled himself to sit through it and politely ask questions as they PowerPointed their way through their range of industry expertise and global coverage and unique offering and impressive client list. Then he could get on with something that mattered.

Not a very auspicious background to a first meeting but not an uncommon one. Some individuals (or teams) will walk out of that meeting having rather drearily confirmed every expectation the potential client had of them going in; others will walk out leaving surprise, interest and even pleasure in their wake. How do we make sure we are in the latter camp?

Where does Making a great impression sit in the client development process?

In first meetings especially, unsurprisingly.

It can also be critical in those situations where you know someone but not well, and because of the nature of the meeting they have particular expectations about your likely message or behavior. Hence it has value in many selling (or persuasion) meetings too.

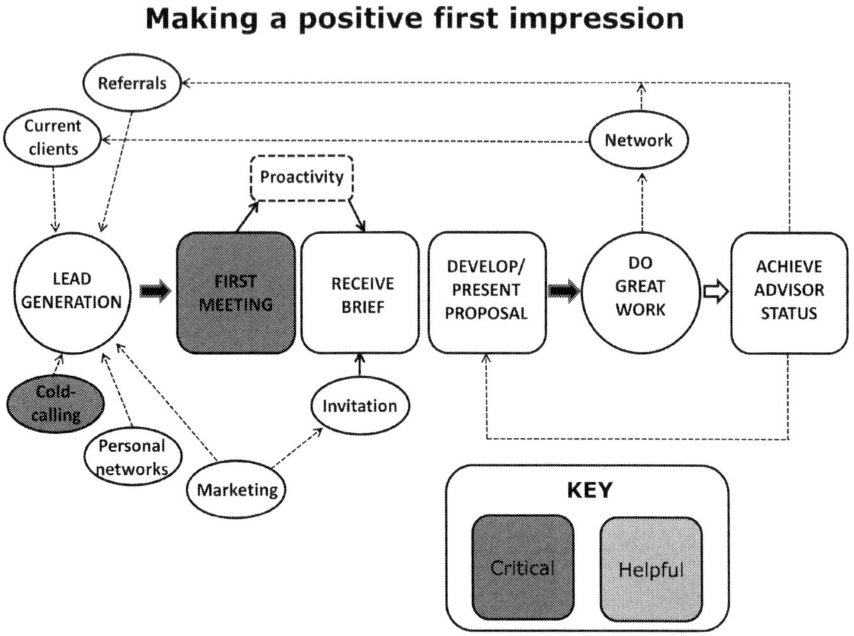

Making a positive first impression

First impressions

We all know we don't get a second chance to make a first impression. Depending on whom you believe, that first impression is fully formed within ninety seconds, sixty seconds, thirty seconds or, according to Malcolm Gladwell in his book, *Blink – The Power of Thinking Without Thinking*, two seconds.

First impressions operate mainly at the subconscious level. When we see or meet someone for the first time our subconscious is busily building up a profile of that person. This can be based on small particulars of how they look, what they are wearing, how they carry themselves, how they sound, what they say and the way they say it. If you want to test how quickly you form an impression of someone, go to a speed-dating event.

Not all first impressions last. They can be changed. But many persist for long after they were first made. The Primacy Effect is our tendency to recall best that information first presented to us. Subsequent events are then viewed through the filter of our initial experience. This effect can be compounded by Confirmation Bias, the propensity to acknowledge only that information which supports our initial perceptions.

It is like being the interviewer of a job candidate: you may be one of those interviewers who can determine the candidate's suitability within a few seconds of their entry into the room. A lot of interviewers claim they can do this. The candidate can of course change your mind in the course of the interview but they are having to work against the tide of opinion which, during the course of the discussion, might even be reinforced as the interviewer looks for data that supports his initial conclusion. How much better instead to start off with a good impression and have that working for you throughout the rest of the meeting?

In 1967 the psychologist Albert Mehrabian undertook a series of experiments in communication which led to the influential 7/38/55 'rule'. This rule is commonly held to say that when judging someone's communication, words make up 7% of the final judgement, vocal expression 38% and body language the remaining 55%. In fact, Mehrabian's studies and conclusions are considerably more limited than that: they refer specifically to judgements of attitude and feeling (like/dislike) in circumstances where there was ambiguity over the content of the overall message.[1]

Mehrabian is the first to say in his subsequent writings that these conclusions are very context- and situation-specific. We cannot expect our potential client to judge us based almost entirely on our non-verbal signals. He must put more credence on our literal words than 7%. But how much? We are unlikely ever to know. But Mehrabian's findings do confirm that our non-verbals contribute very significantly to any assessment of us, especially if the confluence of our words and non-verbal signals give rise to any doubt in the listener's mind.

Managing first impressions

Assuming both teams going competitively into a first meeting with a potential client have equivalent demonstrable hard skills and similar interpersonal and presentation skills (and leaving aside all other soft skills in this book), the successful individual or team will uniquely have delivered on some or all of the following four personal impact skills:

I. Confounding expectations
II. Showing genuine warmth
III. Revealing your personal side
IV. Using positive language

Some of these individual skills apply to the first few seconds of a meeting with someone new, some to interactions during the latter course of that meeting, either confirming the initial impressions or working to repair them, and some are applicable to all meetings.

These skills are not limited to a potential sales call. Any meeting with someone you have never met before, where you hope or expect them to do something you want, has within its dynamics an element of resistance. This is particularly true if the other party has an idea in advance of what you are likely to want. Unless you overcome this resistance your chances of success will be limited. In principle, it is as true of a job interview as it is a sales call.

I. Confounding expectations

You go into an electronics store and the salesman walks up to you. They stretch out their hand to shake yours and offer up their best winning smile. How does that make you feel? Despite the welcoming approach most people will admit to being a little uncomfortable. Some will say something, anything that gets the salesman to go away. What is going on here?

Generally, we have an expectation of how people will behave in certain circumstances – that their behavior will follow a particular pattern based on the motives we assume they have. This expectation may derive from our past experiences, our imagination or from hearsay. In this example we simply expect the salesmen to want to sell us something. When he approaches us, that first step in his behavior indicates that that is indeed what he wants and we might reasonably expect the pattern to continue.

When the salesman offers us, complete strangers, his hand and smiles, he indicates that he wants us to like him. He does this presumably with a view to making the sale easier from his perspective, even if he hasn't read those sales manuals which tell you – correctly – that, all other things being the same, people buy from people they like (Robert Cialdini's fourth Principle of Persuasion in his book *Influence – Science and Practice*[2]). The initial smile and proffering of the hand confirms our expectations of his likely pattern of behavior. As a result, we feel we understand his motives and his plan and if we are not in the mood to be sold to or be subject to a programmed set of actions and responses, we will either raise our defenses, politely ask him to leave us alone or walk out of the store.

Something very similar happens when we walk into the office of a potential client (or any buyer) for the first time. This probably won't be their first experience of such a meeting. In general they expect us to display a pattern of behavior that will encourage them to use our services. Otherwise why are we there? The client's expectations will be colored by his previous meetings of that type which, in general, will have been aimed at impressing him with the expertise and affability of the people involved, so if we walk in and act like everyone else has done, his expectations of our pattern of behavior will be confirmed. He will feel we are therefore like everyone else, our subsequent actions will be predictable and our attempts to differentiate ourselves later in the meeting will simply be that much harder. It sets up a pattern of conscious resistance on his part.

If we can break that pattern of expectation in the meeting, we open up the possibility that he will listen to us with a more open mind and that our meeting will be more positively memorable: a *pattern interrupt*, if you like. A good pattern interrupt will jar the other person's consciousness so it cannot continue with its current expectations and makes it more open to what you do or say next. It works because you do something mildly surprising, something the other person is not expecting. Here are four examples:

i) They expect you to smile on entrance. If they don't, you don't

We smile when we see someone we like. If we want someone we don't know to like us we also smile at them, expecting that their subconscious response will lead to a smile in return, and the smile will contribute to a consequent liking of us.

There is good physiological evidence for this basic human presupposition. The researchers Hatfield, Cacioppo and Rapson in their book *Emotional Contagion* showed that we are hardwired to copy another, what they called 'motor mimicry'. So, when you smile, the other person smiles. Further, however, they also describe a transfer of feelings that can take place, or emotional contagion. So, if you are happy and then smile, the other person smiles back and becomes happy.[3] This sequence is understood by most of us at a very basic level.

However, if we sense that the other person's smile is constructed precisely with that aim in mind, to manipulate our feelings toward them positively, as in the case of the insincere store salesman above, our reaction tends to be more negative.

Our potential client expects us to smile as we walk in. Nearly everyone does. Our intention, however, is to confound his expectations. If our potential client therefore does not smile at us on entry, as is often the case, neither do we. So, before the meeting has properly started, we have a pattern interrupt. (We also have the beginnings of body matching.)

That does not mean we are stern and grim-faced. Far from it. We keep an open, friendly appearance. We simply don't smile as we walk in and as the introductions are made. We don't keep this up for long though. The pattern interrupt has already been achieved. Where I have done this I always then look for an opportunity to smile my warmest smile as soon as I can afterwards, ideally within thirty seconds.

Of course, if your potential client does indeed greet you with a warm and genuine smile as you walk in, you smile your best smile back. You immediately have the beginnings of a good rapport.

ii) They don't expect you to be open about your objectives. If you can, do

Some well-established services firms still operate from the mindset that clients buy from them. They are like stallholders in a market believing that all they have to do is display their wares and customers will beat a path to them. To some extent they have some basis for this belief. After all, they have probably been around a long time and no doubt have an impressive client list. Operating from this mindset can also create an atmosphere of comfortable equivalence between the services firm and their potential client, in which the services firm never feels like a supplicant. Of course, both sides know what the game is – selling – it is just that many people in professional services are uncomfortable being explicit about it.

Ultimately, your objective in most cases is for that potential client to become a client. So, why not tell them that? "Jack, we are here because we really want to work for you [or] We really want you to become a client of ours." If the reasons that follow are specific to that client, and are at least interesting if not compelling, you have a very attentive audience for the rest of the meeting. You will have demonstrated that you are straightforward, open and honest, and your expression of the objective has made what follows very much more personal. By opening yourself up to possible rejection you have displayed your vulnerability. Two minutes into the meeting and you have already marked yourself out as different. You also have a potential client who has experienced something he was not expecting and as a result feels more open to what comes next.

iii) They expect you to take. If you can, give something

It is rare for a potential client to get much out of a first meeting. He may learn about a particular firm, its history and capabilities, and get a sense of its people. But all too often the first meeting takes from the potential client: time and information. Time spent meeting potential new clients for the services firm is time well spent. But for the client, depending on what else is occurring in his or her universe at that moment, there may be big opportunity costs associated.

A common strategy of many services firms in first meetings is to ask the potential client lots of questions about the business and their plans for it. The purpose is obvious: at minimum, to learn more about the company to feed into future approaches; at best, to discover some latent need which that services firm is perfectly positioned to help address. To the host of the meeting it can often feel as if the really interesting information flow is all one way.

The best response is to give something useful in the meeting, something the potential client doesn't expect to get. This can be a piece of work or some information relevant to what has been discussed. Or an insight into his business or industry that he wasn't aware of. Or it can be a document to follow after the meeting. It could be an introduction to someone the potential client would like to meet. Or an introduction for one of his people. Or an invitation to something. Whatever it is it has to be relevant and desirable. Failing all that, finish the meeting a few minutes early if you can and give him some of his time back.

The potential client is going into this introductory meeting expecting to learn something about this services firm that might or might not be useful to know in the future. He knows it will take some of his precious time and he expects that he will be asked lots of questions about his business. He doesn't expect to get anything immediately useful out of it. If he does, he will feel more positive about that expenditure of his time, more positive about the people he spent it with and more open to what they do next.

iv) Take control

It is normal in the first few minutes of a meeting to make small talk. This is simply good manners and serves the purpose of giving people the chance to know each other a little better before settling down to the purpose at hand. In general, it is the host of the meeting who decides when the social chit-chat ceases and it is time to get down to business. There is an understandable desire on the part of most supplicants to let the chit-chat continue for as long as possible because it feeds the sense of human beings bonding and, frankly, it is easier for most of us than having to persuade someone of something. Usually the client expects to be the one to end that part of the meeting and move on.

A pattern interrupt here would be to take the lead oneself in deciding when to end the preliminaries and move on to the agenda. One could preface such an intrusion with something like, "Jack, we know you must be very busy and we are sensitive to time commitments so if it is okay with you we would like to propose an agenda for this meeting." Doing this can feel a little scary at times. We are foregoing the pleasant opportunity to continue chatting without pressure and accelerating the moment when we face potential challenge and rejection. We also have to find a way of doing so which does not sound rude. But after having allowed a decent interval for social pleasantries, the potential client's reaction is invariably one of mild, sometimes pleasant, surprise. They can have the sense that these people are respectful of his time, businesslike and willing to show some leadership.

The one caveat here is if your potential client is female. Women bond through communication, in general, whereas men bond more by doing things with other men. Communication for the two sexes can serve different purposes. Deborah Tannen, in her book *You Just Don't Understand*, describes it thus: "For most women, the language of conversation is primarily the language of rapport: a way of establishing connections and negotiating relationships... For most men, talk is primarily a means to preserve independence and negotiate and maintain status in a hierarchical social order."[4] So, a precipitous ending of a nicely developing chat could badly damage the rapport with a female client. So, in these situations, be very attuned to how the discussion is going before deciding whether to take the lead, or allow your female listener to signal when it is time to get down to business.

II. Show genuine warmth

i) Like the other person

You have two brief meetings scheduled. The first is with a colleague who you know likes you a lot but the issue they wish to discuss is a difficult one. Shortly after, you have your second meeting with a different colleague who enters your office. You are aware that this person dislikes you, though the subject matter is straightforward. Imagining yourself anticipating these meetings, which would you most likely look forward to? Looking back on them, which if either of them are you likely to have enjoyed?

Most people will say they looked forward to and enjoyed most the first meeting with the colleague who likes them, despite the difficult subject matter. We like being with people who like us. How do we know they like us? If the relationship is longstanding there has probably been lots of evidence based on a number of shared happy moments. But if you have just met for the first time, how can you tell?

You could smile to convey that you like them. But if your smile lacks any genuine warmth, conveying no emotion, the other person will sense it. There is the saying: 'They smiled with their mouth but not with their eyes.' There is a physiological basis for this. In his book, *Babywatching*, the anthropologist Desmond Morris describes how babies react to their mother's presence by further dilating the already large pupils in their eyes; the mother responds with an increase in warm, emotional attachment. This is true in adults too. When we see something we like, or are with someone we like, the pupils of our eyes dilate. The other person sees this, or senses it subconsciously, and feels good basking in the warmth of our obvious appreciation.[5]

So, we need to like someone for our smile to be genuine. How can we do that if we have never met them before? If you share the philosophy of the Dalai Lama, who achieves happiness through the practice of compassion to all, then you will probably express warmth in equal measure to all you meet. If your intellectual and emotional makeup, however, isn't quite there yet, then simply like them.

If you cannot just like someone as the result of an act of will, an effective way is to imagine the person you are about to meet is your best friend. Your best friend is the person on the other side of that door. Hold that feeling as you walk in and when you smile you will show genuine warmth in your eyes.

Weirdly, although the 'best friend strategy' does not survive long after initial contact with your client (that is, you can't hold the mental deceit in place for long, given the evidence of your eyes), you will find, surprisingly perhaps, that you do indeed tend to like them. The mind can work in surprising ways. We use a falsehood (we are going to meet our best friend) to convey a genuine feeling (liking), and as a result our feeling becomes unfeigned.

The knock-on of this halo effect, that you do indeed feel actual liking toward the other person, promotes your interest in them. This positive interest is reflected in myriad unconscious ways through your physiology, ways that are largely impossible to control consciously. The other person will sense this warmth of interest and respond positively. As Dale Carnegie wrote in *How to Win Friends and Influence People*, 'You can make more friends in two months by becoming interested in other people than you can in two years trying to get other people interested in you.'[6] In liking someone, your interest in them as a person is greater, your physiology changes subtly to reflect this and they feel comfortably drawn to you in response.

If, however, you are unable to smile with genuine warmth then you risk coming across as the electronics salesman above. In which case make your smile a polite one, necessary and good-mannered, but unencumbered with false promise.

ii) Care, if you can

I once had a client who was in a very difficult situation: a declining, highly competitive market facing the onset of cheaper foreign imports. Worse, the senior management team had their houses invested in the business. I remember thinking how bad I felt for the company and its leadership when I first met them.

We won the work and, as I tended to do, halfway into the project I asked my project manager to set up a chat with our CEO client to get feedback on why they hired us (I found I got better answers if someone else senior from our team asked, without my presence, possibly due to my personal role in the original decision to hire). The feedback said, "You cared more." That was it. I remember being astonished, for two reasons. First, at no point in the process had I expressed my thoughts by saying in some Clintonesque way, "I feel your pain" or anything similar. In fact, throughout, I thought I was my normal, disassociated professional self. Now of course I understand that how you feel shows, in hundreds of tiny verbal and non-verbal signals. But at the time I thought, *How could they tell?*

Second, and more importantly, I was surprised to find out that 'caring' was a decision criterion. On its own it offers no promise of a tangible solution or comfortable process. Yet, if Credibility and a Solution with Value are there, and at least comparable with the alternative offers, then caring becomes a dimension of Liking: it offers the realistic hope, at least, that the carer will feel more motivated to deliver an excellent job and in the process share real feelings of empathy with the client, making them easier to work with. In a world where caring, sadly, can sometimes feel like a scarce commodity, the one who does, stands out.

III. Revealing your personal side

It was once rather helpfully pointed out to me that I am made up of many parts. There is that part of me that is a friend, another that is a husband, another a boss, another a solver of problems, and so on. We bring out that part of us which is relevant to the relationship and the goals we have for that interaction.

We can simplify these many parts by grouping them into two, our *position* and our *person*. Our position is that part of us which relates to our responsibilities and authority, our place in the relevant hierarchy, how we behave given the expectations we set ourselves and the expectations others hold of us. It is largely about achieving results in the relevant context. We can have several positions, one at work which is our professional position, one at home where we may be raising a family and possibly elsewhere too, such as running the scout club or being part of a tennis team. All of these positions have expectations and responsibilities attached to them and some of them can have authority too.

Our person, on the other hand, is that part of us which is everything else: our sense of identity, what makes us happy and sad, our hopes and fears, our loves and wants. Whereas we can have several positions, most of us thankfully have only one person. In each of our positions we always have access to our person and we can choose from which we want to operate. This is most notable at home where, if we have children, we strive to maintain a seemly balance between the two.

At work, however, our position tends to predominate for obvious reasons and we sometimes struggle to know how far to integrate our person into our professional role. In Peter Weir's movie, *Master and Commander*, Russell Crowe as Captain Jack Aubrey R.N. gives a magisterial example of balancing his person and his position as he artfully navigates between his relationships and his duty.

When we present ourselves to a potential client we are usually operating from our position. They see us firstly as part of company X, with whatever brand associations that brings; then as a title or role within that company, which says something about our responsibility and authority, as well as our capabilities and likely intentions; and then as a name. We generally do likewise, seeing ourselves in a role with certain objectives and capabilities and our client as holding a certain position with ensuing needs; our goal is to enable a satisfactory confluence of the two.

Not surprisingly, therefore, early meetings have a high digital content as our potential client talks about his or his company's needs and we talk about our fitting competences. In such interactions our potential buyer expects us to operate from our position. It is entirely normal.

If, however, we can find an opportunity to operate from our person, we can transform how the other person feels about us, leaving them saying to themselves, "This person is not just a self-interested corporate representative, they are a human being, just like me." It promotes empathy.

There are two main ways of doing this. The first is to introduce yourself with a personal story, rather than a list of positional achievements. This is a typical introduction: "I'm John. I've been with ZZZ and Co for five years and I'm responsible for X. Before that I worked for A, B and C. My particular expertise is Y."

While I am sure this is factually correct and no doubt of great interest and pride to the speaker, it can come across to the listener as rather two-dimensional. If a number of people make similar positional introductions it can become downright boring. At minimum, it will be little different from every other services company's team presenting themselves to a new potential client for the first time.

Compare that approach with the following, paraphrased from the real answer when I asked an individual why he worked for his company, a firm of turnaround specialists: "Well, I used to run a large insolvency practice. I did that for many years. After a while I just got sick of having to extract the bits of failed companies, one after another. I wanted to get in before things got so bad and make a contribution that saved the companies and also helped the people who worked for them and the communities they sat in. That's why I joined this firm."

Listening, I felt the drama, the problem and the solution, the personal conviction. I also inferred the level of personal competence required. He could have talked about the well-known turnarounds he had worked on, the two books he had written and his leadership position on the industry body. But he didn't. He just told his story as he felt it. In telling his story he revealed a lot about himself and, by inference, the company he worked for. As a result he didn't need to get into any specifics. And if the client wished to know any more, the opportunity was there to ask. This approach is more revealing and much more engaging. The key is that it is very personal and told as a simple story.

The second way to operate from our person as opposed to our position is to reveal a personal vulnerability. In other words, be *totally honest* about a relevant fear or worry regarding the meeting in general or with respect to a particular point that arose in conversation. Here are some examples that I have heard others say or found myself saying:

> "I have been really looking forward to meeting you and have to say that I am actually quite nervous."
> "This is one of the most important meetings for us this year."
> "We have the capability to do that, though I have to say I am a little anxious at the prospect."
> "I was always very apprehensive about meeting..."
> "Before we started that exercise I have to tell you I was outright scared."
> "The reason I am pausing before answering is because I feel a little uncomfortable..."

To do this with integrity means you have to be honest. Not only is that arguably a 'good thing' in itself but your observation will inevitably invite a request for clarification. If you remain true to your feelings your answer will always be close to hand.

You must also be judicious in your revelations. It is a meeting with a potential client after all, not a tree-hugging session: unrestrained disclosures will only make you look unprofessional and the other person feel uncomfortable. Finally, it needs to be supportive of the positive impression you wish to make, so to appear self-pitying or whining is best avoided.

Done once in a meeting (and no more than twice), at an appropriate juncture and with genuine openness, it can be very powerful. There are three reasons for this. First, few people are brave enough to do it, so you will stand out. Second, it *confirms* your honesty: to be so candid about something personal signifies your veracity in general, that there is nothing important you will hide. Third, it builds a stronger emotional connection between the two of you: the listener subconsciously empathizes, and experiences feeling *safe* with you since you are willing to expose your vulnerability without requiring anything of them in return.

Operating from your person in this selective way demonstrates that you are indeed human. And while you can interact comfortably with the other person from your position and respect their positional requirements, you acknowledge with your sharing that they are a human being too.

iv) Use positive language

If I say to you, "Don't think of a pink donkey!", what are you thinking of? What picture are you holding in your mind? If you are like most people you will have thought of a pink donkey. Why is that, when I asked you not to?

When we are asked not to do or think of something, our mind first processes the positive verb or action statement ("think of the pink donkey") and then the negative action we must apply to it. So, the brain thinks of the pink donkey and then considers not thinking about it. Unfortunately, the process of thinking about the pink donkey in the first place leaves an impression on the subconscious that can stay there for a long time.

The effect of this can be even more unfortunate when said to children. "Jack, don't hit your sister!" Little Jack's mind first processes "hit your sister", then "don't". He then hits his sister again because it was the first thing in his mind and the brain responds most quickly to action words. Most of us who are parents have experienced this scenario or ones very similar to it.

In a meeting with clients the consequences may be less physically damaging though no less serious. If we use negative commands or statements we ensure our listener will process that which we would rather they didn't. For example, "Don't worry about how hard this will be." The listener will process "worry about how hard this will be" first, then the negative "don't". In the same way you are still holding in your mind, subconsciously if not consciously, the picture of the pink donkey, the listener will hold in his mind "how hard this will be" for some time after the statement is made. Possibly for days. Essentially, we are employing a language pattern that is used in hypnosis to plant an idea into someone's subconscious, though most of us are unaware of what we are doing and the possibly counter-productive consequences of doing so.

Here are some other examples:

"You shouldn't <u>concern yourself about the cost.</u>"
"You won't have to <u>ask whether we will do a good job.</u>"

"Don't look at this as a complicated process."
"You won't regret this!"

We have to process action words or verbs, and the resulting electro-chemical changes in our brains are left as an imprint. They can contribute to the sort of subconscious feeling we can have after a social interaction where we say something like, "Yes, good to meet them but there was something about it that didn't feel right." Of course, that gut feeling is going to be influenced by everything else that happened in the social interaction and so the one unnerving imprint we are talking about may well be subsumed into an aura of good feelings from other sources. But if the rest of the meeting is neutral in this regard or there are several other instances of negative commands or statements, you may well leave your client with a nagging feeling of uncertainty about you – the negative feelings you aroused – which they can't quite put their finger on.

The solution is to use language positively. Say what you want the other person to think. The following are the five examples from above with an alternative way of saying the same thing.

"Don't worry about how hard this will be."
"This will be easier than you think."

"You shouldn't concern yourself about the cost."
"This will be better value than you can imagine."

"You won't have to ask whether we will do a good job."
"Rest assured we will do a good job."

"Don't look at this as a complicated process."
"The process is more straightforward than it appears."

"You won't regret this!"
"You will look back and be delighted you made this decision."

Using language positively also has a positive subliminal effect – it contributes to a feeling that the other person is straightforward, upbeat and has a can-do attitude. This feeling persists even if one has doubts about the truth of what is being said!

If you must use negatives in this way as part of your speech, then use them to set up positive thoughts or ideas. So, for example:

"Don't/you aren't going to...

Recommend us/ Buy this proposal/ Set up the next meeting/ Trust me/ See this as the way forward

... before/until/while..."

Here, the mind processes the positive action statement, 'Recommend us', for example, before processing the negative rider. The idea or thought is implanted in the mind and may, subject of course to how the rest of the meeting goes, lead to a residual feeling later on. This a common language pattern used by people who know what they are doing with hypnosis and the mere smell of that association makes me uncomfortable because it smacks of manipulation. Yet we frequently use the negative expression of this language pattern in our everyday speech without thinking about it. We do so regardless of whether it is used by hypnotists or not. It is simply the way language works. Being aware of this means we can choose to take control, structure our language positively and leave only positive associations and ideas behind us, not negative ones.

Making a Great Impression and the Personal Impact Model

The positive impression you create will support your ability to be:

- An Influencer because it facilitates your Communication skills.
- A Persuader because it promotes your truthfulness and honesty, that you are Reliable.
- A Seller because of the integrity and humanity you display, all components of Liking.

If in the first meeting your interlocutor arrives with a set of strong expectations about you or what you are likely to want or do, the steps you can take here will help you quickly confound these expectations and secure Respect.

Summary

This chapter is all about first meetings with someone new. This someone is important to you and your success professionally. That person could be a new boss, a new head of department or even someone looking to hire you or take you on to their team. In all these cases the positive first impression you make will advance your case throughout that meeting and probably subsequent ones too.

The biggest test of first impressions is when you walk in to meet with someone you wish ultimately to have as a client of yours. In such instances not only do you have to make a good impression, it has to be as good as or better than the impressions made by anyone competing with you.

Chapter 5 Takeaways

- First impressions matter:
  - they can form within a few seconds and evolve during the meeting;
  - they can be difficult to change
- You take control of the first impressions you make by Confounding expectations, Showing genuine warmth, Revealing your personal side and using Positive language.

Chapter notes

1. Mehrabian, Albert. Nonverbal Communication. New Brunswick, N.J.: Aldine Transaction, 2008. pp104-9.
2. Cialdini, Robert B. Influence. Boston: Allyn and Bacon, 2001. Ch.5.
3. Hatfield, Elaine and Cacioppo, John T. and Rapson, Richard L. Emotional Contagion. Cambridge: Cambridge University Press, 1994. pp156-8.
4. Tannen, Deborah. You Just Don't Understand. London: Virago, 1991. p77.
5. Morris, Desmond. Babywatching. London: Jonathan Cape, 1999. pp29-30.
6. Carnegie, Dale. How to Win Friends and Influence People. N.Y.: Simon & Schuster Inc., 1982. p54.

6. Listening with Both Ears

Improve the content and quality of what you hear

The introductory meeting had started well. They had presented their credentials efficiently and the client had asked some questions, helpfully allowing the team to elaborate on some of their strengths.

The partner in charge, Dan, waiting for the right moment, then asked, "Jack, we've shared quite a bit of information about us. Can you let us know a bit about the issues you face? What's on your mind?" "Sure," Jack replied. "Let me bring you up to speed with where we are," he added. The conversation then developed as follows:

Jack: "Well, as you probably have heard, we've been growing quite fast."

Dan: "Yup. I think the whole market has noticed how well you have been doing."

Jack: "Yes, we have acquired a number of good-looking companies."

Dan: "Four, right? How's that going?"

Jack: "Pretty well. It's always a challenge when you bring in new companies. You know, there are issues of people, systems, culture that need to be sorted out."

Dan: "Uh huh. We've had quite a lot of experience helping clients with that. I know what you mean. The key thing to us is that whatever you do it needs to be done quickly."

Jack: "Yes, I'm sure. The market is always looking to see the benefits come through fast."

Dan: "Where do you hope to get the biggest benefits from?"

Jack: "There are a number of areas. We've got to get them all singing from the same hymn sheet. We've got to harmonize HR, get financial controls in place and find out what's going on in operations. It's all about systems," he said firmly.

Dan: "Mm," taking rapid notes

Jack: "So, we have our hands full at the moment." Jack shifted slightly to a more comfortable position.

Dan: "Better than not having enough to do!" he said with a smile. "You know, as you were talking I was thinking. We have a team in-house with lots of expertise in financial controls. Maybe they can be of help. Might be a good idea to have them talk to your guys?"

Jack: "Possibly, yes."

Dan: "This is helpful. So, what else is keeping you awake at night?"

Listening

It is hard to be a good listener. For us men especially. We don't have generations of experience bonding with others of our sex through communication, being empathetic. We men like to bond by doing things together. But even for women, who are better equipped than men for good listening, it can be hard.

For a start, our attention span when we are relaxed, for both men and women, is quite short, measured in seconds rather than minutes according to some. Then we start thinking about something else. Even where we resist that temptation to let our minds wander off, if someone is talking to us at an average speed of 130 words a minute, we can listen at a rate of four times faster than that, and think at a rate about ten times faster than that. No wonder our minds want to go somewhere else. Just listening forces our minds to operate in slow motion.

Additionally, we all have a bunch of bad habits, programmed in. We could list these under a variety of headings but here are mine:

- First is pseudo-listening, or not really listening at all. When someone talks to me while I am watching a game of rugby on television that is what I am doing. I might make noises of understanding, I might even try and listen, but not much gets in.
- Second is selective listening, where we only hear that which we want to hear or which interests us. W.C. Fields' response to, "We lived for weeks on nothing but food and water" was "How terrible!" This reflects selective listening.
- Third is not paying enough attention. What is the answer to the following question? Mary's father had five daughters, Nana, Nenny, Nini, Nona

and... What is the name of the fifth daughter? Usually we are not paying attention, simply because we are thinking about something more interesting, or half-listening until we hear something that really grabs our attention. Most people, including me, answer this question, for obvious reasons, with a name beginning with 'N'.

- Fourth is listening to respond or evaluate. We men are especially good at this because of our natural inclination to want to fix things.[2] But both sexes can be at fault because we all tend to listen autobiographically. As Steven Covey puts it in his book, *The 7 Habits of Highly Effective People*, 'Most people do not listen with the intent to understand; they listen with the intent to reply. They're either speaking or preparing to speak. They're filtering everything through their own paradigms, reading their own autobiography into other people's lives.'[3] When selling, we are under further pressure to demonstrate how much value we can add or how clever we are. So, our inclination to listen in order to evaluate, judge or respond in these situations is all the greater.
- Fifth is hearing only what you expect to hear. We are mentally lazy. Not always. But it is hard work operating in top gear all the time and we need to know when to turn it on. For example, answer the following: "You are a participant in a race and overtake the second person. What position are you in?"[4] You might be surprised at how many people get the answer wrong. Answering this simple question requires you to think a little. Perhaps slightly more than you have been thinking as you read most of the other sentences in this book. That is because it is a question which invites you to think. If you were to apply the same level of effort to every sentence you read, you would quickly tire. It's hard to use your System 2 all the time.
- Finally, there is listening to the words, not the emotions. "How are you?" he asked. "I'm okay," she replied. "Good," he said. What people say and how they feel about what they are saying can be completely different. If we listen to just the words and not the feelings or emotions behind them we can be misled about the other person's state of mind. This happens to me a lot at home.

What most of us do, most of the time, is hear but not properly *listen*. Hearing is passive. It is relatively easy (unless I am watching the game on television). It requires almost no effort. Most of the time it provides just enough information to give us what we think we need. But it doesn't give us everything and can leave us misinformed, bereft of a full appreciation. The model of listening proposed here, Insightful Listening, can give us so much more.

Where does Insightful Listening sit in the client development process?

Insightful Listening is a skill that supports success at each stage of the process.

It is critical in first meetings and where a brief is being discussed.

In the course of working with the client, it assists you in keeping the process smooth and navigating potential issues. Likewise, as a Trusted Advisor (or an account manager with Status), it can help you to deepen the relationship while discovering opportunities for you and your client to collaborate on.

The key benefits of Insightful Listening in a professional context are:

First, and most obviously, messages and information are understood accurately, intellectually and emotionally. There is sufficient clarity to allow you to focus discussion where it is of most value. It increases the chance that what you do next will be productive. It can save you time and money.

Second, it can make the other person *feel* valued and respected. Listening

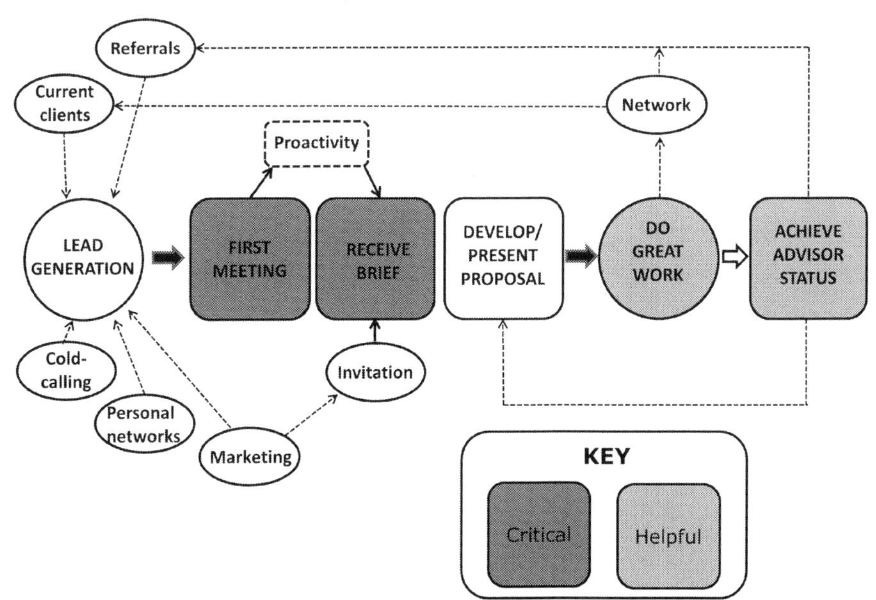

fully to what we are saying is not something we experience every day. Not many people make the effort to understand completely what we mean and feel when we are talking about something. When they do they are conferring a degree of respect to us because it takes some effort on their part. This goes beyond saying, "I value and respect you." Those are just words. But if you can act in a way that communicates that you value and respect the other person, they will experience that feeling.

Third, it can help build the connected relationship. Good listeners are rare. They make us feel good and we tend to like them more. If we feel that their attentive listening helps us to talk about something on our minds, it can actually help us. At minimum, it shows they care. We like people who help us and who care about us.

The principles of good listening

Much of what is understood, and certainly taught, about listening skills today derives from the work of the eminent American psychotherapist Carl Rogers. He found that by listening deeply to the meanings and underlying emotions of a patient's communication he could help them arrive at profound changes in their lives. He called this process 'Active listening'.[5] At its heart was a belief in the efficacy of grasping what the other person was saying and feeling, *from their perspective*: being fully empathetic. Then, and as important, conveying back to them that we clearly understood them.

For Rogers, there were a number of key steps in this approach. First was the imperative that we listen for total meaning. That is more than just the content, it is also the underlying attitudes and feelings. Second was the importance for the listener of responding to the feelings, which were often more important than the content. Third, the need to note all the non-verbal cues from the voice and body language. Finally, the requirement to test that the listener understood the world as the speaker saw it by paraphrasing the speaker's message in the listener's own words.

This sounds easy. It isn't. Rogers describes it as "understanding *with* a person, not *about* her".[6] He himself says it takes much practice. There are a number of challenges for the listener. First is the requirement to *want* to understand, a sincerity and commitment to seeing the world from the other's perspective without which no amount of technique will work. Second is our inbuilt, and in many cases trained, propensity to judge and evaluate someone's statement. Third, especially difficult for a therapist perhaps, but with some resonance for a corporate advisor too, is that we risk being changed ourselves. If we truly come to see the world as the other person experiences it, intellectually and emotionally, we hazard our own beliefs; at minimum, it can feel threatening to us.

When it is successful, good listening promotes good communication, which can be therapeutic. As Rogers describes it: "When I have been listened to and when I have been heard, I am able to re-perceive my world in a new way and to go on. It is astonishing how elements that seem insoluble become soluble when someone listens, how confusions that seem irremediable turn into relatively clear flowing streams when one is heard. I have deeply appreciated the times that I have experienced this sensitive, empathic, concentrated listening."[6]

The theory and practice

There are limits to the applicability of a therapist's model of communication in the world of business. For a start, our goal is not to solve some personal issue, it is to add value or to move something on. We are trained to be evaluative and a lot of the value we can add derives from this ability. When we go into a first meeting with a potential business partner our goal is to win Respect and Credibility and to learn as much as we can that helps us find opportunities to move the conversation forward or add value. Our aim is not to fix their psychological problems.

Nor are we necessarily equipped with the behavioral and emotional flexibility that good therapists require to be truly empathetic. 'Empathy' means 'the ability to understand and share the feelings of another'. I have become better at understanding the feelings of people around me, largely by realizing their feelings matter and then asking the direct question, "How do you feel about that?" But it is still largely beyond me to always *share* those feelings.

Thankfully, perhaps, it is not necessary in my experience. As long as we are able to recognize the feelings of the other and understand how they arise, we are in a position to respond, to be respectful of those feelings and to potentially help. I don't have to feel what you feel in order to appreciate what your feelings are. It might well help but it is not a requirement.

There is much we can take from the psychotherapist and counsellor models of listening. They provide insights and structures that can help us overcome our mostly bad listening habits. They can lead us to a better understanding of our colleagues and our business partners and the issues they may need help with. And in the process they can help us to build better connected relationships.

The Insightful Listening Model

Insightful Listening has as its objective to fully grasp how someone thinks and feels about the relevant issues under discussion. 'Insightful' means 'having or showing a deep understanding; perceptive'. Achieving it means that the listener comes away with as full an appreciation of the situation as possible, in the time available. The speaker feels that they have been heard and their position is fully understood.

Insightful Listening requires us to ask, "How does this person see the situation for themselves?" not "What can I do for this person?". When you fully grasp how they think and feel about the issues under discussion you can then ask yourself, "Now, how best can I help them?"

The four requirements of Insightful Listening are: i) Adopting an attitude of acceptance; ii) Being in a rapport; iii) Asking good questions; and iv) Reflecting understanding.

i) Adopting an attitude of acceptance

Adopting an attitude of acceptance means we respect the other person's thoughts and feelings for what they are, theirs. We already know that, unless they have exactly the same Representation system as us, they will process information differently. Additionally, their evaluation of a situation may be very different to how we might evaluate it. Their feelings about matters will also be unique to them, colored by how the situation makes them feel validated, affirmed or appreciated. Their feelings will almost certainly be different from our feelings, from how we imagine their feelings to be and from how we imagine we might feel were we in their shoes.

Insightful Listening requires us to let go of our natural inclination to listen autobiographically, to evaluate what we hear through the prism of our own beliefs, to 'add value' or evaluate information for the opportunities it can present to us. Intruding into the flow of information too early with our perspectives, judgements or analyses will simply hinder the quality of information we receive.

Adopting an attitude of acceptance has two main benefits. First, it increases the chance that we will hear everything that is said. We won't miss content or feelings because what we hear is less likely to be filtered by the prism of our own experiences.

Second, the other person will feel moved to talk with us. We are giving him the space to share with us what he wants. He will feel our respect for his words and for him. He will feel more comfortable sharing with us. As the American psychiatrist Karl Menninger put it, "Listening is a magnetic and strange thing. The friends who listen to us are the ones we move toward, and we want to sit in their radius."

ii) Being in rapport

Physiological rapport is essential to good listening. The sense of harmony created between two people makes the speaker more inclined to talk and the listener more inclined to listen. It helps the listener to sense, to intuit what might be felt behind the words.

When listening, the physiology of rapport may have to be adapted to accommodate the overriding requirement of encouraging the speaker. If you have already achieved rapport earlier in the meeting then these adaptations should be easy and comfortable.

Adopt as open a posture as possible, especially with the arms. This communicates that you are receptive. So, if the client is sitting with arms folded as they talk, keep your arms by your sides. Cross-match by perhaps crossing your legs instead. Or hold your hands together on your lap or on the table.

Second, remain as still as you can, minimizing the danger of doing something that distracts the speaker. So, if the other person is tapping their pencil on the desk or gesticulating a lot as they talk, ignore it. If you can match their breathing instead – easier to do when listening because you simply breathe out as they talk and in when they pause – you will find you maintain rapport despite the more obvious physiological mismatch.

Third, maintain eye contact. This communicates you are being attentive, that what they are saying is important to you. It means that you do not spend a lot of time writing notes. Occasional scribbles are fine but keep them short. If you are one of those people who likes to have lots of notes and you have colleagues with you, let one of them take the role of recorder. Your job is to maintain rapport and listen. If you fear you will forget something important, the techniques in 'Reflecting understanding', below, will help.

Make low-key gestures showing your involvement and interest. Nodding gently and smiling occasionally, as appropriate, communicates that this is a two-way engagement. That you are following what is being said. That you are interested. That you want to hear more.

iii) Asking good questions

Good questions in the Insightful Listening Model are those questions which propel the conversation forward in ways that the client feels encouraged to continue. Because good questions prompt and shape the kind of information we listen to, and have the capacity to affect how the other person feels about us as we listen to them, they are the twin to listening skills.

Types of questions

The most useful kinds of questions to promote a speaker-led flow of communication are open ones. "What's on your mind?', as Dan in the opening story asked. They invite the other person to start where they want, to focus the communication on what matters to them. Open questions can lead the conversation into a new area, such as, "Can you talk more about the people issues you mentioned?' but they still leave the speaker in control of what they wish to say.

Probing questions, such as, "Can you be more specific about the people issues?', and closed questions which invite a yes/no or factual response, have their place but should be used sparingly. If asked, they should be quickly followed by another open question or a lead back to something the speaker had felt was important, "You were talking about the systems?"

Leading or hypothetical questions, such as, "Wouldn't it have been better to...?", are best avoided since they introduce the listener's view of the world into the conversation and can be seen as a misplaced attempt to demonstrate Expertise by someone not in full possession of all the facts. If risked, it should be when the discussion has gone well and the listener is reasonably confident of a favorable answer.

The power of questions

Good questions have the ability to propel a conversation in a constructive, informative way, helping the other person to discuss matters in ways he is most happy with. But they are more than this. Questions also have a unique power. Let me ask you, reader, a question. How do you rate this book so far, on a scale of one to ten? Think about it. Now write the answer down. What is your reason for the number you wrote down?

When you have finished reading this book I guarantee you will remember that question. Possibly you will remember it for some time afterwards. If you really thought about your answer and had to delve into the pictures, sounds and feelings you hold inside to answer it, you will remember it for longer.

Now, another question: "What was the statement you read just before the question I asked you?" **Avoid looking.** Hardly anyone will be able to answer that question. The answer in fact is: '*Questions also have a unique power.*' The simple fact is that people remember questions more than they remember statements.

Why do people remember questions much better than they remember statements? A statement is, in general, received passively, processed rapidly by the intellect and then passed over. (The exception of course is if the statement is surprising or controversial.) A question by contrast requires a response. Many times, that response will involve accessing a mix of pictures, sounds and feelings as the neurotransmitters in our brain fire-off and electro-chemicals swirl around, leaving a slightly altered emotional state. Even if that is not exactly the whole reason, and no-one I am aware of knows for sure, the fact remains that questions which require us accessing some inner part of ourselves to answer, we remember. And we remember who asked them, the circumstances, and the feelings they aroused in us too.

A question which can be answered entirely digitally, however, without thought, might leave no impression. So, asking, "What is your planned turnover next year?", might generate an answer but little memory of the question. But a question requiring us to process an answer internally, to think about it, or to access our pictures, sounds and feelings, stays in our memory much longer than statements which don't. So, in addition to providing helpful information, 'good' questions make the recipient *think*. They will remember those questions and the fact that you, in asking them, made them think.

The second, related power of questions is that they have the ability to leave the respondent feeling good, bad or indifferent. If a question requires accessing some inner part of ourselves to answer and taps a particular emotional response, then that is how we will feel when we answer it. So, if the answer to the question, "What is your planned turnover next year?", prompted feelings of,'I feel terrible about the numbers' or 'I feel great we are doing so well', the question will be remembered *with* the associated feelings.

If we were to know in advance which emotional responses would be tapped, we could ask only questions that left people feeling good or, at worst, indifferent. We certainly would not want to ask lots of questions that left people feeling bad. They would remember the questions, the feelings they promoted and of course associate those feelings with us.

Of course, we cannot always know, or guess correctly, in advance how a particular question will make someone feel. But we can think about it. We can be sensitive to it. We can make sure our good questions are thoughtful, relevant, respectful and move the conversation forward in a productive way which leaves the client feeling good.

Avoiding two words – Why and But

In asking our questions, we avoid the use of 'Why'. Why? Because when we ask someone to explain or tell us something with this interrogative adverb they can feel defensive, on the back foot or a requirement to justify. None of these are positive feelings. They make us feel bad. A whole meeting full of questions led by 'Why' can contribute to the questioner being associated with a lot of unhelpful negativity. If Steven Covey is right when he talks about leaving a legacy, in *The 7 Habits of Highly Effective People*, that we choose to spend time with the people who make us feel good, then we can be sure that our colleagues and potential clients are unlikely to want to work with us if we make them feel bad, even if they can't explain why.

Instead we ask process questions, such as "What led...?" or we ask "How did...?" So, "What led you to this decision?" rather than "Why did you make this decision?" "What led...?" is a process question and promotes a process, not a justificatory answer. The same is true for 'How'. The answer tends to be formed as a series of process steps, "first this, then that..." because the question leads the brain to think about what came first, then second, and so on.

The word 'But' is similar to 'Why' in that it usually sets up a direct question or a statement advancing a different point of view, inviting a justificatory response: "I hear what you are saying but what about...?" The problem with its use is that it disempowers that part of the sentence that precedes it. It is as if you had never said the words, "I hear what you are saying..." The listener often stops listening to what you say as soon as they hear the word 'But'; they are instead concentrating on framing their response.

When someone hears the word 'But' they can feel on the back foot, forced to defend their earlier statement. If someone does this rather too often in a meeting it can feel to their interlocutor as if they have few redeeming qualities at all. Rapport is lost. Instead, if you want to acknowledge what has just been said and link it to a question, either drop the 'But' or use the word 'And'. "I hear what you are saying... What about...?" or "I hear what you are saying. And [thinking about that] what about...?"

Some might argue that asking tough, direct questions in a no-nonsense manner has benefits. It shows we are straight talkers, not afraid to say what we think. That is undoubtedly true to a point. Certainly, if rapport is very good, perhaps with an established client or longstanding colleague, one could be more direct and ask 'Why' and 'But' questions with less or little risk of building friction. In a first meeting with someone new, the rapport level usually starts around some midpoint. As rapport grows in the meeting one can be more probing or take more risks with the questions asked. In such cases it becomes a careful balance based on a highly tuned sense of how the meeting is going. When in doubt, don't.

Arguably, as the graphic below illustrates, if you are in a meeting with someone where the rapport is very low and unlikely to improve for whatever reason, you have little to lose by asking the questions which will most help you most quickly.

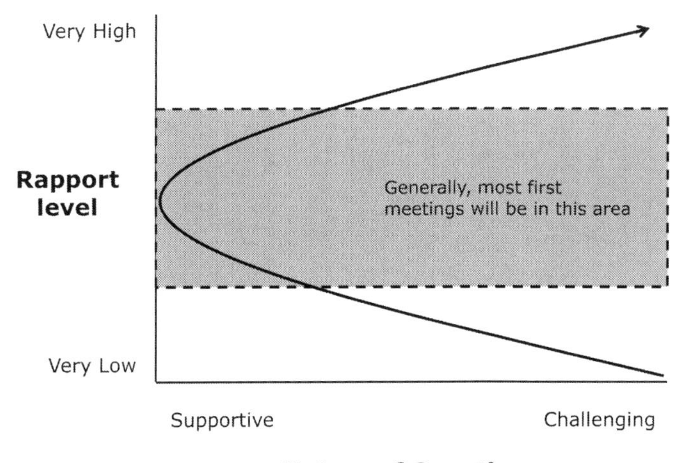

Good questions propel the conversation forward in ways which inform us about how the other person sees (and possibly feels about) his world, while leaving him feeling good about us.

iv) Reflecting understanding

The final part of the Insightful Listening Model is Reflecting understanding. This provides a technique to help us listen better and a process to ensure we communicate that understanding back to the client. To do this we first backtrack, then backtrack and clarify, then paraphrase.

Backtracking

This is the process of repeating back the words used by the speaker as we confirm our understanding of what they just said. So, in a hypothetical conversation, someone says to you, "I like rainy days in the morning." Your response would simply be, "You like rainy days in the morning." They might then say, "Yes. Everything feels fresh and smells green." Following the model literally you would then respond with, "Everything feels fresh and smells green." And so on.

We generally choose the words we use because they have a particular meaning for us. By matching the precise words chosen by someone, we communicate that we understand their position fully, because they will invest those words with the same meaning that they have for them. In doing so we deepen rapport. Of course, their meaning might be very different from the meaning we attach to those words. So, we must distinguish between backtracking to deepen rapport and other methods to confirm our understanding, principally asking questions and paraphrasing.

I was talking about vacations with a friend over a beer, what sort we went on and why we chose those holidays over others. It transpired that we both had an almost identical (digital) list of very important criteria, including variety, good weather, somewhere interesting and, given we both have young families, a range of activities, in that order. We immediately bonded over the idea of going on a joint holiday with our families the following summer. The idea didn't last long. As we got into the detailed options it became evident we meant completely different things from exactly the same words. Here are some of the differences:

'Variety':

Lots of different activities available	*Different places to see and visit each day*

'Good weather':

Sunbathing hot	*Sunny but not sunburn sunny*

'Somewhere interesting':

Large amounts of choice in what to do	*A different culture, with good food*

'A range of activities':

Things for each member of the family to go off and do on their own	*Different activities which the whole family can do together*

One of us would be very happy with an activity holiday at Club Med on an island in the sun while the other would much prefer a sightseeing holiday in a warm foreign location noted for its culinary tradition; the alternative holiday on offer filled each of us with dread.

If a holiday company agent was trying to sell to myself or my friend they would, however, benefit from using exactly the same words to each of us, at least initially: "So, you want a family holiday with variety, good weather, somewhere interesting and with a range of activities?" "Yes, that's it!" we would both say. If the holiday company agent had used different words or phrases, like 'lots to do' instead of variety, or 'unusual' instead of 'somewhere interesting' they would be interpreting our words and replacing them with their words, words which have a totally different meaning for us in the context of this discussion.

Hearing someone use our own words back to us communicates they understand exactly what we want because we attach the same meaning to the word 'variety', for example, in this context, whether we say it or they do. Talking with someone who gives us the feeling they completely understand what we are saying makes us feel very well disposed to that person and encourages us to continue. It makes us feel that they are listening closely to us and understand what we are saying *completely*.

Exercise

'Backtracking' is simply the process of repeating the other person's words back

to them. Here is an exercise you can play with an unknowing colleague (their answers are probably going to be different):

You: "How was your weekend?"
Them: "Good."
You: "You had a good weekend?"
Them: "Yes. We took the kids to Disneyland!"
You: "You took the kids to Disneyland?!"
(By now you may already be feeling like a parrot and getting a little self-conscious – they, however, are enjoying your obvious attention, your taking a deep interest in their life.)
Them: "Well, they have always wanted to go. And it was good fun."
You: "It was good fun."
Them: "Yup. They loved it and I have to admit I did too. Sort of like finding your inner child again."
You: "You found your inner child."
Them: "I did! I don't know where it has been hiding all these years but it felt good."
You: "It felt good."

And so on. You will surprise yourself at how long you can continue a social conversation in this way without the other party feeling uncomfortable.

You will also notice two other things. First, you will be able to remember almost everything they said, word for word, for quite a long time afterwards – days certainly and sometimes for weeks. The process of engaging in this way reinforces our memory. It can replace the need to take notes. Second, you will feel tired. The first few times you do this exercise, depending on how long you do it for, you may even feel exhausted. Listening with this degree of attention and engagement takes effort.

Your colleague, on the other hand, will feel that you are paying very close attention to everything she is saying and each time you use her words back to her she will experience a connection with you that goes beyond a mere exchange of words: she will bask in the warmth of your understanding because it feels full of acceptance and free of judgement. Long past the point you start to feel uncomfortable – because being a parrot feels unnatural or because you want to interrupt with an interesting point of view or talk about something more important to you or just would prefer to have her listen to how your weekend went – she is still reveling in your focus and your newly welcome depth of interest. And she will want to talk more.

As a further exercise, you can test how it feels to be on the receiving end of backtracking by soliciting the help of a friend or a colleague. Brief them on what you are testing out and ask them to keep a conversation going with you by simply repeating or echoing your words or statements back to you. If they do a half-decent job you should feel the closeness and warmth that comes from being with someone who takes such a profound interest in what you have to say.

In the business world, however, if you keep going for too long you will eventually indeed sound like a parrot and your colleague will start to wonder about your sanity. But in the context of most business conversations you wouldn't maintain such a one-dimensional conversation for long; you would instead pepper your dialogue with comments and questions to add dimension, variety and meaning. By continuing to backtrack as a *part of your dialogue* you will build rapport and reinforce your depth of understanding.

With experience, you will find that you don't need to backtrack verbally all the time. Instead you will occasionally backtrack mentally, repeating the speaker's words in your head to yourself. This achieves the same benefits of recall as backtracking verbally, without testing the speaker's potential patience.

In addition to deepening rapport, backtracking is a helpful discipline to avoid the mistake of trying to add value or specificity too soon.

Backtrack and clarify

If the words being used in the conversation are straightforward and not open to much interpretation there is little requirement for clarification. However, if the words refer to desired outcomes or deliverables, or values, then the specific meaning the speaker attaches to them could be very different from that of the listener's.

The following is an almost exact summary of the tail end of a conversation I had with the buyer of a series of training courses, the senior partner in a professional services firm. He started by summarizing as follows:

"So, I want this training course to **motivate** and **empower** people on it… I want them to be able to take away **course materials**… and I believe that **discussion groups** are important…"

"I understand. We will ensure this course is inspirational. There will be handouts throughout… and we will also make sure brainstorming sessions on how to apply the learning are built in," I replied, helpfully adding specificity and value.

"No. That's not what I want."

"Okay. To be precise, you want this course to be **motivating** and **empowering**. You want **course materials** for people to take away and for them to participate in **discussion groups**."

"Exactly."

The issue, of course, is that I was then left wondering what the words 'motivating and empowering', 'course materials' and 'discussion groups' actually meant to this buyer! They meant a range of possible things to me and, like any brief, I still had to go and design a proposal that met this buyer's needs. Of course, this was not a concern in the mind of this buyer who felt comfortable that I had completely understood what he wanted.

So, we have the situation of a deepening rapport based on the other person's feeling that we have listened well and fully comprehend, yet we have not in fact understood because backtracking alone does not enable us to clarify, where we need to.

To resolve this, we backtrack and question. Essentially, we bond and then clarify. We do this by playing back the exact words and then asking a respectful question. For example:

"So, the first thing is to **motivate and empower** people on this course. Can you expand on that a little? For example, what would tell you that the course had succeeded in this objective? How would we know?"

"Can we talk about the **course materials**? There are a couple of options here: we can send an electronic version of the slides out after the course finishes, give people paper handouts of the key concepts as we go through, have a book tailored to the needs of each participant, which they can use throughout, or a mix of the three. What would work best for your people? Or did you have something else in mind?"

"The **discussion groups** are an important part of this exercise. What do you feel are the most important objectives of these discussions? That could affect how we run them."

We retain our rapport while opening up the path to greater understanding.

Paraphrase

Finally, we use our own words to confirm our understanding, by paraphrasing what we have heard the client say.

Carl Rogers argued that, when paraphrasing, the listener should use the speaker's words because of the specific meaning they attach to those words. Yet the listening objectives of the therapist and the corporate advisor are different. The first is attempting to create an environment of emotional support and understanding, allowing the patients themselves to arrive at solutions which work for them. The corporate advisor, on the other hand, is seeking to elicit an understanding of needs and requirements which allows him to go away and design something, a process or a solution. To do that he requires absolute clarity in his own mind. The only way to do that is to check his understanding with that of the client by paraphrasing in his own words.

A paraphrase from the example above might be something like the following:

"So, we need to design in specific examples that relate to people's work here, give attendees a concise 'everything on one page' summary which they can keep to hand and refer to easily, and structure the days so they can formally share examples with each other of real-life opportunities. Have I missed anything? Okay. Anything else?"

The key to Reflecting understanding is to build rapport and comprehension by **backtracking**, then **clarify** where necessary with questions, and finally confirm our joint understanding by **paraphrasing**, if required, in our own words.

The Insightful Listening Model at work

How might the conversation at the start of this chapter with our potential client Jack have developed if Dan had been employing the Insightful Listening Model? We can never know for sure but it might have sounded something like the following (note, in addition, how Dan uses Representational language):

> "Jack, we've shared quite a bit of information about us. Can you tell us a bit about the issues you face? What's on your mind?". "Sure," Jack replied. "Let me bring you up to speed with where we are," he added. The conversation then developed as follows:

Jack: "Well, as you probably have heard, we've been growing quite fast."

Dan: (sitting still in an open posture and nodding): "You've been growing quite fast."

Jack: "Yes, we have. We have acquired a number of good-looking companies."

Dan: "What made them good-looking?"

Jack: "Well, they all had good market positions in growing sectors and were well run."

Dan: "So, each company was in a growing sector, had a good market position and was well run."

Jack: "Yes."

Dan: "Okay. You've grown fast based on acquiring a number of – four, right? –companies, each of which is in a good position. Sounds good."

Jack: "Yes. Our challenge now is how best to integrate them."

Dan: "So, now you need to look at how best to integrate them."

Jack: "Yes. You see, the real challenge for us is how to get integration benefits without losing the strengths that led us to acquire them in the first place."

Dan: "Getting integration benefits without losing the strengths," he said thoughtfully, jotting a quick note.

Jack: "If we can't find a way to do that relatively quickly the market will punish us."

Dan: "I see. You feel you need a plan relatively quickly. What sort of progress have you been making?"

Jack: "Well, there's the challenge because we don't really have anything detailed enough…"
Dan: "You don't have anything detailed enough."
Jack: "No."
Dan: "What do you need?"

At first glance all this can seem a lot to do when compared with the seductive advantages of just hearing passively. Yet the benefits are considerable, especially in a first meeting with a potential client where critical impressions of you are formed and you may get only that one chance to learn something useful. Yet the value of the Insightful Listening Model continues throughout the relationship. Being a good listener ensures you have the best information throughout. As your relationship develops from transactional to having Status to Trusted Advisor, your listening skills will help deepen the quality of your interactions and provide you with the knowledge and insights to continually add value.

The Insightful Listening Model and the Personal Impact Model

Insightful Listening is a core part of our Communication skills: it promotes Respect.

Because of the feelings it engenders in the speaker, the warm sense of being fully understood and acknowledged, it fosters Liking. They feel, *This is someone I can work with.*

At all three levels of Influencer, Persuader and Seller, Insightful Listening supports our hard skills because it helps give us more accurate information about our interlocutor's thoughts, feelings and needs. These hard skills you will recall are Expertise, skill in Presenting arguments and a Solution with value. Insightful Listening is an enabler that allows us to deploy our hard skills with greater effect.

Summary

The Insightful Listening Model requires us to listen differently, not passively as we so often do but with energy and a little effort. It requires us to: Adopt an attitude of acceptance, opening ourselves up to the speaker's view of the world; maintain Rapport, promoting a feeling of comfort and openness;

Ask good questions, moving the conversation forward constructively, while leaving the other person feeling neutral at worst, good at best, about us; and Reflecting understanding by backtracking, clarifying and paraphrasing.

In this way, we hear what they have to say and possibly what they feel, and we will recall that information for longer as we leave them feeling they have been listened to and understood.

Chapter 6 Takeaways

- To hear when you listen is hard work.
- Use the Insightful Listening Model to improve the content and quality of what you hear by:
    - » Adopting an attitude of acceptance;
    - » Being in a rapport;
    - » Asking good questions; and
    - » Reflecting understanding.

Chapter notes

1 The answer is, of course, 'Mary'.

2 For an accessible and entertaining description of the differences between men and women, especially in matters of communication, John Gray's book *Men Are From Mars, Women Are From Venus* is hard to beat.

3 Covey, Stephen R. *The 7 Habits of Highly Effective People*, London: Simon & Schuster, 2004. p239.

4 You will then be in second place.

5 A summary can be found in Carl R. Rogers and Richard E. Farson's 'Active Listening'. In Newman R. G. et al. (eds.), *Communicating in Business Today.* D.C. Heath & Company, 1987. (Available online.)

6 Rogers, Carl. 'Experiences in Communication'. Lecture given to California Institute of Technology in Pasadsena, C.A. 1964. (Available online.)

7 Rogers C. R. and Roethlisberger, F. J. 'Barriers and Gateways to Communication'. *Harvard Business Review.* July-August 1952.

7. Developing a Powerful Voice

Use your physiology to change how others respond to your words

It was South Africa versus New Zealand, early into the game. The referee seemed just about to blow for a penalty when there was a screech from the next room. I turned up the volume but the twins' screams were shriller and louder than the announcer's voice.

"Get off me!" I went in. My delightful daughters were rolling and wrestling on the floor. "Girls, I'm trying to watch the rugby match and I can't even hear it! Would you please play quietly, as I asked you to? Just until the rugby's over?" Emmelien got off Levina, they both nodded solemnly and I went back to the match.

New Zealand kicked to the corner, the ball went infield and then back towards the touchline just as a crash – clearly, something heavy falling over – came from the kitchen. This time when I went in I just stood there, weight evenly balanced on both feet, face expressionless. Only when they'd both stopped talking and were looking at me a bit apprehensively did I say, "I won't ask you again." I closed my mouth firmly, intonating down at the end of the sentence. "Okay, Daddy," Emmelien said, smiling expectantly. I didn't smile back. Face still expressionless, "No more noise," I said. This time, they did as I asked – until half time anyway.

How we talk, and the associated physiology, can have a profound effect on the way a listener responds subconsciously to us. It really is a case of not what you say but *how* you say it.

Children can provide a demanding test case – their impulses are strong, sometimes controlling. Directing children to more desirable behavior, without the explicit threat of punishment, can be challenging, to say the least! In the situation above I used two contrasting voice patterns, with their associated physiology: the first – an Approachable voice pattern – achieved little; the second – a Credible voice pattern – achieved much more in the circumstances. The patterns convey different impressions and elicit different, subconsciously powerful, responses from the listener.

In the adult world using these voice patterns appropriately can support our objectives of building relationships and getting things done. The Approachable voice pattern draws the listener in, helping them to feel comfortable with us. The Credible voice pattern conveys authority, even stature, reinforcing the belief that we know what we are talking about.

As we have seen, clients buy into us when they feel we are Credible, have a Solution with value and we are Likeable. They believe we can do the job and feel that the process of working with us will be agreeable enough. We can communicate these feelings non-verbally by adopting voice patterns that congruently reinforce these capabilities of ours.

Where do Voice patterns sit in the client development process?

Voice patterns promote our ability to communicate that we know what we are talking about. Hence they are critical in first meetings. Because they can

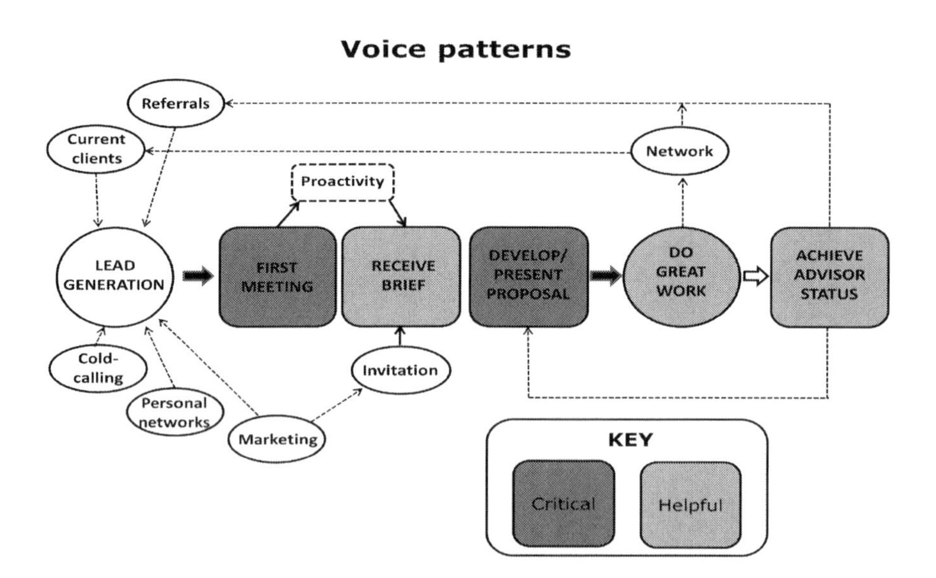

additionally communicate that we are good people to work with, they are as important when we are selling ourselves. This combination of supporting our Credibility and Likeability helps us to do great work.

Finally, maintaining the communication benefits of voice patterns, as a relationship manager, supports our ability to sustain Credibility while promoting Intimacy.

Credible and Approachable voice patterns

A voice pattern is a repeatable sequence of (largely) auditory behaviors that results in a predictable response. The two we shall focus on are the Credible voice pattern and the Approachable voice pattern. I lift these terms straight from the work of Michael Grinder who, over several decades, has studied and classified non-verbal behavior. Although I have adapted them somewhat for the world of professional services I am indebted to him for the core concepts and the insights they reveal.[1]

Imagine you have just boarded a plane. As you sort out your bag and disentangle the various electronic devices you want to use on the flight, the captain's voice comes over the PA system:

> *"Good morning," he says, in a firm, calm voice. "I'm Captain <u>Bob</u>. I'll be your pilot for this short flight <u>today</u>," he adds, with the emphasis on the last word of each sentence. He pauses briefly. "We'll be leaving <u>shortly</u>." Pause again. "We shall be flying at an altitude of thirty thousand <u>feet</u>." Emphasis at the end. Another brief pause. "I expect us to arrive at our destination on <u>time</u>." Pause. "I will now hand you over to <u>Adam</u>, who is in charge of our in-flight <u>service</u>." Pause again. "I wish you a pleasant <u>flight</u>."*

> *"Good morning, everyone? I'm Adam, your purser?" Adam introduces himself in a rhythmic, sing-song tone, full of energy and enthusiasm. He intones up at the end of each sentence, making it sound as if he is asking a series of questions. "I'll be looking after you on this flight today? And helping me will be David and Jean?" he continues with barely a breath. "We'll be making your flight as pleasant as possible? If you need anything do be sure to let us know? And we'll be happy to help?"*

This is an example of contrasting verbal styles that most of us have experienced at one time or another when flying. The pilot comes across as in control; he knows what he is doing. We feel reassured. We trust him. We are happy to put our lives in his hands. He does not, however, come across as particularly friendly; in fact, he might sound slightly intimidating. But then we don't really care much about such things since we don't expect to interact with him personally as he concentrates on getting us safely to our destination.

The purser by contrast comes across as a likeable person with whom we would feel quite comfortable chatting. We feel drawn to him and might even look forward to the chance of interacting with him later in the flight. Their verbal styles promote a response in us that is entirely in line with our needs as airline passengers: to feel safe on the one hand, and to enjoy the experience on the other. We can test that by imagining how we might feel if the pilot sounded like the purser and the purser sounded like the pilot...

The Credible voice pattern

Much like our pilot, when someone speaks in the Credible voice pattern they talk in a flat tone but intonate *down* on the last word of every phrase or sentence. Their mouth is firmly closed as the sentence is finished. They drop their chin at the end of a sentence. There is a short pause between sentences, when they raise their head again. Otherwise, the head (indeed the whole body) remains quite still. If they gesture, they do so with the palms of their hands facing down. If standing, their body weight is evenly distributed across both feet.

A listener on the receiving end of a Credible voice pattern is loath to interrupt. The speaker is sending information. The listener listens. The speaker looks and sounds as if he knows what he is talking about. He has considerable confidence in what he is saying. He is very believable.

When listening themselves, people with a Credible voice pattern sit straight and very still. They remain silent as they listen. When they want to speak they are comfortable interrupting.

The Credible voice pattern communicates that the person is in control and can rely on their own strength. They know the answers, are factually oriented and sell by giving the required information. They are like presenters.

The person talking in a Credible voice pattern blinks much less than the average fifteen to twenty times a minute. At times, like Brad Pitt giving his new recruits their pep talk in the film *Inglourious Basterds*, they can appear to hardly blink at all. This conveys greater intelligence compared to someone who blinks frequently. This is especially important when first meeting someone and when delivering important parts of a message.

At its best, the Credible voice pattern communicates self-confidence and mastery, and builds confidence on the part of the listener. At its worst it can be intimidating, even scary.

The Approachable voice pattern

Much like our purser, when someone speaks in the Approachable voice pattern they talk in a rhythmic tone. They intonate *up* at the end of phrases, as if asking a question (much as teenagers sometimes do). They talk more quickly, with little pause between phrases, and their mouth often remains open at the end of sentences. Their head bobs up and down as they talk. They make more gestures, always with the palms of their hands facing up. If standing, their body weight rests predominantly on one leg. They shift their weight from one leg to another frequently.

A listener on the receiving end of an Approachable voice pattern feels drawn in. They feel the speaker is implicitly requesting their engagement. The speaker sounds like someone who is very easy to talk to, who is flexible and amenable. Unsurprisingly, many interviewers on television have a good command of the Approachable voice pattern because it is their job to get others to open up to them. One of the best examples is the American comedienne and television show hostess Ellen DeGeneres (as famous for her voiceover as Dory in the film *Finding Nemo*).

When listening themselves, people with an Approachable voice pattern lean forward, nod their head encouragingly and frequently murmur their agreement as if silence must be avoided at all costs.

The Approachable voice pattern communicates that this person relies on the strength of others. They aim for influence by knowing the right questions and being sensitive to the other person. They are flexible. They seek information and interact well with individuals. They sell by getting information and facilitating change. In a business context they are like process consultants.

At its best, the Approachable voice pattern communicates affability, even likeability, and promotes a desire on the part of the listener to engage. At its worst it can convey doormat levels of weakness or even desperation.

These traits and the associated physiology are summarized in the graphic below. Of course, the descriptions represent extremes: in fact, there is a continuum of behavior between these end points and one can mix them as appropriate even within the same sentence.

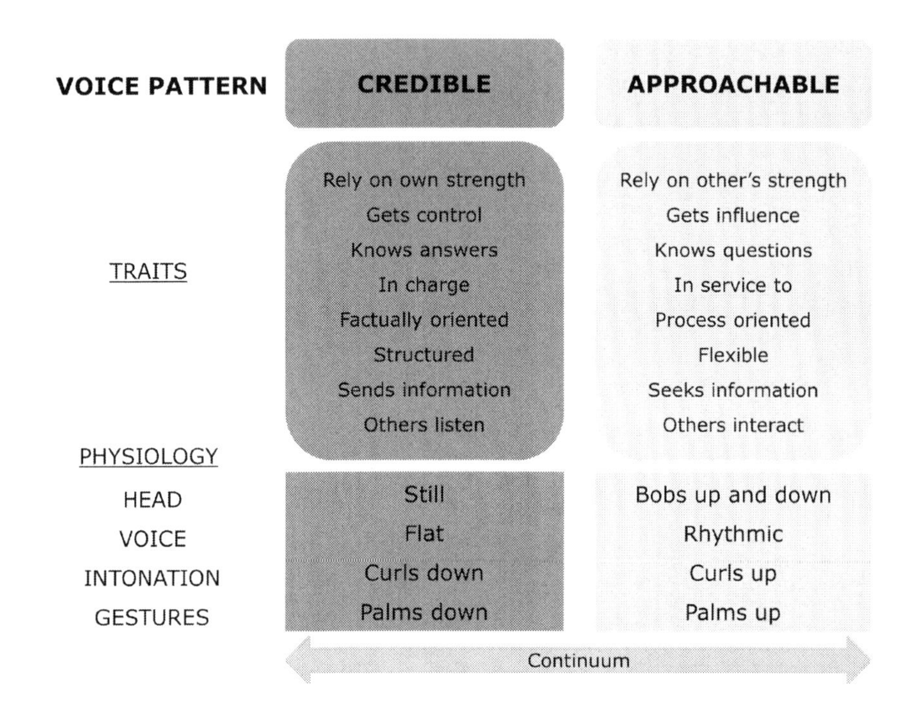

Implications of the voice patterns

The two voice patterns communicate very different things and elicit very different responses from listeners. Simplistically, the person with the Credible voice pattern is the one you would give a job to but you would probably avoid spending an evening with them in the pub. The person with the Approachable voice pattern is the one whom you would think carefully about giving any job to, except perhaps airline steward, but you would almost certainly look forward to an evening over drinks with them.

The voice patterns can even be thought of with regard to robots. Think of R2-D2 and C-3PO in the *Star Wars* films. If you had to have a drink and chat with one of them, which would it be? If you wanted an important job done, which would you choose? R2-D2 incorporates many of the behavioral elements of the Credibility voice pattern, while C-3PO, with all his befuddled charm, has much of the Approachability pattern about him.

The Credible voice pattern is very effective in supporting the impression that you know what you are talking about, that you are a serious person who should be taken seriously, that you can be relied upon. People listening to you will be more respectful and attentive. In a large meeting you can hear a pin drop when someone is speaking well in the Credibility pattern. But you are probably not much fun to hang around with.

By contrast the Approachable voice pattern is very effective in supporting the impression that you are easy to get on with, a good and sympathetic listener who is easy to talk to and a pleasure to have around. But you are possibly something of a pushover, even a lightweight.

There are some people who are all Credible, all of the time, and some who are all Approachable, all of the time. It is easy to see how and in what circumstances each might be successful, or not. Most people fall somewhere between these ends of the continuum and some show both patterns at different times even if they are unaware of it. Men, in general, tend toward the Credibility pattern, while women, in general, tend toward the Approachability voice pattern. It would be a mistake, however, to characterize these patterns as gender stereotypes since many women operate comfortably toward the Credibility end of the continuum and many men also operate comfortably toward the Approachability end.

Circumstances call for different voice patterns at different times, supporting the desired impression we wish to convey or the results we aim to achieve. For example, in a first meeting with a potential client we need to be Credible when talking about credentials and experience and Approachable when discussing the business and encouraging our potential client to talk. If we are Approachable when presenting our experience, we risk failing to win Respect; if Credible when asking questions, we could seriously hazard the rest of the meeting.

Similarly, over a longer timeframe, such as preparing a proposal, we would wish to be Approachable while in discovery or fact-finding mode, to encourage the flow of information and Credible when presenting our plans.

Sometimes, as a Trusted Advisor in meeting with our client, we may need to switch from one voice pattern to another many times in the same discussion, as the conversation switches between us seeking input (Approachable) and giving information (Credible).

Controlling our voice patterns

If you tend strongly toward one end of the voice pattern continuum you will experience some difficulty in adopting the behavioral characteristics of the other. Our voice patterns are part of who we are and it can feel quite alien at first to force ourselves into another pattern.

There is, however, a simple and wonderful solution. You control your voice pattern, and a large part of the accompanying physiology, just by holding the palm of your hand in front of you, face down or face up. Depending on your dominant pattern and how pronounced it is, this may have a moderate or a large effect on your voice pattern. In either event it is noticeable and, compared to where you start, sufficiently different.

Exercise

Stand up. Hold one hand out in front of you, palm facing down to the floor, fingers together. Now say, "Hello. My name is Jack/Jill [or whatever it is]. Welcome to the meeting." Notice how you sound and feel.

Now turn your palm face up, fingers loose. Repeat: "Hello. My name is Jack/Jill. Welcome to the meeting." Notice how differently you now sound and feel.

If you find it hard to notice differences in how you sound, get someone to listen to you and then have them do the exercise while you listen to them.

Some women with strongly Approachable voice patterns find that holding their palm face down with fingers straight and together almost physically impossible. If you are one of these try holding your hand sideways with fingers extended and together, like a karate chop. This should have a very similar effect for you as holding your hand palm down. I have yet to meet someone who can't do this comfortably.

Some men with strongly Approachable voice patterns find that if they drop their head slightly on the last word of each phrase and ensure they close their mouths firmly, they accentuate their downward intonation and sound much more credible.

Exercise

Practice switching from one voice pattern to another quickly. Have a conversation with yourself (or a willing accomplice) about those times you need to be Approachable and those you need to be Credible. For example:

Palm down. "When I present work to the client I need to be Credible."
Palm up. "When I am interviewing a candidate for a job I have to be Approachable?"
Palm down. "While I am at work I tend to be Credible yet [palm up] as soon as I get home I must remember to be Approachable?"
Palm up. "When I am considering something with others it helps if I'm Approachable? [Palm down.] Though when I have to make my decision and explain it, I carry more weight if I'm Credible."
And so on.

Switching between palm up and palm down allows you to pretty effortlessly switch between voice patterns instantly without having to think about any of the other physiological characteristics. The palm position controls them. It is also easy to do in a meeting, depending on whether you are seeking or sending information, since the movement of the hands becomes just another part of the normal gestures people make as they converse with each other.

As with many of the soft skills in this book, seek out low-risk situations in which to practice, before inflicting them for the first time on someone important to you.

Breathing and voice patterns

Interestingly, your breathing has a number of important effects on how you feel, how you sound and how the other person feels when they are with you. As far as voice patterns are concerned, how you breathe, or more specifically *where* you breathe, impacts the message you convey in both Credibility and Approachability patterns.

Where we breathe in our chest cavity affects how we sound. When we breathe low down we tend to speak slightly slower and deeper. When we breathe high in our chest we tend to speak faster and sound slightly breathless. The different impressions communicated by the two voice patterns when breathing high or low can be summarized in the graphic below.

VOICE PATTERN	Communicates...	
Approachable	APPEALING	PLEADING
Credible	AUTHORITATIVE	ANGRY
	Low	High
	WHEN BREATHING:	

For the voice patterns to be effective it is important that you are not breathing high in your chest cavity. It is for this reason that some people, when talking in the Credible voice pattern, can sound angry or even scary and some people speaking in the Approachable voice pattern can come across as pleading or even desperate. They are breathing high as they speak.

Given that we tend to breathe high when we are nervous or scared – the former, at least, a common occurrence prior to important meetings – it is important to have a quick technique to get control of our breathing. In such situations do the following:

Exercise

Stand up. Notice where in your chest you are breathing. Now place a hand on your tummy, just below your belly button. Imagine that you have a small metal ball in your chest, at the center of where your breathing is located. The ball can be of any size or color you want (mine is a white billiard ball, for instance).

Now, imagine your hand has magnetic qualities. As you breathe out, visualize the magnet in your hand drawing the ball, and with it your breathing, down. It stops as you breathe in. Then as you breathe out again it draws the ball (and your breathing) a little lower. Continue until you feel your breathing comfortably within your solar plexus region.

You should now feel more relaxed, your voice tone will be a little lower and your pace of speaking a little slower.

With practice you can do this quite quickly. These days it takes me only two or three seconds to get my breathing low. I have known some people, Kinesthetics probably, who with some practice can achieve this just by thinking about it. Being a Visual, I need the prop of something I can see in my mind's eye. If you are strongly Auditory you might find it helps to give the ball a sound of some kind, so you can imagine hearing it as it descends.

Combining voice patterns

When you have got a decent command of both Approachable and Credible voice patterns, and you can switch seamlessly from one to the other as required, then you can experiment, developing your own personal style using elements from both. Some of the most effective communicators incorporate elements of each voice pattern in their own style.

Barack Obama tends toward the Credible voice pattern with his trademark pause, stillness, firm closing of the mouth at the end of each sentence and his low breathing, yet incorporates the intonation up at the end of a phrase when he is seeking agreement. When he is making a serious point he emphasizes the Credibility elements more; when he is being lighthearted he gestures more frequently and his hands are held in an open, upward-facing posture. He is dancing up and down the scales, almost certainly unconsciously but with great effect.

Another interesting example is James Corden, on *The Late Late Show*, who is rooted in a moderate version of the Approachability voice pattern. Yet when he wants to say something important his hands turn sideways instead of palm up, he moves around less, there is a telling pause at the end of the sentence and his intonation drops a couple of octaves. Occasionally he combines opposing elements at the same time – intonating up at the end of the sentence while gesturing with his palms sideways or down; this has the effect of maintaining our connection with him emotionally while making us more receptive to his authority on that point.

In both these examples the switch in communication objective is mirrored by small changes in physiology that are fluid, seamless and entirely natural. Neither is at the extreme of the voice patterns but the changes are sufficient to elicit supportive responses from us, the audience. Each style is very much that person's; each works for them in those circumstances.

Voice patterns and the Personal Impact Model

Voice patterns principally support Respect and Liking.
The Credible voice pattern helps build confidence in your Expertise because it reinforces the impression you know what you are talking about. The Approachable voice pattern supports your Communication skills because it encourages people to share information with you. The combination of the two patterns in one conversation can make you a better Influencer. They help you to convey your authoritativeness while retaining your personableness. They support your attainment of Respect.

Liking is the sense of being comfortable with the idea of working with someone: that they are capable and agreeable. The interaction of Credible and Approachable voice patterns conveys that this is someone who knows what they are doing, yet is easy to talk to and prepared to listen.

Summary

Becoming skilled at switching between Credible and Approachable voice patterns as needed will make your communication more effective.

With practice, you can become naturally fluent in the two voice patterns and you will find many of your work and personal relationships improving. When you are Approachable people will want to talk with you; when you are Credible they will listen more carefully to what you say. You will find yourself thinking more about the object of the interaction and tailor your voice pattern, driven by your palm position, accordingly.

Because most people lack this behavioral flexibility it can make you stand out: someone whom people want to be with and, with your Expertise, to work with too.

Chapter 7 Takeaways

- Your voice pattern determines how people respond to you and what you say.
- Controlling your voice pattern strongly influences the interaction.

- The two most notable voice patterns are Credible and Approachable: they convey different impressions and ask for different responses from the listener.
- You can comfortably switch from one pattern to another by simply altering the position of your palm.

Chapter note

1 See Michael Grinder, The Elusive Obvious: The Science of Non-verbal Communication, available at www.michaelgrinder.com, for this and the other twenty non-verbal patterns he has classified. Along with his other main work, Charisma – The Art of Relationships, his thought-provoking insights come near to genius in my view.

8. Mastering the Art of Empathy

Put yourself in another's shoes

James and Andy were young lawyers, two years in with their Manhattan firm and doing well (even if their private lives had taken something of a hit). But they were both working on a team they hated and they wanted to get a move to something more interesting. "I'm going to see Sarah; she runs the resourcing on legal teams and I'll get her to move me. Anyway, she knows my dad. It should be a cinch," James declared. "What about you?" he asked Andy. "Well, I doubt Sarah would want to know my dad," Andy replied, "but I'll give it a go."

A couple of days later James came out of Sarah's office looking crestfallen. He passed Andy going in and said, "No chance, she's in a foul mood." When Andy came out a short while later with a bemused smile and thumbs up, James was agog. "What did you say?" "Well, I'm not sure it's so much what I said," Andy replied, "it's more how I said it. You know the story of the North Wind and the Sun? – I think it was a bit like that." James was exasperated. "What do you mean?" he asked. "It's a fable from Aesop, you know the Greek, who told of the North Wind and the Sun arguing over who was the strongest? So, there was this traveler on the road and the North Wind said he could get the traveler's cloak off him. He blew and blew but the harder he blew the tighter the traveler wrapped the cloak around him, until eventually the North Wind gave up. Then the Sun had a go and he gently warmed the traveler until he was uncomfortably hot wearing his cloak and he just took it off himself." "Okay, so what?" James demanded. "Well," Andy replied, "I just made Sarah feel good about moving me." "And how did you do that?" James almost shouted. "Ah," Andy mused, "I guess I just tried to look at it from her position."

Where does Mastering the Art of Empathy sit in the client development process?

The empathy skill covered in this chapter helps us generate insights into how someone is likely to be thinking and feeling.

As such, it is critical in situations where we are hoping to persuade or sell, most obviously in proposal meetings. It has significant benefit in helping us do excellent work for our clients as it helps us anticipate needs and concerns. Finally, as a Trusted Advisor or relationship manager it can aid us in anticipating where our client is coming from at that moment, allowing us to adapt our supportive approach accordingly.

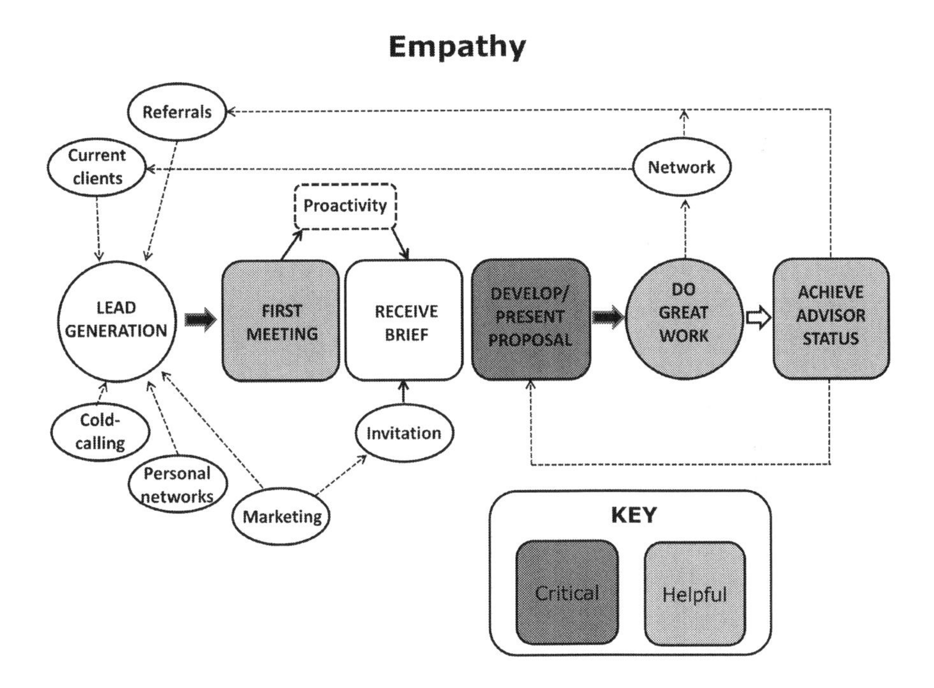

The challenge

The basis of all modern selling and marketing is the requirement to understand what the customer wants. In some fields, consumer goods and automotive, for example, very considerable sums are invested to acquire this knowledge. Potential customers are interviewed individually, in focus groups and with standardized questionnaires to answer every conceivable question from the marketer's perspective. Only then is a product developed or a pitch designed. Often it is then tested, the results researched again and any revisions incorporated. Sometimes this cycle can go on for years before the eventual product is launched.

In professional services the situation is slightly different. Our product is largely determined already, whether legal or marketing services or some variant of consultancy. The more our product is a function of hard-won expertise, the harder it is to change. In that sense it can feel sometimes that when we go to sell as individuals we are not much more sophisticated than the proverbial hammer looking for a nail. Of course, most sensible client handlers before a first meeting will ask themselves some basic questions: What has the company's performance been like? What do their brokers think are the main issues? What is the media saying? And so on. From that, one may be able to hazard a guess at what might be on our prospective client's mind but it often is little more than that.

The bottom line is that usually before the meeting we have little or no idea of what is on our prospective client's mind and all our guesses could be wrong. We may feel that might matter little since the purpose of a first meeting is to elicit all that information. The first meeting is in effect all about personal introductions and customer research. To some extent that is true. However, as we design our general, introductory pitch we have little idea of where and how to focus our messages, so they tend to become a shopping list of our firm's capabilities and we hope that somewhere in the list of 'hammers' we describe, the client has one or two 'nails' that need banging in.

Then there are the practicalities. I remember weeks when I might have had two or three client presentations that needed preparing, reviewing and delivering, as well as several first meetings with prospective clients. And that was on top of all the other day to day responsibilities of a senior partner, such as recruiting, training and dealing with the myriad management issues that present themselves in any people business. Essentially, time is short and pressure is high. In this context, with limited scope to change the product, limited hard information about where the potential client is coming from and limited time (as well as head space), our focus becomes ensuring that our hammers are all well-polished for display. Unfortunately, that is unlikely to differentiate us much.

This problem of not knowing enough about where the other person is coming from – the issues on their mind, their concerns and feelings – is not restricted to first meetings. Follow-on discussions with a potential client and continuation meetings with an actual one all benefit from varying degrees of knowledge about the person and the issues but they present additional challenges. In the case of follow-on discussions with a potential client, the closer we get to being invited to pitch, the greater the specificity of the issues in the client's mind, structural and analytic as well as psychological and emotional. Unless we can get the potential client out to dinner where he or she will reveal all to us in a trusting download of everything on their mind (possible but unlikely in this situation in my experience), we are left to grope forward with a mix of data, intuition and hope.

Continuation meetings with an actual client present their own challenges. If they are focused around a piece of work, the client's reaction has ideally to be considered, taking into account the practical, political and emotional dimensions from their perspective if the work is to be judged a success. Not all of these may immediately be apparent and the three limitations described above, scope to change the work, understanding of all the client's likely reactions in the absence of full disclosure and limited time, all remain pertinent to some degree. Finally, if the meeting is not project-related and covers something else, such as the client relationship in general or a new area for potential assistance or something else on the client's mind, the situation may not be that far from what is experienced in a first meeting.

How can we hope to gain further understanding and insight given the situations described? How can we improve our understanding of where our clients, potential and actual, are coming from so we can better focus our efforts and solutions?

Mind Reading

The solution to these questions is a simple process that helps us to stand in someone else's shoes. I have called this process Mind Reading. It is not a magic bullet solution since no-one can fully understand what another is thinking and feeling without sharing their skin. However, it can go a long way, certainly much further than any alternative I am aware of. And sometimes the results of this process can be staggering.

The Mind Reading process derives from work done in the 1980s by therapists working to help their clients adapt to and resolve relationship issues with others. These therapists developed something called the Perceptual Positions model. Their aim was to find a way to help their client take a step out of their own world to see the world from another's point of view, to metaphorically walk a mile in their shoes. Doing so, the consequent insights could change how their clients feel.

For our purposes I have adapted and simplified the Perceptual Positions model to suit the needs of client handlers in professional services. Our environment is different from that experienced by professional therapists. Also our time is often shorter. Finally, we are not in the business of engendering transformational change in others but simply seeking to better grasp another's standpoint.

For these reasons I have given the process a different name. Therapists would be horrified at my use of the term 'Mind Reading' to describe it, since that is (probably) impossible to achieve and the belief that you can could lead to all sorts of erroneous conclusions. Nevertheless, it remains our goal and if we can only go some way up the path, never quite reaching the door itself, that is progress compared to standing at the gate. My hope is that the value and simplicity of the Mind Reading process will encourage you to use it, or one of its variant forms, before each and every client meeting you have and all other important non-client meetings too.

The Process

This works best with someone to help you. Think of a meeting you have coming up. It may be a first meeting with someone new or a continuation meeting with an existing client. Now get your friend to assist you. We will call this person 'the Guide'. Find a quiet room somewhere with three chairs. Place each of the chairs facing the others at the three points of an imaginary triangle on the floor.

One of these chairs will be 'you' (or '1st position'). The second will be 'the other person' (or '2nd position'). These two chairs face directly toward each other. The third chair will be 'the observer' (or '3rd position') and will broadly face both chairs one and two.

When you are sitting in 1st position this is 'you'. At the start you bring with you all your existing thoughts, ideas, aspirations, fears, perceptions and any other feelings as they relate to your upcoming meeting.

When you are sitting in 2nd position you imagine yourself to be the other person with whom you are planning to meet. You make a creative leap to understand the world as they see it, at least as far as it relates to the upcoming meeting. You imagine sitting there as the other person and looking across at yourself.

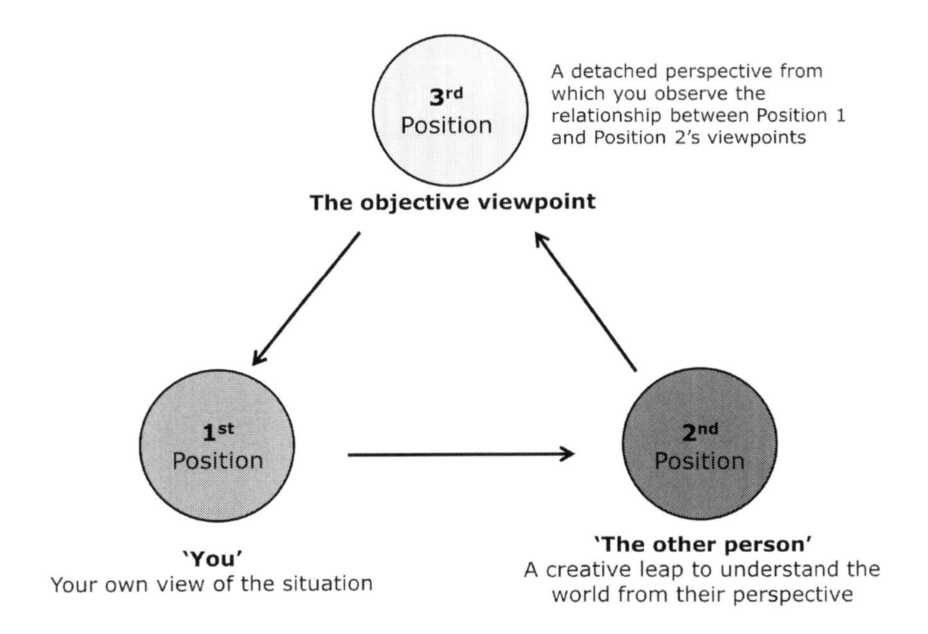

When you are sitting in 3rd position you are the fly on the wall. This is the position of the objective observer, listening to, watching and perhaps feeling what is going on between 'you' in 1st position and 'the other person' in 2nd.

The process requires you to sit in each chair in turn and think about and then answer a number of questions your guide asks you, using the script below, as you take your place in each.

1st position/you

You are sitting here looking across at an empty chair but doing your best to imagine that sitting there before you is the other person you are planning to meet. Your guide then asks you the following questions, each of which you think about carefully before answering aloud.

"What is your goal for this meeting?"
"How will you know when you have got it?"
"How will you structure the meeting?"
"What will your manner or style be like?"
"What, if any, will your fallback goal or position be?"

Having answered these questions, when you are ready, walk across to the 2nd position chair. As you move between the chairs 'shake off' the original you by waving your hands and making a silly noise as you shake your head. This helps the transition from being one person to becoming, imaginatively at least, the other.

2nd position/the other person

When you sit down you imagine yourself becoming the other person. Put yourself as fully in their shoes as you can. If you know them already, adopt as far as you can their posture, their tone of voice and any mannerisms they have. If you don't know them, imagine what they might be like from what you do know about them. Take a moment to 'become' the other person in your mind and, if you can, in your physiology too. Look across at what you imagine to be 'you' still sitting in 1st position and think about the upcoming meeting. For the purposes of this exercise we shall call you Jack or Jill. Then answer aloud the following questions.

"How do you feel toward Jack/Jill?"
"What is your goal or likely intention from this meeting?"
"What will your manner or style toward Jack/Jill be?"
"What are you thinking and feeling?"

Having answered these questions, when you are ready, walk across to the 3rd position chair. As you move between the chairs again 'shake off' 'the other person' you by waving your hands and making a silly noise as you shake your head.

3rd position/the objective observer

When you sit down imagine yourself as a fly on the wall at this meeting between Jack/Jill and the other person. Observe them and the interaction. Remember what each has said. Now answer aloud each of the following questions.

"What is likely to happen in this interaction between these people?"
"Will both parties get what they want?"
"If they don't, what will have to change?"
"What advice would you offer to Jack/Jill?"

Having answered these questions, when you are ready, walk back to the 1st position chair. As you move between the chairs again 'shake off' the 'objective observer' you by waving your hands and making a silly noise as you shake your head.

1st position/you

As you sit down you become yourself again. Take a moment to re-associate with yourself. Then, when you are ready, your guide asks you the original set of questions, which after reconsideration you again answer aloud.

"What is your goal for this meeting?"
"How will you know when you have got it?"
"How will you structure the meeting?"
"What will your manner or style be like?"
"What, if any, will your fallback goal or position be?"

It is very rare for someone to answer the original set of questions in the same way as they did when they were first asked at the beginning of the exercise. Nearly always, the process results in a set of new insights, ideas and approaches. Invariably, the 'you' in this process goes into the meeting with more confidence, even if, in the rare case, your original approach has not changed substantially.

Some years ago, I got an introduction to the CEO of one of the biggest food companies in the world. The source of my introduction was the audit partner, who planned to join us in the meeting. Needless to say, this was a big deal for me. I could find out quite a lot about the company; but what I spent most of my preparation time doing was talking to the audit partner about what the client was like and then thinking at length about him, his concerns, feelings, doubts and hopes. A lot of it was guesswork, obviously, but I consciously put myself in his shoes, concluding that this was a man of great feelings with many deeply felt worries. I knew I had only the one shot.

When I met him a few days later in an office that could be best described as occupying the floor, not just a corner, he sat there, a big man behind an enormous desk. The audit partner was there too, waiting for me to be impressive and so justifying his recommendation, making him look good too. I felt like I had just been thrown to the lions.

The client's voice was as big as he was. "We employ the best, or certainly the most expensive, advisors in the world, like your friend here. I have never even heard of you." He leaned back in his chair, clasping his hands behind his head and looked straight at me. "What on earth makes you think you can do anything for us?" My stomach was turning somersaults but I held to my instincts about the man. I refused to let myself blink as I held his eyes and blurted out the cliché, "I don't know. What keeps you awake at night?" A long silence ensued which I resisted filling. Then, after what felt like a lifetime, he dropped his hands and started talking. (He eventually became our biggest client for the next five years.)

Why does Mind Reading work?

Some of the benefit must come from simply taking time out and stopping to think for a moment. Some from the forced adoption of the other person's position, requiring you to put yourself in their place, which can promote better understanding. And some must come from looking at the situation dispassionately, as the objective observer. The scripted questions, though simple (and one could extend them in detail and complexity as much as one likes, though I have found little extra value in doing so), require you to be logical and comprehensive.

But this straightforward analysis falls short of how powerful this process actually *feels* when you do it. There is an emotional component as well as an intellectual one. You feel very different afterwards. Maybe as someone once tried to explain it to me, we mirror the structure of our external relationships internally with a particular set of pictures, sounds and feelings; when we re-examine and change our perception of the external structure, all of our subconscious internal representations change too.

Like most of the soft skills in this book, enlightenment comes from doing rather than reading so please give it a go to really experience the results for yourself. You can obviously practice for an upcoming client meeting. Do it once and notice how it changes you and your planned approach. Alternatively, practice with other relationships that may be troubling you, with a family member perhaps or a colleague. The process works equally well with any relationship.

Executional observations

1. The role of the guide in this exercise is just that. They are a facilitator whose only role is to ask the questions. They are not there to add value with their own ideas and observations, much as they will be tempted to do so. This is not about having a discussion. It is about you, thinking deeply about the meeting from three different perspectives. The answers, and their value, come from within. If there is a desire for discussion then that can take place *after* the process has been completed.
2. It is important to fully 'disassociate' yourself from the previous position before you move into the next. Hence the 'shake-off' with silly sounds and movements. Make them as silly as you can. They help to physiologically distance you from the previous position. If you don't, you carry some of the previous position with you as you sit down in the next.
3. It really is helpful, if you know the person, to adopt as much of their physiology as you can. I have often seen people doing this exercise, quite dramatically become another person in how they sound and look; they are convincing even to colleagues who know both them and the person they are about to see. At minimum, it helps you to more fully associate with the other person and the resulting answers will be more useful. For this reason, even if you don't know the person, it is still worthwhile adopting what you *imagine* their physiology to be. In the case of my story above, the audit partner had in advance painted a pretty good picture for me of what the client looked and sounded like.

Practical variations

Doing the Mind Reading exercise in this form can take as little as ten minutes. It could be the most valuable ten minutes you ever spend on that client or meeting. But sometimes it may not be possible to do it fully as described because you are on the road or there are no chairs around or no-one available you would be comfortable having as your guide, so you might be tempted to leave it. However, in my experience it can have value in any circumstance; it is just that the full potential might be constrained by those circumstances. The following are my own variations depending on where I am:

- Best is where I have a room, chairs and a guide.
- If no guide, I ask myself the questions.
- If no chairs, I stand as I move from one position to the next.
- If no room, or because I am in a taxi or plane, I do the whole process in my head.

In fact, if I think about the number of times I have done this process, the vast majority would be as the last variation, in my head. A lot of that is due to the fact that now I often work on my own without the colleagues and partners to share preparation with, and the fact that I do it before every meeting. Nevertheless, I know that, where circumstances allow, I would always choose the room, chairs and guide.

Mind Reading and the Personal Impact Model

Mind Reading is a soft skill which develops empathy, supporting each of the four levels of the Personal Impact Model:

As an Influencer, it helps you target the content of your Expertise in ways your listener will find most helpful.

As a Persuader, it informs how you position your information, so improving your skill at Presenting arguments.

As a Seller, it helps you develop the most appropriate Solution with value.

As a Trusted Advisor, it can guide you to act in ways your client will find most supportive.

Summary

The Mind Reading process helps you to better understand where the other person is coming from. As a result it gives you more choices in how you approach your communication with them. At minimum, even where you have never met the other person before, it gives you more confidence as you consider the meeting. It makes you think, increasing the chances of a positive outcome, and it makes you feel more confident having done so.

Chapter 8 Takeaways

- To Influence someone, you need to *know where they want to go*, then show them how you can help them get there.
- To Persuade someone, you need to *know what their concerns are*, then show how they can be overcome.
- To Sell to someone, you need to *know what they want*, then offer it to them.
- Mind Reading forces you to delve into these questions; the feelings of empathy arising will generate insights and potential answers which can radically change your thinking

9. Telling a Compelling Story

Capture their hearts and minds with BIOBA

Bob had a tricky problem. He needed to go to his new client, at whose company he led an important piece of work, and tell him he was now unable to finish on time. The reason for this was that some key members of Bob's team had to be taken off the project for a few weeks to work on another client's project. As a result, Bob was going to miss the agreed deadlines. Bob could guess how his client was likely to feel. What could he say? How best should he say it?

Where does BIOBA sit in the client development process?

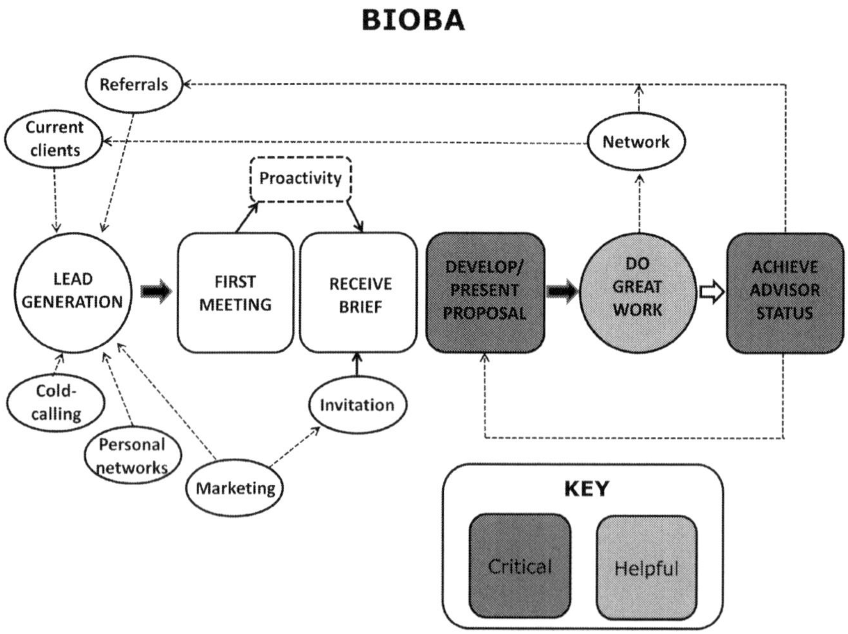

BIOBA

Referrals
Current clients
Network
Proactivity
LEAD GENERATION
FIRST MEETING
RECEIVE BRIEF
DEVELOP/ PRESENT PROPOSAL
DO GREAT WORK
ACHIEVE ADVISOR STATUS
Cold-calling
Personal networks
Marketing
Invitation
KEY
Critical
Helpful

BIOBA is a way of organizing information to persuade anyone, anytime. It can be critical when presenting proposals. It is also very helpful when working with clients in order to facilitate the process and convince them of the results. Finally, it assists the Trusted Advisor or relationship manager to add value by ensuring information is always well thought through and compellingly presented.

Background to BIOBA

To get things done you have to persuade people. To get them to agree to something new or different you have to convince them that the path you are proposing is the best or right path or perhaps that they have no real choice. To induce them to buy from you, you need to secure their agreement to the transaction. This happens in our professional lives all the time but also in our personal lives. For example, how do you persuade your partner that where you want to go on vacation is the best choice?

In each case, having figured out what you want and what you want to say, you are left with the question of *how* to say it. Do you just come out with it? "Darling, I want us to go to Timbuktu this year. How about it?" To your client above: "Jack, we aren't going to meet the deadline on this project. Sorry. Why? Well, another client has nabbed some of the team."

You could always fall back on the time-honored way of structuring presentations that professionals everywhere use: Situation, Complication and Solution. So, to your partner you might say:

> Situation: "Darling, we need to decide on where we go on holiday this year."
> Complication: "There are loads of choices."
> Solution: "I want us to go to Timbuktu."

That may or may not be successful, depending on how your partner feels about Timbuktu, and probably about you at that moment.

With your client Jack, using the same framework, you might say:

> Situation: "Jack, as you know we have been making good progress on the project so far."
> Complication: "We have a problem now in that we will be shorthanded for a while because we have lost some of our team."

Solution: "That means that we will have to put back the deadline by a few weeks in order to finish it all to your satisfaction."

Of course, there are many ways of putting it. There are also different ways of framing the complication. In each case, however, you risk leaving the audience potentially feeling that your 'solution' is not what they would want. Even if they are forced to agree with you, they could be left less than happy.

So, what is the best way of organizing information in situations where you have to persuade, that maximizes the chances of your audience saying "Yes" *and* feeling good about you at the end?

Idea of BIOBA

The best way to organize information in order to persuade is the five-step plan, or for those who, like me, benefit from the use of a handy acronym, BIOBA. This stands for Background, Idea, Operation, Benefits and Action.

Operation of BIOBA

Using BIOBA presupposes that you have thought hard about what it is you want to say. Also that you have given thought to the audience, where they are coming from and their likely reaction. Ideally, you will have completed the empathy-generating Mind Reading exercise earlier. This preparation is not part of the BIOBA structure itself, although thinking through the steps will help prompt you to do it if, for some unaccountable reason, you have neglected to.

It will assist you considerably in the meeting if you are in physiological rapport and breathing low. Finally, if you start with the Approachability voice pattern while discussing the Background, then switch to the Credibility voice pattern for the Idea, Operation and Benefits sections, and back again to Approachability for the Action section at the end, you will be more engaging and convincing.

There are five simple steps in BIOBA, each of which requires some thought to execute well. In my own experience, writing down what you want to say in each section will help clarify your thinking. The overall structure is shown below:

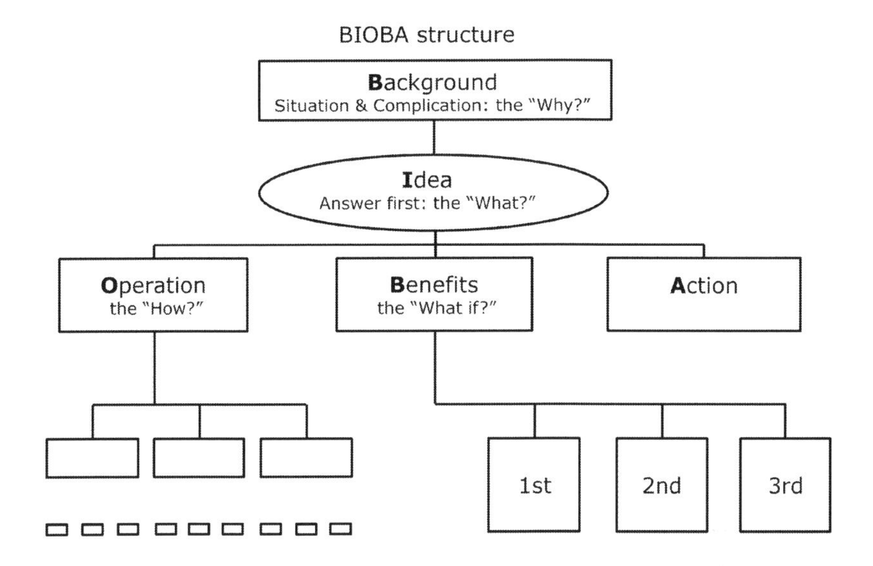

1. Background

The objective of the Background section is to introduce the subject matter. In doing so our aim is to create a climate of agreement before putting forward our Idea or proposal.

We can start by headlining the purpose of the discussion or by raising the subject area in more general terms:

> *"Darling, can we talk about our next vacation?" or "Darling, vacations."*

> *"Jack, I need to talk to you about the progress of our project" or "Jack, can we talk about the project?"*

In introducing the subject matter, we want to ensure that our audience has all the information relevant to the Idea we wish to propose. They need to know the 'Situation' and the 'Complication' elements of the situation. We would like them to feel, at minimum, that the Idea, which we raise next, is at least a logical solution to this Background information. Ideally, we want them to feel that the Idea is also attractive, although this is not always possible at this stage. It all comes down to how we position the Background information.

"Darling, vacations. As you know, we have nothing planned yet this year. And you said you wanted us all to go again, if we could afford it. We have had a good year so it looks like we can. We need to choose where to go and I have a suggestion I hope you like, if you would like to hear it?"

"Jack, can we talk about the project? You will be aware that things have gone pretty smoothly so far. The last update meeting went well and I can tell you we have now addressed all the points raised by your team in that meeting. So far, I am pleased and I hear you are too? Unfortunately, for a bunch of reasons I have now had some of my team taken away from me for three weeks. I think it is manageable, though clearly not ideal, and I would like to get your agreement on how I plan to handle it."

Consciously, it is important to avoid raising anything in the Background that could be contentious. We wish the audience to agree to our Idea; if they start arguing or disputing something we say in our opening remarks, we may never get to present our Idea and, if we do, it may be in the unhelpful context of disharmony or dissent. Instead, we want our audience sympathetic, supportive or feeling in accord with our Background remarks.

I call this careful structuring of our opening comments 'creating a climate of agreement'. Subconsciously, we want our audience supportively nodding as much as we can during the Background phase of our proposal. The more people agree with you on the small things, the more they are likely to agree with you on the big thing. This is a principle well understood by door-to-door financial products salesmen in the 1960s and timeshare salesmen today. The more someone says "Yes" throughout, the more likely they will say "Yes" at the end. It is called the 'Yes-set'. It echoes Robert Cialdini's second principle of persuasion, 'Consistency', in his book *Influence: Science and Practice*.[1] If you can get someone to make small commitments, they are more likely to make a bigger one later. In this case, 'commitments' are statements, gestures or feelings of agreement.

Happily, our clients in professional services are not so susceptible to such simple acts of manipulation as the 'Yes-set' but they *are* affected by any positive feelings aroused, since they are only human. The more the other person says "Yes" to himself or herself as they listen, the more likely they are to feel they should say "Yes" at the end. However, being independent thinkers they may well nod amenably all the way through your discourse and still say "No" at the end. Even so, we should still aim to create this climate of agreement in which to discuss our idea than the opposite. In our two examples above, we structured our Background section to secure three likely 'yes' responses, consciously or unconsciously. In practice, we could probably have gone for even more.

Where we can, we also aim to head off any likely objections that we can anticipate in the Background section. If we can *clean out* possible objections before the Idea is presented, we create the possibility that our audience will listen to the Idea and what follows with a more open outlook, uncluttered by potential obstacles jostling for mind space. So, in the quoted examples above, our partner may have had a concern about affordability, which we have hopefully headed off. And our client Jack may have had doubts about progress following the update meeting, which we put to rest. They may well have other issues and objections, especially when they hear our Idea, but they are now, at least, fewer than they would have been.

The Background section also gives you the opportunity to think about how you wish to position, or frame, your proposal. Things presented in different contexts give different meaning. Imagine I were to ask you, for example, whether you feel your life is like a glass half-full, or instead ask you whether you feel it is like a glass half-empty? The facts of your life remain the same. Yet how you feel about each description would be very different. Similarly, if a doctor frames a procedure as having an 85% success rate or a 15% failure rate, far more patients will elect to go forward if presented with the first frame than the second.[2] Politicians commonly present issues in a way that favors their political persuasion. Journalists often include a 'spin' of one kind or another in their reporting; some argue it is impossible not to.

Kahneman and Tversky, whom we met earlier, found that, under circumstances of uncertainty, how you frame a choice can determine the outcome along very specific lines: people avoid risk when a positive frame is presented and seek risk when a negative frame is presented. They also discovered that the outcome can be affected by where you start from (which they called 'Anchoring'), sometimes in surprising ways.[3] For example, people asked to pick a ping pong ball with a number on it and then asked how much they would be willing to pay for a bottle of champagne gave prices in line with the size of the number on their ball. There is a long list of interesting findings from the fields of social science and psychology that document how we respond to information differently presented. But you don't need to be familiar with it all. Just put yourself in the other's shoes and think how *you* would respond given the alternative positioning choices you have.[4]

Finally, the Background section gives you the chance to think about what the issue and the Idea actually are. You can choose to presuppose certain areas and focus on others. For example, in the Background section to Jack above, the question is all about how you plan to manage the situation, not why the team has been denuded and whether that can be changed: the issue of the team going has been assumed as a given and the focus for discussion is now on your plan to deal with it. Whether Jack will let you get away with this presupposition, you will find out, but at least it has allowed you to frame the discussion positively. Presuppositions have their place, though they need to be used with care and with the awareness that your audience may call you on them.

2. Idea

This is the shortest section. Just say what your suggestion or proposal is in clear, simple terms.

"Darling, I would like us to vacation in Timbuktu."

"Jack, we will use the extra time to make sure all your team is ready to start executing when we finish."

As you write the Idea down on a piece of paper you find yourself considering the words you use most carefully, and their implications. What *is* the actual proposal here? Regarding your partner, is it that you would like to go on the vacation and have them accompany you, putting up with it for your sake? Or do you think they should go for reasons that would benefit them? The precise wording you use can also have an effect. 'Want' has a different meaning and implication to 'should' or 'could', for example. The differences are subtle but arouse differing emotional and intellectual responses. The words you choose to define your Idea set questions and possible objections that you must deal with later. Writing the Idea statement requires you to *think* about all this carefully.

It is also called an Idea, rather than a proposal or pitch or plan or sell, for a reason, unrelated to the ease of constructing memorable acronyms. An 'Idea' is a possibility, open to shaping. The more definite linguistic alternatives imply something more formed and finished. Emotionally, you feel more relaxed about your pitch when it is an 'idea'; you are open to the possibility of it being revised or developed in conversation. Your mindset is one of constructive improvement in a situation where the ideal outcome for you is win-win.

The more definite alternatives, such as 'plan' or 'proposal', lock you psychologically into the inevitability of a binary outcome: acceptance or rejection. Fear of failure can lead you to feel nervous and, during the presentation itself, defensive. In practice, of course, it may make no difference – your Idea may be accepted in its entirety. But if you meet resistance you are more likely to adapt and, if facing outright rejection, be better equipped to positively consider other ways to achieve what you need or what your audience wants. Emotionally, you are still in the game.

3. Operation

This is where you explain how your Idea works. It is the nuts and bolts of your proposal.

> *"Darling, we would fly there as a family and stay in a nice hotel, of which I have found several. Once there, we can do some things together which we all like, such as sightseeing and shopping in the souk, and there are some activities I know you will want to do, such as the great spa, and some I am especially excited about, like desert trekking. We can book some things in advance and some things when we get there."*

> *"Well, Jack, the way this would work is that I would commit to meeting with each member of the team individually. I can listen to their issues and help them find ways to overcome them. That will take me about three weeks. At the end they should all be on board and have a plan of action they can implement. If you wanted, we could even include those plans in the final presentation and have them present them?"*

If your proposal is a simple one in execution, say you are requesting that something stays the same, then the Operation section is where you will put forward your reasons.

Having given some thought to where your audience is coming from, your description of the Operation will address predictable concerns and possible objections, highlighting areas to which your audience will feel well disposed.

The Operation section needs to be as full and complete as you can make it. It is obviously helpful if you can structure the section in a logical way. The best tool to help achieve this in my view is the Pyramid Principle. It was developed by a former McKinsey partner, Barbara Minto, for the firm, and is available in various published editions and on the Internet. The Pyramid Principle starts with the 'Answer first', corresponding to the 'Idea' in BIOBA, then requires you to lay out the supporting arguments in a logical, hierarchical sequence. It helps you ensure, in the language of the Pyramid Principle, that your description or argument is 'Mutually Exclusive and Comprehensively Exhaustive' (MECE), which to me always meant that I had to have all the bases covered. It is easy to learn, mind stretching to execute well and always time well spent.

The Operation section is likely to be the place where most questions are raised or points discussed. That is fine. You need your audience to feel good about it and part of that requires them having the opportunity to raise whatever is on their mind. If you are well prepared, there should be little or nothing raised that you are unable to address. If there is and you are unable to deal with it, you may have to go away, reconsider the material (part of 'Expertise', one of your hard skills) and re-present.

4. Benefits

The title of this section presupposes a very important component of your pitch: that there are indeed one or more benefits for the audience. If you find yourself planning your pitch and come to this section with your locker empty, then find something to fill it. This may require changing your pitch or the expectations you have for the outcome. But if you wish to persuade or sell something to someone, there generally needs to be something in it for them.

This is the section where you highlight these benefits, reinforcing and elaborating those you think they will consider the most important from your description of how the Idea works.

> *"Darling, I think there are three main reasons why Timbuktu: I really, really want to go; it's completely different and it will be a great escape for both of us. The other big one is that I think you'll love it; the hotels look great and have all the things you go for, and the reviews are amazing! But the biggest reason*

I think is that we can get to do the same things we love doing in other places while deciding if we want to try some new stuff together."

"Jack, there are three reasons why I think this is actually a benefit for the project. First, we get time to meet with your other guys on the team which previously we didn't have schedule time for; that means their input gets into the presentation along with their support. Second, you avoid having to get them on board yourself once we have finished. And third, perhaps most importantly, we will have action plans drawn up ready for your go-ahead. Over the long run, that might save you a lot of time."

In general, keep the number of benefits to three. Although the psychologist George Miller argued that our working memory can hold between five and nine items of information (the rule of 7+/-2 or 'Miller's Law'), in practice you will find that the more benefits you highlight, the greater the dilution of each benefit's impact.

By contrast, less than three benefits feels like you have missed something out. This may have something to do with the attachment we have to the number three. We find it everywhere in religion, everyday usage ('on the count of three...), analysis (twice could be a fluke, thrice could be the beginning of a trend), and classical rhetoric (where ideas and arguments are traditionally grouped in threes). And if you ask people to choose a number between one and four, most will choose three.

For whatever reason, we are attached to it. Sometimes, of course, there may indeed be only one or two benefits. In which case, fine – don't try to invent benefits if they don't exist, or add trivial benefits to a major one.

Be clear that you are in fact highlighting benefits, not features. In principle, the difference is straightforward: features describe some aspect of the Idea; benefits describe what that aspect does for the audience to improve their life. For example, a feature of this book is that it describes lots of soft skills; a benefit of this book is that learning these soft skills can make the reader more successful. When you come to choose the benefits you intend to highlight, always ask yourself, "How does this *help* them?" The exception is where the advantage offered by a feature is self-evident. So, taking Internet speeds, for example, saying a particular speed is fast or even faster is a feature, not a benefit. Nothing is said about what that does for the user. Yet nearly everyone will understand the plethora of benefits arising without you having to remind them.

When you present the benefits, think carefully how best to position them so they are as motivating as possible. Put yourself in your audience's shoes and imagine how different ways of positioning the benefits would affect you. There are some broad rules of thumb affecting motivation that can help. In the early years of NLP, researchers discovered that similar people given the same set of inputs could arrive at very different decisions. They developed the idea that we have preferences in how we subconsciously sort the myriad sensory inputs we receive; these sorting preferences guide our thinking and our behavior. The researchers called them 'Meta programs', internal mental strategies we run which operate in the background like pieces of software. Today, they would be called 'heuristics' and 'cognitive biases'. But whereas most of the heuristics of recent behavioral science research, like loss aversion or hindsight bias, apply in general to most people, most of the time (if only under certain circumstances), Meta program results can differ considerably from person to person.

Around fifty different Meta programs have been researched, which range from how we tend to think, in big picture or small (chunk sizes), whether we tend to look for similarities or differences in things (match versus mismatch), whether we are driven by opportunities or lack of choice (possibility versus necessity), to whether we like to work on our own or with others (self versus proximity).[5] Of course, like much of NLP, there is very little, if any, scientific underpinning, although there are areas of alignment with some of the research on heuristics. Nevertheless, when tested against one's own thinking processes, one finds a surprising degree of traction.

There are two Meta programs in particular which can offer some insight in to how best to position the benefits of our proposal. The first of these is 'Toward/Away from'. When you decided to read this book were you hoping to get something new for yourself or did you want to change a bad situation you found yourself in? When you go on vacation, are you seeking new happy experiences or escaping from your normal life? We can ask these sorts of questions with regard to every decision we make. They make you think. I find myself discovering that some things I have done have been driven very much by 'Toward', seeking something new, and some entirely by 'Away from'. And some were a mix. While I tend to assume that everyone else in the world is like me, with the same sense of balance, reason and similar obvious motivations, when you ask others about their actual motivations, you discover how different people are.

Our client (or partner) will also be driven by either a desire to move toward or away from something and, if we know it, we should express the benefits in those terms. It will hit a very hot button emotionally. Expressing a benefit as, for example, 'Toward', when in fact their motivation is 'Away from', even though the material (or factual) gain is the same in each case, will simply not feel motivating to them. If you are unsure, then think about expressing the benefit in both ways: "You will get this and avoid that". In the case of our client example above, we have expressed the benefits in terms of him getting something (support, buy-in) and avoiding something (time wasted, personal effort).

The second Meta program to think about is 'Internal/External reference'. When you come to make a decision about something, are you generally pretty sure it is right based on your own judgement and analysis or do you usually want to hear the thoughts of relevant others? In what sorts of decisions are you at one end of this spectrum and in what sorts the other end? In what kinds of decisions are you a mix? That is, you are pretty sure but would still like some external confirmation.

I have had successful CEO clients who were at opposite ends of the spectrum for similar business issues. Some people *just know* when something is right based on an internal reference; others need the reassuring input of friends, colleagues, experts or some other authority. Where they are on this spectrum can of course change depending on the type of issue or decision. They might be 'External' at work and 'Internal' at home. Or 'Internal' on some types of business issues and 'External' on others. If with regard to the objective of your persuasion you are clear that your audience is at one end of the spectrum, then use that as the frame to position the benefit.

In the case of our partner and the impending vacation, we offered her the reassurance of good reviews ('External'); similarly, with our client we suggested that our proposal would get him the support of his team ('External'). Again, if you are unsure what their motivating bias is here, then think about it. How has your audience talked about it? How have they explained making similar decisions in the past? You always have the possibility of positioning the benefits along the lines of, "This will get you to where you want to be and is also endorsed by every expert we know", or similar. In which case, your audience will hear that which is motivating and ignore that which is not.

These two Meta programs, or biases, can have real motivational power. When you try, for example, to sell someone the best holiday in the world, placing the benefits at the 'wrong' end of the spectrum of their two biases, "Why am I doing this and how will I know it's the right thing?", they will remain unmoved. So, it is worth thinking carefully about your audience and their motivational biases. Sometimes, where they are on the spectrum will be obvious; in which case, ensure you position the benefit accordingly. At other times it will be clear as mud. If so, consider positioning the benefit both ways if you can do so crisply.

5. Action

This section is where you tell your audience what they need to do to get the benefits. The objective is to make it as simple as possible for them to say "Yes".

> *"So, darling, if it looks/sounds/feels good to you too, I can book it today. Okay?"*

> *"Jack, if you are okay with that/agree with me, all I need is for you to cast your eye over this revised schedule and I will ensure it happens."*

We include a query in the Action statement: "if it sounds good", "if you are okay with that". The query checks for their agreement. It allows our audience the opportunity to raise anything on their mind. We do, however, position the query ("if it sounds good", "if you agree with me") in positive language, the importance of which we saw earlier. The fact that the query is there, allows them to raise any further questions, which if they have, we want to hear. It is in positive language so that if they are minded to agree, it is easier for them to do so.

Cheeky salesmen have, over decades, developed a variety of ways of 'closing' their customers by playing on the way words and our minds work. Many of these closes involve a presupposition that the audience has already agreed and the only question now is how best to go forward. For example, "Would madam like it wrapped in pink or blue?" (the 'Alternative close'). Or in the case of our client above, we could avoid the first half of the sentence and simply say, "All I need is for you to cast your eye over this revised schedule and I will ensure it happens" (an 'Assumptive' close where you take their agreement as given). Or you put forward two options, both of which are acceptable to you, and recommend one of them; the discussion then is about the options, not the supporting case. There are others. None of them are advisable if you wish to preserve the relationship, since they are easy for smart people to see through. We might, however, feel emboldened enough with our partner, should we be feeling lucky, to end with something like, "So, which of these two hotels do you like most, darling?"

Finally, we structure the action required so that it involves the minimum effort for our audience. The bigger the pay-off to us, the more we are probably willing to do to make it easy for them. Our partner simply has to say "Okay". Jack has just got to look at and approve the revised schedule we have prepared. We have made it very easy for both of them to say "Yes".

Benefits of BIOBA

There are three benefits of using BIOBA:

1. The main benefit is that it is powerfully persuasive.

When you are on the receiving end of a proposal couched in the BIOBA format, you feel drawn to say "Yes" – emotionally, *you feel you want to agree.* This remains true even if you eventually say "No" or "Yes, but" for whatever reason.

BIOBA works in this way because it is structured to give information in the way we like to receive it. In her early 1980s book, *The 4MAT System*, Bernice McCarthy presented her discoveries from research into how children learn, showing that we have four different learning styles. These are:

Discussion: Needing reasons and explanations – the WHY?
Teaching: Requiring data – the WHAT?
Coaching: Wanting to try it out for ourselves – the HOW?
Self-discovery: Needing to test it out or explore the limits – the WHAT IF?

While everyone processes information in each of the four learning styles, children especially, but some adults too, can have a strong preference. If you have to present information to a mixed group or to one well-educated adult who processes information in all four styles, there is an ideal sequencing for the information you give:

1. Start with the 'WHYs' – these people won't listen further until they have the reasons to do so.
2. Then the 'WHATs' – these people need to have the base information before they can proceed further.

3. Then the 'HOWs' – the way this works or how they can use this information.
4. Finally, the 'WHAT IFs' – what the consequences are of following or not following this information.

There is an intuitive, perhaps logical, appeal to this sequencing, which matches the BIOBA structure of Background, Idea, Operation and Benefits exactly.

The BIOBA sequence also addresses our best understanding of how people are motivated. All motivation starts with having a 'need' we want to satisfy. In the 1930s, Alan Monroe, professor of public speaking at Purdue University, came up with his 'Motivated Sequence' for making persuasive speeches. He had five steps: 1) Get attention; 2) Establish that a need exists; 3) Satisfy that need with a solution; 4) Visualize what the future will look like when the need is satisfied; and 5) Tell the audience what they must do to get that future.

Alan Monroe's sequence is little different from the slightly truncated acronym well known to advertisers worldwide, AIDA, which stands for Attention, Interest, Desire and Action. Nor is it a million miles away from the four steps of classical Greek rhetorical structure: 1) Introduction (raising the subject in reference to the audience, location or recent event); 2) The Narrative (a story setting up the issue and the audience's motivation); 3) The Argument (the logical proofs supporting the case, normally organized into three parts); and 4) The Conclusion (being more a call to arms than a dry summary).

Each of these motivational structures, both of which arguably have passed the test of time, are encompassed within the BIOBA format.

BIOBA presents information in a way in which we like to receive it and which we are most likely to find motivating, which is why it is effective.

2. The second benefit of BIOBA is that it is very versatile

BIOBA gives you an effective tool that you can adapt to circumstances. It lends itself to the quick and informal ("Darling, let's go to the movies. As you know..."), as well as the most momentous and complex of issues. In fact, I have yet to come across a circumstance it cannot be successfully adapted to, including the structure of major client presentations.

This chapter follows the BIOBA structure, and so do all the other chapters in this book (although the 'Action' component at the end may more appropriately be presented as a summary, or a general call to arms in some cases).

Finally, with regard to versatility, you may sometimes find yourself making it all the way through your presentation with little or no interruption, right up to the point when they say "Yes" (or "No"!). At other times the presentation can be hauled off in all sorts of directions with questions and issues raised – if so, BIOBA provides an easily remembered structure for you to pick up the reins again. It works in all types of meetings and social situations.

3. The third benefit of BIOBA is that it makes you think things through

BIOBA forces you to consider *how* you present your Idea given *their* likely starting point, increasing your chance of success. Where are they coming from? How can I structure the Background to create a climate of agreement and deflect some of their possible objections? What is my Idea and why will it work? How can I summarize the Operation in a logical way for them? Will it be enough? What am I asking them to do at the end? Is it easy for them? Does it move us to where we want to get to? Do I think they will say yes? If not, what else do I have to do?

Because BIOBA *forces* you to ask these essential questions you are more likely to arrive at the meeting with answers to hand.

BIOBA and the Personal Impact Model

BIOBA aids you with the Skill in presenting arguments. It is the single tool that, having established Respect, can make all the difference when it comes to becoming a good Persuader.

Because BIOBA forces you to think carefully about what it is you are proposing and how you propose it, BIOBA can help you generate and present Solutions with value.

Action

Getting started with BIOBA is simple. Practice at home and with colleagues at the office. Keep to low-value situations first (going to the movies with your partner, for example, or organizing an office social event). Consider how it went afterwards. What could you have done better? If you weren't successful, why not? Then do it again, and again. After a while it becomes intuitive.

As you practice, you can even use the BIOBA headlines to help remind yourself of the structure of your proposal, by articulating them. So, you could say something like: "The Background to what I want to talk about is... Now, given that, the Idea I have is... The way this could Operate is... Now, there are three main Benefits of doing this as I see them... So, all we need to do to Action this is..." Revealing your schema in this way has no negative impact on how your audience feels about what you say. If anything, because you headline your talk or proposal in this way, it makes it easier for them to follow.

Chapter 9 Takeaways

- **B** You need a way of organizing what you want to say when you seek agreement.
- **I** BIOBA is the best framework with which to do this.
- **O** It involves five simple, easy to remember steps: Background, Idea, Operation, Benefits and Action.
- **B** There are three principle benefits:
  - » It works;
  - » It is flexible; and
  - » It makes you think.
- **A** You can easily put it into practice the next time you have to persuade someone.

Chapter notes

1 Cialdini, Robert B. *Influence*. Boston: Allyn and Bacon, 2001. Ch.3.

2 Kahneman, Daniel. *Thinking, Fast and Slow*. London: Penguin Books, 2012. p367.

3 Ibid. Ch.11.

4 Framing needs to be grounded in a reality your audience shares. I witnessed one grizzled old sales director reminded by his worldwide CEO of the somewhat clichéd corporate frame: "There are no problems, only opportunities." "Well," he replied after a moment, "this is an insurmountable opportunity."

5 Shelle Rose Charvet's book, *Words That Change Minds – Mastering the Language of Influence*, Dubuqe, Iowa: Kendall/Hunt Publishing Co., 1997, is an accessible description of the major Meta programs applied to the world of personal motivation and work.

10. Controlling Your Emotions

Keep cool in hot situations

Some years ago I was in a London taxi speeding home from hospital where my wife and prematurely born daughters were all in intensive care. I was rushing home for a scheduled Skype call with a man in New York to whom I hoped to sell some training services. Frankly, my head was all over the place – premature birth had not been on my mind when the call was set up.

I was also very nervous. Andrea was an intimidating man: head of the North American arm of the fastest growing turnaround specialists in the world. He himself was personally credited with saving one of America's most iconic companies. I didn't expect an easy ride from him as people who turn around companies generally don't take prisoners. Finally, I hated the idea of meeting him for the first time over a Skype call, where I would have little chance of developing any physiological rapport.

I rushed in, dumped my bags and switched on the laptop to find I had a call coming through. There he was in a smart suit and open-necked shirt in a small room full of other people busy around him. Uh oh, not even his full attention, then. The pleasantries were brief but he politely allowed me to finish my short presentation. He then enquired, "So, what do I get out of this?" I thought about the question for a moment and said, "I will improve your senior guys' ability to win new clients by fifty percent." He nodded absently as he looked down at some papers someone had stuck under his nose. So, then I said, "And I will improve your own ability by the same." He stopped still for a moment before looking up and staring at me. Then he said slowly, "You have cojones."

My children eventually came out of intensive care, followed by my wife a week later, and I have been working with Andrea's company – one of the nicest groups of people it has been my privilege to meet – pretty much ever since.

Most people will convey some aspect of their inner emotional state during the course of a meeting. Some of this may be obvious, such as nerves affecting speech or gestures. A lot will be subliminal. If what we feel is communicated, we need to control what we feel.

Where does Controlling your emotions sit in the client development process?

It sits everywhere.

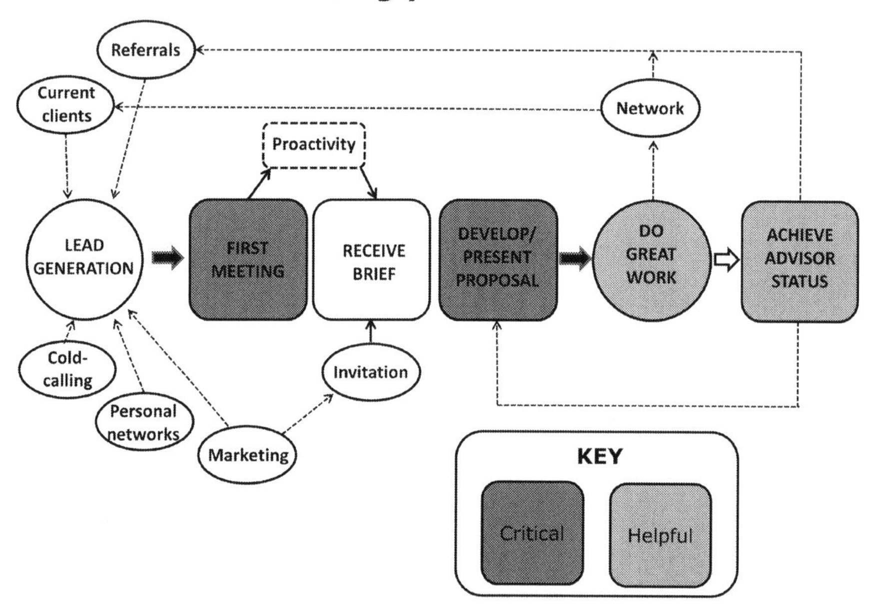

Most critical is where the stakes for you are high and the ensuing worries and concerns you might have are correspondingly elevated. Hence it is vital in first client meetings and anytime you are selling. During the course of working with your client there may be emotions you are experiencing which might affect your performance or the reaction to you of those you are working with: frustration, annoyance, dislike, and so on. You need to have these under control. Even at the level of Trusted Advisor you must ensure that any negative or unconstructive feelings you might have – all of which could be entirely explainable – do not infect the positive relationships you have built up.

How you feel, shows

The American psychologist Paul Ekman claims to have identified ten thousand facial expressions, three thousand of which relate to emotions which can be read, if only subconsciously, by the viewer.

It may well be that our ability to read the emotions of others has a neurological basis. In the early 1990s at the University of Parma, Italian scientists observed that monkeys automatically simulated, in their own brains, the mental processes occurring in other monkeys when they performed an action. They advanced the idea that monkeys had in their heads 'mirror neurons' which mimicked the mental patterns of those around them. Further, they found that the monkeys' brains reacted differently depending on what they read as the *intention* behind the action. So, they could copy in their minds, empathize and intuit.

Since then, researchers claim to have discovered something similar in humans – the existence of a general mirror system, if not yet the existence of individual mirror neurons themselves.[1] While many of these claims about how we come to 'know' what another is thinking or feeling, from 'face reading' and emotional sending to mirror neurons, are still subject to counterclaims and further research, it is hard to resist the conclusion of David Brooks in *The Social Animal* that, 'Minds are intensely permeable. Loops exist between brains. The same thought and feeling can arise in different minds, with invisible networks filling the space between them.'[2]

Does it matter if someone can sense how you are feeling? If you are feeling positive, energized, helpful and empathetic, then no, not in a negative sense. In fact, in a professional environment it could only be beneficial. And even some degree of nervousness can be helpful too: it can be an antidote to complacency, a spur to effort and good preparation. But if you were feeling unconfident, fearful or downright terrified, then your audience, if they sense it, might have reason to wonder at your potential effectiveness, your ability to work with other people in powerful positions, your ability to persuade, to lead and to build effective relationships. It might even make them feel uncomfortable too.

Possibly you are one of those people who are so well centered that the good and bad consequences from your actions are there to be learned from but have no impact on your generally positive, optimistic and empathetic approach to dealing with people. I have known some lucky souls who live in this happy state. Unfortunately I am not one of them. My own anticipatory response to meetings of consequence, the results from which can materially impact my success, is inevitably one of nervousness and some fear of failure. Most people feel something similar to one degree or another. Even seniority is not always a cure for personal insecurity.

Many successful people have developed their own strategies to deal with their fears when it comes to performing well in meetings of consequence. In so doing they avoid their fears becoming their performance. In addition to excellent preparation, they do something or think something that changes how they *feel*. This changed emotional state may not outlast the day but it usually survives the meeting. They decide how they want to come across and then do something that helps them to achieve that. We could call these actions *emotional strategies*: controllable ways to manage our feelings and consequent behavior. We do something that avoids a feeling we are uncomfortable with or which we feel will lead to undesirable consequences, or we do something which makes us feel the way we want.

These strategies are, in practice, little more than mind games we play with ourselves. Yet their effect on our feelings and behavior can be profound. At minimum, they can help ensure we control our fears; at best, they can give us the emotional platform to be comfortably Credible. The following are a selection. They fall into two categories:

1. Eliminating nerves.
2. Equipping yourself with the necessary skills or behaviour to enhance your performance.

Some of these strategies are 'quick and dirty' emotional fixes that are very situation-specific; others are more involved and require a little effort.

1. Eliminating nerves

That sense of worry as you are about to enter a meeting is an uncomfortable one. It is hard to pin down a specific cause, other than fear of failure, or rejection. Most of us, even those who have played some form of the Mind Reading exercise previously, experience it. Here are four helpful strategies to manage these fears, which can be used in isolation or collectively.

i) Predictive anticipation

One reason we feel nervous is the (correct) sense that we are not in control of how the meeting will go! Of course, this is especially true of first meetings and those times we are proposing something. One solution, therefore, is to imagine all the possible reactions, lines of discussion, questions and issues that could arise, and determine your responses to each. 'If they say X, I will mention Y.' 'If she asks us that question, my response will be this.' 'If he brings that up, we can say this.'

Depending on the time and energy you devote to this preparation you might have dozens of possible scenarios worked through in your mind. The effect is to give you a sense of greater *control*. Because you believe you have anticipated every possible important angle, you feel well prepared. Of course, there may always be something you had not anticipated but if it is only one or two things then you can probably deal with them as they arise. You may still have some nerves wobbling around somewhere but they will be a lot fewer.

ii) Breathing low

If you change your physiology you can change how you feel.

A simple way of demonstrating this to yourself is to imagine something very sad. You will probably notice your physiology changing as your head drops, your shoulders slouch and your breathing moves higher in your chest as you start to feel sorrowful. Now, keeping that sad thought very much in your mind, stand up, raise your arms to the ceiling and smile. It is virtually impossible to continue feeling sad as you hold this posture, regardless of what thoughts are in your head.

The most powerful way to change your feelings through your physiology is via your breathing. When we are anxious we tend to breathe high up in the chest cavity, a natural response which helps our body produce the chemicals and physiological preparedness for 'fight or flight'. When we are relaxed and happy we tend to breathe low down in our chest cavity, producing a different set of chemicals and a happier emotional state. Consequently, it follows that if we are nervous and breathing high, we can immediately eliminate those feelings by breathing low. To do this, we follow the exercise described earlier, placing a hand just below our belly button and imagining a ball in our chest, where our breathing is, being magnetically pulled down each time we breathe out.

> *You can try this out yourself by thinking about something that you find deeply worrying or stressful. Notice how high your breathing is. Now bring your breathing down, using your hand below your belly button as a magnet. When your breathing is low, how do you now feel about that thing that was troubling you? I bet the price of this book that you now feel a lot less worried about it.*

There is another powerful effect of breathing low: it centers us. In Asian martial arts the point below our belly button is considered the center of our life force, our 'chi' (though it is called different things in different places). Exponents of these arts are trained to center their consciousness on this point, partly through breathing exercises. As a result, you see little old men in white pajamas resist all attempts to move them, and then push with one hand some giant across the room.

> *You can test this less dramatically, but no less persuasively, yourself. Have someone help you. Stand tall and breathe high; then ask your friend to gently push you on the shoulder to see how easy you are to move. Invariably they will find you pretty easy to push around. Next, get your breathing low, using your hand just below your belly button to help drag your breathing down; then ask your friend to push you again. Usually, they will find themselves having to use significantly greater force to achieve the same effect.*

Being centered in this way changes your whole posture. As we saw earlier it changes how your voice sounds. But in fact it changes everything about you. You just feel different. If you were worried or nervous about something before, those feelings will drain away or diminish considerably. If you still have residual nerves before going into a meeting (or any presentation, for that matter) this is the most effective strategy I know to get them under control quickly.

iii) Remembering they are a person, not just a position

Many times, the source of our pre-meeting nerves stems from the fear of an unknown but important individual. We are going into a lion's den and are unsure of how the lion will react – they can cuddle up to us and share their food, or bite our heads off. It is the lion and its power we are wary off, and we engage with that set of perceptions.

Yet the lion has a personal side too. It is possibly a father, a husband or partner to someone and definitely a child of someone else. They have hopes and fears of their own. As one very successful (and an important 'lion' in his own organization) put it to me, "I always consider their very human frailty" before meeting someone important for the first time. Doing this means you engage with them as a human being and your fears of their positional behavior can lessen.

I think of this as the Dalai Lama strategy. I don't necessarily have to believe, as the Dalai Lama does, that the purpose of life is happiness and the route to finding it is through feelings and acts of compassion. And yet starting with compassion, even for someone I have yet to meet, changes my mindset positively and the associated feelings I have about them.

Similarly, it helps to hold positive views about the other person in general. Your subconscious tends to engage with that part of them you believe them to be. This is best imagined in reverse: if you believe someone is a fool or some other negative characteristic, you tend to deal with them as if that were the case. Likewise, if you believe the person you are about to meet is in all probability a good human being trying, like most of us, just to do their best in sometimes difficult circumstances, that is the part you will engage with. It affects how you feel about them and, subconsciously, it affects your behavior.

The logical extension of this approach is simply to be empathetic. Plato suggested, 'Be kind, for everyone you meet is fighting a hard battle'. If you can actually bring yourself to care, you simply feel more positive about the other person.

iv) Jumping to the end

Nerves are also rooted to fears about outcomes. 'What will the result of this meeting be?' We cannot predict the end, with any certainty, so we populate the doubt with all our foreboding. We become, and remain, nervous.

We can, however, pretend. The mind cannot distinguish between something that is real and something that is strongly imagined. If you doubt that, then you have never woken up from a terrifying dream. If we strongly imagine the outcome we want, we can eliminate the fearful feelings about what the outcome will be.

The simple way to do this is to visualize yourself after the meeting. See yourself in the future, walking out of the meeting. In your mind's eye you look back at the meeting you have just had, happy that it went as well as it could have. Feel that level of contentment. If you are with colleagues, hear their positive expressions about the meeting too or listen to yourself telling someone else that it went well. If all that is having only a marginal effect on how you feel, make the pictures bigger and more colorful, the sounds rich and louder, and send those warm feelings out to the tips of your fingers and toes.

The mind is a funny thing. You can trick it into feeling that something yet to happen has happened and, as you are about to experience it, the feelings of having already done so accompany you into it. So, while of course you really have no idea at all how the meeting will go, because you have visualized a positive outcome and looked back from the future on its success, you will feel good going into it. How useful is that?

2. Equipping yourself with the necessary skills or behavior

It is one thing to have nerves. It is another to wish you were better at something which could help you in the meeting, or just to be at your best. Fortunately there are very effective mind games we can play here too.

i) Being at your previous best

Most of us can think back to times when we were good at whatever it is we are now, again, contemplating to do. In fact, the more I get on in life the more I come to identify with the bumper sticker, 'The older I get, the better I was'. Some of it I probably imagine but some of it was definitely true. In fact, for most things I have to do professionally or personally, I can think back to at least one exact or similar event in my past in which I performed well, successfully. Most of us can. Even if this were our first client meeting, we have probably had experiences that approximate this event, such as a good interview or a great presentation we led. But how can we help ensure that we come close to replicating or emulating our best performance? How can we be at our best?

We do that by reliving the good or excellent example we have in mind, shortly before the meeting. We rerun it in our minds, as vividly as we can. Something like the following:

Think back to a meeting you had where the outcome was successful and where you handled yourself well. Picture yourself as you walked in, introduced yourself, chatted, presented, interacted and closed the meeting. Make the pictures big and colorful. Listen as you hear yourself in the meeting and the positive words from the client at the end. Make the sounds loud and clear. Feel what you felt as you sensed the meeting going well and the sense of accomplishment (or whatever it was) you felt at the end. Lock those feelings in and consciously send them all round your body. If you are actively doing this as you read these words, you will almost certainly be feeling different now. Likely you are experiencing an upsurge in quiet, understated confidence. If you were now or soon about to walk into a new meeting, you would take those feelings, and confidence in your likely behavior, with you.

Doing this should take about thirty seconds.

The key to doing this well is to make the sensory recollections as rich and as vivid as possible. This is a simple skill which through practice you will get better at. It will of course never guarantee that the upcoming meeting is as good for you as the one you have recalled but you will go into it with greater self-belief, which simply increases the likelihood that you will indeed perform well.

This is also a useful, quick skill with benefit in lots of other areas: for example, a difficult meeting with a colleague, giving a speech or even gyrating on the dancefloor when you should really have left such things well behind you.

ii) Step into someone else (temporarily)

I have never been very good at making small talk at the start of a meeting with someone I am meeting for the first time. Partly this is due to the fact that I am just not good at small talk, period. Partly it is my own insecurity leading me to believe that if I can get into the substance quickly, then I am more likely to have a good meeting. Of course, this is a weakness in me – introductory chit-chat is necessary to help people get to know each other in a relaxed way and often it is expected. In some cultures it is essential. So, for a long time I struggled with it and as a result was always a little uncomfortable in the early stages of meetings.

By contrast I had a partner who was just excellent at small talk. He could keep a whole meeting going making what seemed to me just idle conversation.

In fact, sometimes I thought that that was all we were going to achieve. What surprised me, though, was just how well the other person often warmed to him, while I sat there silently to the side, steaming with impatience.

So, when I went to introductory meetings on my own I 'became' my partner for a short while. He had a distinctive size and shape, always wore the same type of suit and had a very noteworthy smell of deodorant (Paco Rabanne, if I recall). I imagined him in front of me and then consciously in my mind I stepped forward into where I imagined him to be. Being taller than me I felt my physiology lengthen to match his; I held my shoulders as he held his; I imagined I smelt the same. Then I imagined myself/him walking into the meeting and hearing myself chat in polite, productive and engaging conversation. Then I entered the meeting. For some early part of the meeting, a part of my behavior was not me entirely, it was him. I won't say that my small talk was ever as good as his but it was a lot better than it had previously been and I certainly felt more relaxed engaging in it than I had before.

Writing this down I am the first to admit that it can sound a little weird. How can you 'become' someone else, if only in part and if only for a while? Well, I have seen highly intelligent, confident and assertive people become someone else under hypnosis. Indeed, I have put people into a hypnotic state in which they completely believed they were someone else. Through their words and actions they almost convinced me too. I guess this technique of 'stepping into' someone is not so different. We just use the power of our mind and imagination to believe something about ourselves and, for a time at least, it becomes true. Perhaps it is as Henry Ford said, "Whether you think you can or you can't, you are right."

We could use this technique, at least in theory, to temporarily acquire any characteristic we find ourselves in need of – confidence, the ability to be humorous, being more empathetic, a better listener, and so on. In my experience, however, it helps to have a very distinctive role model in mind, someone who evinces the needed characteristic strongly. But if you do have someone in mind, and their skill or characteristic is one you feel in need of, then this is an astonishingly quick and surprisingly effective way to 'upskill' yourself, at least for a while. The more you do it with a particular characteristic, the better you actually become at it. So, nowadays, I am much better at and more comfortable with idly chatting away at the beginnings of meetings. Thankfully, I no longer have to fill my nose with the memory of my former partner's deodorant.

iii) Gathering your best bits together

Sometimes your previous best is not enough. You want or need to be better than that. You may well have been good in parts at past meetings but never as good overall as you would like to be.

There is a way to marshal all those characteristics or attributes that we desire to have, so we are better than we have been. Say we have a new client meeting coming up and we need to be as good as we can be. Let's pretend that the characteristics we want, being the ones we feel we are weakest at, say confidence and a sense of fun, are also the ones you most want to be better at in this particular meeting. Then do the following:

Imagine a shape on the floor in front of you (any shape you want, it is your shape; mine's a circle). Now step into that shape on the floor. Remember an event where you were supremely self-confident. Visualize yourself at that event. Make the pictures bright and colorful. Listen to yourself speaking with confidence and the positive responses of those there. Make the sounds loud and resonant. Then recall how you felt. How good it was. Feel that emotion, enlarge it and send it out to the tips of your fingers, up to your head and down to your feet. Have it swirling all around you. When your good feelings are at their most intense, touch some part of you, such as your earlobe or nose, or clasp hands or press finger and thumb together, anything definite. Then step out of your shape on the floor.

If you have more than one event you can recall where you were self-confident, repeat the exercise while recalling that event. Do it for as many similar events as you can remember.

Now you wish to add a sense of fun. Step into that shape on the floor. Remember an event where you were happy and amusing, and where those around you enjoyed your lighthearted company. Visualize, as you did previously. When your good feelings are at their most intense, again, repeat the gesture you chose in the first iteration. Then step back out of your shape on the floor.

Repeat this for as many similar events as you can recall.

Now, step into your shape again, make the same physical contact or gesture (say, you touched your earlobe) and hold that for a moment. The feelings of confidence and sense of fun will infuse you. Release the gesture and step out of your shape. Then, immediately before your meeting, imagine the shape in front of you on the floor, step into it and repeat your gesture. The feelings of confidence and sense of fun will return.

In theory, you could add lots of different personal attributes, though I have found that more than three or four starts to dilute the intensity of the others. That may just be me. Play around with it yourself.

The benefit of making the physical gesture is that it acts as a trigger to recall those feelings when you need them. It is called an 'anchor'. It works in the same way as walking into a particular room or place or experiencing a certain smell can release a set of feelings (and sometimes memories) that your subconscious associates with that place or smell. In this case we are simply making that association deliberate. The shape on the floor and the gesture work well together, though for some people it would be possible to just have the shape or the gesture. Because it is likely that you will be recalling this mix of feelings when you are in a public place (outside the office of your client, for example), it is a good idea to make the gesture one that is quite natural and low-key; in my case, I press my thumb and forefinger together.

What is happening here is similar to what method actors do in order to get into their role. Traditionally, classical acting had it that to convey an emotion, you simply emulated the physiological manifestation of someone feeling that emotion. So, if the part calls for me to be angry I imagine what angry should be like for the part I am playing and configure my face, body and sound to communicate that. In the Lee Strasberg Theatre & Film Institute in New York, method acting, by contrast, requires the actor to experience the emotion, to actually *be* angry. Students are taught to recall an event in their own experience where they had felt anger, relive that experience in their imagination and then carry it over to the part they are playing. The look, physiology and sounds would then naturally be evident.

The effectiveness of this exercise depends very much on the vividness of the memories you recall. 'Exaggerating' the pictures, sounds and feelings in the way I have described, increases the emotional intensity and makes it easier to summon up the feelings when required. Repeating the exercise for the same attribute seems to build up the bank, making it easier to recall.

With practice, you can get to the position of recalling those necessary skills or attributes just by thinking about them. So, nowadays, if I need to be more lighthearted or passionate or caring or witty or anything that I feel is required and which I am most definitely not feeling at that moment, I think about the attribute I want, remember what it feels like, and then I am. It is as simple as that.

In part, the value of this exercise for me has always been that it demonstrated that how I felt, or my way of being, if you like, was to a large extent within my own control. I could take charge of myself, my emotions and to some extent those behaviors which have an emotional underpinning. That is not to say that I always do so (as my wife will attest); I have some human frailty too. But when I come to an important event where my feelings are not in accord with how I believe I need to feel for that event, I can and often will think about changing those feelings in my mind. Often this will require me to recall a similar positive event and to relive those feelings. I am then more likely to behave in a way that is successful for me and those around me.

For this reason, I recommend the exercise, although it undeniably feels a little cumbersome at first and more time-consuming than the others. It can give you a mix of attributes and feelings at one time and place that are helpful to you, as you determine. But more than that, it can open your mind to the possibility that control of all your feelings, when you need them, is within your grasp.

iv) Becoming the best of someone else

Sometimes we just want to be like another person. If you are relatively junior in your organization, with little experience of going to important meetings on your own, no doubt you will have gone along previously as part of a team or with someone who was the lead for that meeting. Most people in this position will probably have worked with a more senior colleague who just seemed to have it all. They were relaxed, confident, knew what to say when, built a good relationship with the client (or potential client), asked great questions, were appropriately amusing and all round were just the bee's knees. It is not one or two things that made them stand out, it was everything. These people can be intimidating. They lead you to wonder, "How can I ever be as good as them?"

The following technique allows you to acquire some of whatever it is they have. Not necessarily all of it, but more than you feel you have at present. Of all the techniques in this section, it is the one that is most overtly a visualization exercise, involving a positive mental rehearsal to enhance your performance, as many successful athletes do. In principle, it works the same way: the rehearsal triggers an array of neural firings in the brain which create a mental blueprint. Whereas for the athlete the neural firings are weighted toward the body, creating muscle memory, for those of us seeking to improve our social performance, the effects are largely on our emotions and our subconscious. Although we might call it a visualization exercise, in practice it is a sensory one. Its power comes from the full employment of all five senses: visual, auditory, kinesthetic, olfactory and, possibly, taste too. It helps with this exercise, though, if you like going to the movies.

> *Imagine you are the projectionist in a cinema, sitting in a little cubicle up behind the circle seats. You can look out of the cubicle across the rows of seats below you to the screen. You are in control of whatever movie plays on the screen. This movie is called 'The new client meeting'.*
>
> *The film runs. You see your superman colleague walk into the meeting room in his usual friendly, confident way and greet the client. They chat, and then sit down and the meeting commences. You watch as your colleague makes his presentation, then leads the discussion constructively and enjoyably (or however he does it) to a very satisfactory end. At each stage you imagine what he sees, what he is saying, how he is saying it, how it sounds and what he is feeling. You then rewind the film back to the beginning.*
>
> *Now rerun the film, except this time imagine floating out of the projection booth, across the seats below and superimposing yourself onto your colleague. You see what he sees, say what he says, hear what he hears and feel what he feels. Then rewind the film back to the beginning again.*
>
> *Finally, this time, as the film starts, float out of your projection booth across the rows of seats into the movie itself. You are now the star of this film. You experience what is happening directly. You notice how it feels, sounds and looks at each step of the meeting from start through to very successful conclusion. Then at the end float back to the projection booth and reflect on what you have achieved and how it feels.*

You can, if you wish, run it again and again. With each repeat, you will become more comfortable with the exercise, and the characteristics of the person you are modeling will increasingly become your own. Of course, none of this changes who you are, but the *way* you are will subtly change to encompass those characteristics. Eventually, your skillset will have changed and it will all feel quite natural. To paraphrase Mahatma Gandhi, your thoughts become your actions, which become your habits, which become your life.

Controlling Your Emotions and The Personal Impact Model

Getting control of your feelings allows you to be at your best at the times most important for you. Consequently, it supports you in all the roles: Influencer, Persuader, Seller and Trusted Advisor.

Unsurprisingly, it has most effect on how you come across with regard to the relevant soft capabilities: your Communication skills, the extent to which you are felt to be Reliable and your Likeability.

Summary

At the end of the day, many of the exercises in this chapter are just mind games based on the principle of imagination and the ability to recall or create strong sensory experiences. But they can completely change how you feel and, in some cases, how you behave and come across. They give you control over your feelings, allowing you to harness them to a specific goal.

Some people may dismiss such self-management as insincere, fake, or lacking in personal authenticity or even integrity. Others may feel that it is all too close to those self-help platitudes one comes across, along the lines of 'Think successful and you will be successful'.

I take a different view. I am made of many parts, some of which are better developed than others. My major part is my introversion: my happiness being on my own, my love of the outdoors. Another major part of me is my desire for success, personally and professionally. The two don't always work well together. I learned in my early twenties, when I worked as a tour guide taking busloads of fifty or so people around Europe, an employment essential to my remaining at college, that to make that work for them, and as a result for me, I had to be the person they needed me to be to have a safe and enjoyable holiday. A college friend, seeing me at work, would have said I was a 'different' person. I was not. I was the same. I just brought out those aspects of me that I had previously suppressed or which lay dormant or unexercised. So, I became this ultra-organized, high energy, lighthearted and emotionally engaging source of all knowledge. I was a very good tour guide; I had to be.

Similarly, as a partner in a consulting firm, I had to be the person my clients or my team needed me to be. I wasn't always successful at this just 'being me'. Oftentimes I had to deal with or change my emotions, to highlight particular characteristics and downplay others.

Even these days, when I still occasionally run training courses, I need about half an hour beforehand to get myself into the right emotional state, dealing with my nerves and the skills I need to bring to the fore. This allows me to do my job as well as I can. Using a mix of the techniques covered in this chapter can help you to do your job as well as you can too.

Chapter 10 Takeaways

- You are how you feel, so control how you feel.
- Think, see, hear and feel the way you want to be and, with practice, you will feel that way.
- This applies to Eliminating Nerves as well as Equipping yourself with the Necessary Skills and Behaviors to be successful.

Chapter notes

1 Some of the claims made for mirror neurons are striking. Daniel Goleman, author of *Emotional Intelligence*, suggests, for example, that they explain and are proof of the existence of empathy; the eminent academic V. S. Ramachandran is reported to have said that they are to psychology what the discovery of DNA was to medicine and biology. And so on. Yet their precise role in humans appears hard to nail down due to the invasive research techniques possible on laboratory monkeys but not yet on human subjects. Nevertheless, the field is undeniably exciting. If found to be as important as hypothesized, the existence of mirror neurons in humans might confirm that people can indeed sense the intentions behind another's words or actions, no matter how gifted they are at hiding it.

2 Brooks, David. *The Social Animal*. London: Short Books, 2012. p48.

11. Engaging Conversations

Add value even when you lack expertise

A client of mine, the CEO of a business services conglomerate, once called me in and said, "Julian, we are thinking of going into the prison building and management business. What do you think?" I knew absolutely nothing about that business. My first thought was, 'Why is he asking me?' What should I have said to him? "Good idea, Jack. I like it. Good additional revenue stream. Contract services are the growing thing. Big market. We can help you with that. When would you like the proposal?" It might even have worked. But, knowing the client, I was sure he didn't want me to just agree with him. He wanted me to help him think.

I asked lots of questions and walked out without any work. How could I have managed that conversation to ensure I had taken the right approach? Should I have been pushier? Did my firm get any value from the time I spent, given I emerged from the meeting with nothing in hand? How could I know?

When a client raises a potential need with you, your heart probably gives a little leap. *Is this an opportunity for some more work?* you invariably think. That is always an uplifting prospect. But what if you know nothing about the subject, perhaps less than your client? What if you are unsure whether the issue has even been defined correctly, or worry that your client has not thought it through enough?

What if, in your heart, you know that even if there is a tangible project in the offing you and your firm are not the best equipped to take it on? Finally, what if your client is simply floating an idea and is unsure themselves of the substance behind it but is reluctant to admit that they think about anything in a half-baked way?

Where does Engaging Conversations sit in the client development process?

This chapter describes a methodology which assists us to manage client conversations around issues or potential issues. It leaves the client feeling helped, regardless of whether any work is forthcoming as a result. As such, it can add considerable value.

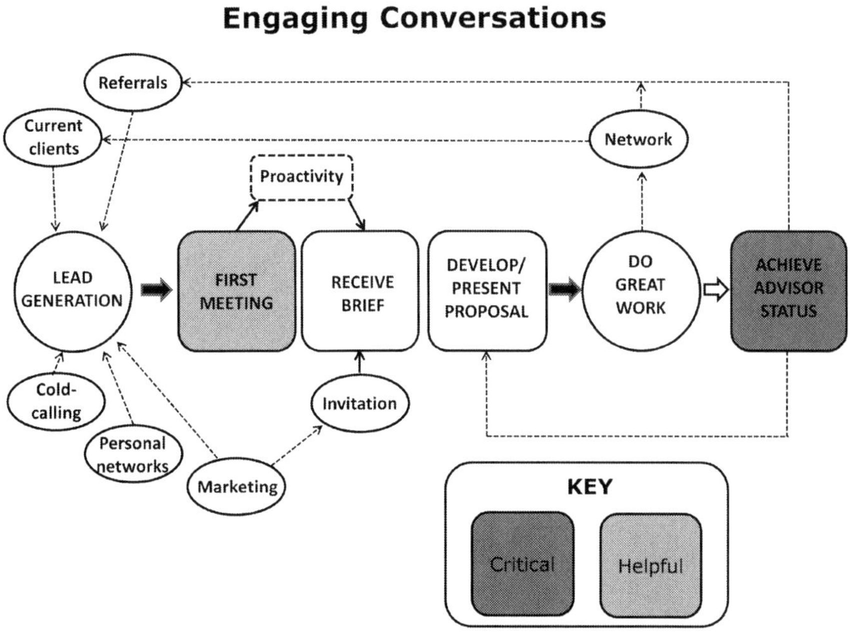

It is most critical for relationship managers: its effective use can be a stepping stone to Trusted Advisor. In first meetings, it can also be a helpful tool to structure the opening discussion about the business and help frame the sorts of questions that are asked.

Adding value without selling

There is often a balance to be weighed in client conversations about a potential issue. On the one hand, you want the business if it is there. If a need is outlined then the promulgation of Alec Baldwin in the film *Glengarry Glen Ross* is seductive, "Always be closing!" Why not? After all, you come across as responsive and helpful. You give your client what they want.

On the other hand, the issue in question may not be properly framed, or pursuing it in the client's best interests, or resolving it the best use of their resources at that time. Or it is just an idea.

This may be less of an issue with a first-time client, where a proposal is unlikely to be on the table without proper prior scrutiny; in any event, you probably lack sufficient Status at this stage to question it. But with an existing client you have a responsibility to act in their interest and the Status to do so.

This balance is even more acute when the conversations are informal. There are two categories here. First are those meetings where, with a previous or existing client, you are walking the halls and drop in to see how things are going. Your aim is to solidify personal relationships and surface any issues your firm can help with, should they exist. How pushy should you be? Too pushy and your client's defenses get raised. Too retiring and the meetings remain social. How best to negotiate your path between those unproductive extremes?

The second category of informal conversation is when your client calls you in to discuss an idea. It is not yet a need or an issue but a possibility. In fact, to be so called says much for the strength of your relationship and the high regard your client holds you in. It may be an idea in a field you know much about. Or it may not.

When we find ourselves in the fortunate position of having a discussion with a client, we want to ensure we are helping them. That help might well result in a clearly defined project which we are most suited to work on. It might not. If so, we will still have spent time chatting the issue over with our client. If nothing tangible (for us) comes from the meeting, we nevertheless want our client to feel we helped him, perhaps to think the issue through, or by adding value with some good ideas. The alternative is to leave him feeling that the meeting with us was largely a waste of his time or, worse, worn out from batting away our unwelcome revenue-hunting attentions.

Getting this balance right, between managing a conversation which leads to a defined project without being pushy, and managing the same conversation to leave our client feeling helped in the absence of such an outcome, is a challenge good client managers face all the time.

Always be asking, with the SPINE in mind

The solution to this conundrum is to think and operate as a good coach would, while keeping to a fixed structure which helps navigate the conversation in a logical way. Doing this ensures that you cover all the likely issues and opportunities, while leaving your client feeling helped and empowered at the end.

Achieving this requires a little attitude shift: from being someone who tells, based on your undoubted expertise, to someone who asks a lot – putting the client's needs first while leaving your own interests to be considered only at the end. Because this is not a pitch, it is a conversation, you leave that part of you which is the super-salesman at the door. There are two important elements to this approach: 1) Always be asking; and 2) SPINE.

1. Always be asking

If you have ever benefited from the attentions of a good coach, you will have noticed that they asked a lot of questions. These questions made you think deeply. The coach rarely, if ever, offered you advice or solutions. A good coach operates on the principle that you have all the answers you need somewhere inside yourself. They see their job as helping you find those answers by leading you to explore your options and challenge your assumptions, to consider your emotions and the source of those feelings.

Done well it can leave you feeling re-energized, positive and with a strengthened sense of purpose. It can even make you feel happier. This sense of renewal many experience may well be the result of satisfying an issue Ralph Waldo Emerson noted when he said, "Our chief want in life is someone who will make us do what we can."

The principle technique employed by a good coach is asking pertinent questions and listening very carefully to the answers. Asking questions as a means of helping someone think, or even to teach, is not new. In the 5th century BC, the Athenian philosopher Socrates taught by asking questions. The 'Socratic Method' was a dialectic enquiry which examined someone's beliefs by asking questions to identify any contradictions in their position, which then would lead to an alternative hypothesis. In this way, a person's thinking would be refined to the point where they reached an answer. Although the Socratic Method is 'negative', in the sense that it looks to disprove a position before moving on (unlike scientific method which is more open-ended, advancing a hypothesis and then testing it), the aim was to ensure precision and completeness in someone's thinking so that they could move forward.

The best questions are open questions, allowing the listener full scope to answer as they want. These will usually start with 'What', 'When', 'Who', 'Where' or 'How'. Closed questions, which result in 'Yes' or 'No' answers or a short statement or fact, have their place, but should mainly be used as probing questions to seek clarification. Leading questions, which steer the listener to agree with the questioner, should obviously be avoided.

A conversation propelled by largely open questions might, if one listened only to the questioner, sound something like the following:

"So, how are things?"
"How is that going?"
"Where will that get you?"
"What does that mean?"
"What does that assume/am I right in thinking that assumes that...?"
"Can we explore that some more?"
"What will that give you?"
"How do you feel about that?"
"How will you know when you have reached it?"
"What are your other options?"
"Can you tell me more about that?"
"What is stopping you?"
"So, what would you need to make that happen?"
"What would that look like?"
"Do you have what's needed or the resources to do that?"
"What would your action plan be?"
"Where do you go from here?"
"Tell me, how does all that feel to you?"

Using these sorts of open questions, most good coaches will follow a five-step process, asking their questions in the following order:

1. What do you want? (What direction are they going in and is it the right one for them?)
2. When do you want it? (Is there some time element or target?)
3. What will that give you? (This is the source of their motivation; is it enough?)
4. How will you know you have got it? (What is the evidence they need to know they have achieved it?)

5. What step will you take to start the process? (Do they know what they need to do and do they have the right resources in place?)

The majority of questions will be open, many will be probing and some closed. The key is to ask questions which clarify matters from the client's point of view. Because you are thinking as you listen, the next question should naturally present itself to you.

Avoid questions that start with 'Why', as explained earlier in Chapter 5, Making a Great Impression, unless your relationship is a strong one. Similarly, avoid asking for an 'opinion' or 'point of view'. This invites someone to state a position from which it may prove hard to shift. By contrast, asking for their 'feeling', which relies on an emotion, or their 'thoughts', which relies on analysis and so is open to argument, keeps the field free for maneuver as required.

In practice, you will find it expedient to be a little more flexible with your client than in the coaching process example presented above. You are, after all, a professional services advisor not a coach. So, to be known as the depository of all wisdom on your subject and then to be suddenly content-free in your first open discussion, might feel a little strange to your client. If, however, you preface the conversation with something like, "Jack, that's very interesting. Do you mind if I [first] just ask you some questions?", you orient the client to your changed approach while also getting their permission. Similarly, if you happen to have a blinding insight or game-changing piece of information which you can volunteer, you probably should.

By asking good, largely open questions in a structured way you can help lead someone to a solution or a way forward which they own completely. This is revelatory for both sides: for the client, a new sense of purpose from only one conversation allied to a revised appreciation of their questioner; for the 'coach' (you), the staggering realization that you can really help someone with a problem in an area outside of your expertise or without sharing any of it.

Of course, it may be that at the end of such a conversation your client needs some external help to move forward, in which case you are well positioned to talk about how best to do that. But it is important to keep in mind that this is *not* the goal – the objective is to help your client in whatever direction that takes him and, in the process, leave him feeling good about you, your contribution and your help. To go into such a conversation with your own interests in mind will, subconsciously at least, tend to skew your questions and responses in such a way that the 'answer' arrived at may not be the best for the client and will leave them feeling rightly suspicious about your motives.

To make such a conversation work well for you and your client requires you to do three things well:

i) **Be in physiological rapport.**

The more your client feels subconsciously comfortable with you, the more they will be happy to open up. Further, your ability to ask potentially intrusive questions or to open up difficult subjects will be tied to the success you have with getting and keeping rapport. A key part of this is using the appropriate representational language to either match your client's preferences, Visual, Auditory or Kinesthetic, if known, or a mix if not.

ii) **Leave your ego at the door.**

This is not about you, it is about them. All your lifetime's experience and wisdom may have value at some point but not, in general, during this process. The more you interject with your own opinions and knowledge, the less your client will feel that they have come to the answer themselves.

Moreover, each time you 'add value' in this way, you raise a question in their mind about your purpose. If they feel you are selling, confirmation bias kicks in and defenses get raised. Naturally, there may be instances in such a conversation where a piece of knowledge or insight from you can help the process, or you may get asked a question; if so, then briefly give the information and move back to the process of asking.

This is all about you being interested in them and their wants. It is a good idea to get yourself firmly into the right emotional state using some of the techniques in the last chapter, being curious and helpful, before you walk into the meeting.

iii) **Listen deeply.**

Employ all the skills covered earlier in Chapter 6, Listening With Both Ears.

Additionally, start to listen out for 'fuzzy' language. This refers to the tendency we all have of not always saying what we mean or saying something that presumes an unstated belief. The linguist Noam Chomsky describes this distinction as the 'Surface structure' of our language, which is what we say to others and to ourselves, compared to the 'Deep structure', which is the underlying meaning of our words, containing information not expressed or known consciously.

The most common expressions we use which signal that something else is going on in our minds are: i) generalizations; ii) imperatives; iii) vague descriptions – words or statements missing information; and iv) negative assertions, or 'blockers'.

Challenging such surface structure expressions can be difficult, even embarrassing, as it can reveal imprecise thinking on the part of the speaker. Hence it should *only* be done where a strong rapport has been established, and with respectful phrasing. I have found it best also to ask with a raised eyebrow and a wry smile. Listening for these expressions and challenging appropriately can open up whole new possibilities. Examples abound:

i) Generalizations: "That sort of thing never works" is a generalization which, like many generalizations, could limit thinking. It is best challenged directly: "Never?"

ii) Imperatives: When someone says 'must', 'should' or 'ought', they are reflecting an outcome driven by someone else and as a result these words are often expressed with feelings of tension. All these words require probing to understand the underlying driver: "Who says?"

iii) Vague descriptions: "They/people/workers/management won't let us..." is an example of a large, possibly un-addressable category being cited as a causal factor in something. Information is missing. Who specifically is being referred to? Similarly, unspecified nouns such as 'profits', 'productivity', 'growth' and 'improvement' raise a number of questions about definition, size, reference point, and so on. Precision in language reflects precision in thinking.

iv) Negative assertions: Words like 'can't', 'shouldn't' and 'mustn't' presuppose some limiting factor. Removing these 'blockers' can create options. They are best explored by countering with, "What is stopping you?" or "What would happen if you did?"

Few of us become good at this – helping by always asking questions –

overnight. Men, with our DNA-driven desire to fix things, find it hardest. It requires practice. But, having the desire to help, rapport, leaving your own ego at the door and listening deeply, it is surprisingly doable.

Start practicing at home with your partner or children. The process is helpful with anyone who wishes to talk about a problem, an opportunity or a situation they are facing. Use the five-step coaching process described above as your guide. It can at first require an immense amount of self-control to change the habit of a lifetime and not simply tell them what to do or proffer advice! When you succeed, however, you might find the quality of your relationships at home actually improving. Also practice in the office. Informal chats with colleagues about career options or even plans for the holidays all work. Some argue (a 'vague description' if ever there was one) that coaching skills as described here may even be critical for better managing and motivating subordinates.

2. SPINE

'SPINE' gives us a guide to the sequencing of our open questions. It stands for Situation, Problem, Implications, Need and Empower.

S	**SITUATION** Background and contextual questions: "How is the plan looking?"
P	**PROBLEM** Questions to identify issues: "How satisfied are you...?"
I	**IMPLICATIONS** Questions to draw out the consequences of a problem: "What is the effect of that?"
N	**NEED** Questions about the nature and value of solutions: "What would be the effect of doing that?"
E	**EMPOWER** Questions about moving forward: "Who needs to be on board?/Do you have all you need?"

SPINE is based on the approach first described in *SPIN Selling*, Neil Rackham's book published in 1988.[1] This book revolutionized big-ticket sales calls by advocating a question-based, problem-solving approach to selling, which at the time was new. It is still widely used in B2B selling, from office computers to outsourcing.[2] Most more recent sales approaches based on 'consultative' or 'solution-selling' processes are derivatives of it. Although originally intended as a sales aid, SPIN is easily adapted to our purpose here, as a conversational tool.

Why use SPINE as the basis for structuring our client conversations, especially when we have the five-step coaching process described above? First, compared to the coaching process, SPINE is business- and issue-focused. The coaching process works well where the issues are more personal and the discussion can rove into all sorts of areas. In the three types of client conversations covered here (existing client with a need; existing client with no apparent need; existing client with an idea), we are seeking to surface (or respond to) a problem and help move our client to a solution – a very specific aim.

Second, as a tool for managing an issue-driven conversation, SPINE has a simple, memorable logic which is very effective.

Finally, with little change (in fact, by adding just one letter to the original acronym and focusing on the solution-finding rather than selling aspects of the SPIN model), SPINE can facilitate both types of likely conversational outcomes in the client environment, those where the client goes forward on their own and those where the advisor is co-opted to help.

The five steps in SPINE are as follows:

i) Situation

These are the easiest types of questions to ask.

In a formal conversation, where you are talking with an existing client about a request for proposal (or RFP), Situation questions are aimed at understanding the reasoning behind the declared need: "Can you tell me how this requirement came about?"

Similarly, if you are being invited in to talk about a specific issue, like entering the prison-building business, Situation questions can be directed to the background behind the subject: "So, what led you to this idea?"

If you already know the client and are just popping in for a chat, you probably already have some prior knowledge about the business and can focus your question specifically, for example, "I saw the last progress report and wanted to hear how you felt about things." Asking knowledge-based, introductory, open questions is always helpful, although you need to check that the area in which you have knowledge is also the area in which the client may have the biggest issue. Hence there can also be value in asking more generic open questions, such as, simply, "How's business?" Sometimes the best solution is to do both, along the lines of, "I wanted to talk to you about how X is looking but first I hoped to get a sense of how you feel things in general are going?"

ii) Problem

Problem questions are aimed at eliciting causes of dissatisfaction.

In the case of the RFP discussion, Problem questions are probably confirmatory because the Need has been specified. But they can still be asked in an open way: "So, what would happen if you did nothing?"

Talking with your client about prison building (or whatever the idea on their mind is), you are hoping to understand what the problem is for which prison building is an eminently good solution. This may arise naturally from the client's description of the Situation (he is probably trying to justify it, after all). So, again, your Problem questions are likely to be confirmatory but can be asked in a way which opens the subject up: "Given what you have just said, is the problem (or opportunity) here sales, margin or return on capital?"

Chatting to your client chum about the business, the Problem questions you can ask are straightforward: "How satisfied are you with the situation?", "Any issues?" or "What's getting in the way?", for example. If a Problem emerges, questions can then be asked to better understand it: "So, what is driving this problem? Can you give me some examples of how this works?"

Following up the answers to these initial questions with further enquiries will likely arrive at a definition of the problem. This answer may be in line with what the client had in mind at the outset. Or it may not. In either event, you must be wary at this stage of confusing the Problem identified with the Need, and so rushing to the solution. It may be a 'problem' but it may not be the main one or there may be other ways of addressing it other than tackling it directly or, on its own, it is insufficiently big to warrant much if any effort. Clarifying this is the purpose of the next step in SPINE.

iii) Implications

The purpose of Implication questions here is to establish the significance of the Problem and the broader consequences of it not being resolved. Most importantly, in clarifying these consequences and the options for managing them, the definition of the Problem itself may change or it may go away; sometimes one of the Implications is identified as capable of being managed and so that becomes the focus of the Need that follows.

In our RFP discussion, Implication questions could be as simple as, "If this is not resolved in this timeframe what would the consequences be? Can you put a number on that? Which of these consequences would be the most pressing for you? Are there any related issues? How best could you handle these?"

With our prison-building client we might ask, "So, how big is the hole if nothing is done? Have you thought about any other options? Would you like to brainstorm ways around this? If you did this, how would that impact the balance sheet? Which do you feel are the best alternatives we have here?"

Shooting the breeze with our client chum, we are trying to understand whether the Problem they have just defined is a real one. The key is to ask questions which link the expressed dissatisfaction to an effect, or series of consequences. "So, how does that affect sales? What is the link? Can we quantify that? Can we address the problem here by looking at those links? Are there other ways of coming at this?"

The value of Implication questions is two-fold. First, they help confirm where the real problem is and the routes to tackling it. Second, they quantify the effects of the problem, ideally in financial terms. In the case of our shooting-the-breeze discussion, this can establish whether a desire for a solution exists (in selling terms, 'the bigger the pain, the bigger the gain'); in our other two types of discussion, where a need or an idea is already on the table, this can help confirm whether the expressed requirement or idea is an appropriate solution to the client's Problem.

iv) Need

Need questions are very closely related to the meaning of the word. They are designed to clarify what sorts of actions or resources are necessary to arrive at a solution, irrespective of the services available from you, the advisor. In so doing they confirm the precise nature of the Need.

In all three of our discussion types, we have previously arrived at the Problem (whether it is as originally stated or not), we understand it's financial, any other implications and the area we need to focus on to provide a solution. Now we ask questions about how to solve it. "What needs to happen? What options do you have here? What are the main upsides and downsides of each? How do you feel about that? Who could do this? What would they need? What is the best process?"

At this point in the conversation, it will become clear whether, as in the case of the RFP discussion, your services are indeed appropriate and you can progress to the next stage. In the case of the other two conversation types, the casual chat in your client's office and the more specific idea-consideration discussion, you may feel that you and your firm are well provided to help deliver the solution. In which case, if appropriate, you can ask, "Could our resources be of help to you here?"

v) Empower

Empower questions are designed to ensure that the client has all he needs to successfully move forward, with your help or without it.

If your client is moving forward on their own, or with help potentially from some other party, you want to ensure that they feel they have all they need. "Are you comfortable with what has to happen? Are you clear on your next steps? Is there anyone else you need to be involved? How do you feel about where we have come out? Is there anything further I can do to help?"

SPINE is a versatile tool to help guide your thinking and questioning. When using it, you may find yourself jumping around from Situation to Problem and back to Situation, or Problem to Implication and back to Problem several times. It is a framework but it needs to be used as a flexible guide driven by the course of conversation. Common sense will dictate. It can be an invaluable tool to frame your thinking and guide the questions you ask, but it remains just a tool, which you decide how best to use in the circumstances.

Because of its simplicity and ease of recall, SPINE is simple to practice. You can use it with almost any issue you and a colleague may be discussing. Initially, practice using it just to help the flow of your thinking: ignore the 'always be asking' aspect to start with and be as content-driven as you like. When you are comfortable with the structure (and it will quickly become second nature), when a colleague comes to you with an idea or an issue you can then start being question-driven too.

The advantages of 'Always be asking with the SPINE in mind'

There are three main benefits from using a question-driven, structured approach to managing client conversations.

1. It gets to the heart of the matter, as the client sees it.

By asking questions, you find out more thoroughly what is on the client's mind. By probing with good follow-up questions, you can discover what may be behind their thinking and insights they themselves may not consciously be aware of at the time. Keeping to the asking discipline, you restrain yourself from the natural tendency to be content-driven, to continuously 'add value' through your own expertise and as a result potentially lead the client's thinking astray. It should lead to a better understanding of potential problems and a more successful set of processes to resolve them.

2. The questioning process itself adds value and leads to greater feelings of a connected relationship.

By asking good questions in a structured way, you help the client to think for himself. Sometimes the questions alone will lead to the client arriving at the solution, without any further intervention. In doing so you are adding value. Because this process requires no quid pro quo, *your involvement becomes a gift to them.* You are demonstrating in what you do (not what you say) that you are truly interested in them and you put their interests first. Their resulting (re)appreciation of you can be profound.

3. It is sufficiently flexible to be used in all situations.

The model is frequently useful in discussions with colleagues where they need help thinking something through. It provides a framework to diagnose a situation and to discover issues should they exist. With existing clients, it also gets there without any danger of contaminating a good relationship by evoking concerns about your agenda. If there is an issue in the other person's mind, the SPINE model is a helpful tool to begin analyzing it.

Even in first meetings with potential clients, where they are prepared to discuss their business openly with you, it can be a useful way to learn about them and at the same time distinguish yourself from others.

It is perhaps with existing clients, where you are invited to discuss something about which you know nothing, that its value is the greatest. Even though the discussion may be about something which is well outside your area of expertise, the model enables you to add value in a way that can be entirely content-free. This ability, along with a demonstrated commitment to put the client's interests before your own, is the hallmark of a Trusted Advisor.

Managing Conversations and the Personal Impact Model

'Always be asking with the SPINE in mind' is a conversational tool that most notably helps you build and maintain Respect. It makes you a powerful Influencer.

Because the tool helps you to add value outside your area of hard Expertise, it adds to your Expertise overall.

At more elevated levels of client relationship management, it enables you to Add value continuously, a key component of becoming and retaining a position as Trusted Advisor.

Summary

'Always be asking with the SPINE in mind' gives you a structure and style to manage all issue-related conversations with your colleagues and clients. It leads to good outcomes that leave people feeling good about you and how you have helped them. Taking this forward and building it into your own skillset will have career-long benefits.

Chapter 11 Takeaways

- Asking good questions makes the listener think and feel differently.
- You will add more value by asking good questions in a positive framework than by sharing everything you know.
- The SPINE framework provides the most effective structure within which to ask good questions in a business environment:
  - Situation
  - Problem

    - Implications
    - Need
    - Empower
- Asking good questions which lead the other person to a sense of being empowered can create a profound and lasting debt of gratitude.
- It enables you to add significant value in areas outside your traditional expertise.

Chapter notes

1 Rackham, N. *SPIN Selling*. New York: McGraw-Hill Inc., 1988.

2 Nor is it restricted to product sales. The management consultancy McKinsey & Co. employs a conversational sales tool which they call 'SOIG'. This stands for Situation, Opportunity, Implication and Goal; a minor revision of the original acronym.

12. Presenting with Soft Skills

A masterclass in action

Jill had a tough day ahead of her. She had three presentations to give, all on the same subject. First, she had to meet with her main client, Jack, and tell him in a one-on-one meeting that the project was behind schedule – a difficult message. Second, she had a call lined up with the site manager, Bob, who would be most impacted by the news. Finally, at the end of the day she had a meeting with the heads of the client project team to give them the same message in more detail.

Jill's grasp of the facts was probably better than anyone else's, which gave her confidence. But she had three different formats to deliver the message in: paper slides over the table with Jack; a phone call with the site manager who expected to receive the slides in advance via e-mail; and, finally, a stand-up PowerPoint run from her PC with the heads of the project team (a number of whom she thought might be difficult). Jill had built some good relationships over the course of the project. Everyone said she had great soft skills to go along with her expertise. But she felt that this day was really going to test her.

Introduction

Up to now we have talked about individual soft skills and how they contribute to us becoming a more effective Influencer, Persuader, Salesperson and Trusted Advisor.

Meet Jill. After reading this chapter some readers will feel she is superhuman. Jill is going to influence, persuade and sell to three different audiences with different needs, in three different presentation formats, one after the other. She expects resistance certainly, hostility possibly.

To achieve this, Jill is going to incorporate almost all the soft skills covered in this book. The fact that she is presenting, as opposed to merely engaging in conversation, will require her to think carefully about what she wants to achieve and adapt her skills accordingly to the different presentation formats.

Finally, because she expects some resistance (nobody wants to hear a disappointing message, after all), she will introduce us to some new skills which help her to preserve her relationships going forward.

Jill's masterclass will touch on situations we find ourselves in across the whole client development process and often within our own organizations too. Her excellence may be a stretch too far for us to emulate every day but it gives us a benchmark we can all aim for.

The Soft Skills Meeting Plan

As Jill thinks about and prepares for each upcoming meeting or presentation, she will follow a five-step process called the Soft Skills Meeting Plan:

i) Plan the content and your style
ii) Manage yourself emotionally
iii) Determine the best way to achieve rapport quickly
iv) Identify and aim to manage potential problems
v) Use supporting voice patterns systematically

Some of the soft skills are common to all three types of presentation situation Jill will encounter. Some are tailored to the different formats because the choreography of physical delivery is different in each case.

Jill has to make a one-on-one presentation to Jack first, followed by a telephone update to the project leader, finishing with a group stand-up presentation, so we shall see how she adapts her Soft Skills Meeting Plan to each situation in that order.

One-on-one presentations

i) Plan the content and your style

Jill first has to meet with her overall client. She needs to think about three things: where he is coming from; given that, how to organize the information she needs to give in order to get the outcome she wants; and, finally, how to use her soft skills to best present it.

Jill has met Jack on a few occasions but couldn't say she knew him well. So, the first thing she does is get a colleague to help her and, with three chairs, goes through the Mind Reading process a couple of times. She infers that Jack has high expectations for the project, will be deeply disappointed by lack of progress but is likely to be more interested in the steps to get it back on track than in laying blame. She reminds herself that Jack likes things straight and doesn't tolerate fools for long, so it is likely there will be little preliminary chit-chat. That leads Jill to think carefully about the focus and brevity of the message.

Jill then considers how best to structure the message. What does she want out of it? Well, she needs Jack's agreement and support for her proposed next steps. How does she want Jack to *feel* at the end? That the next steps are in safe hands, that Jill is not the cause of the problem (she is not) and that he can easily contact Jill if he is worried down the road. Using the BIOBA structure (Background, Idea, Operation, Benefits, Action), Jill lays out her script in outline as follows:

B "It's nice to see you again, Jack.
You asked us to report on the progress of the MG project.
I have looked at it in detail and want to share with you the results.

I Well, we have a new plan.

O The results show progress is way behind. This is because of A, B and C.
So, what can we do about that?
We have a plan to fix it which involves doing X, Y and Z.

B Doing this has three benefits:

- First...
- Second...
- Third...

How do you feel about that?

A I am talking with the project team later today and with your approval I can update everyone when I see them."

Of course, the exact words may change during the course of the conversation but Jill wants to ensure she is clear at least on her opening and closing remarks and has the headlines at each step firmly in her mind.

Jill then thinks about how she wants to come across. What will be her style? She decides that being sympathetic, businesslike and action-oriented will work best with Jack in these circumstances. She thinks about some strategies she can use to get her in that frame of mind before the meeting. Jill runs a visualization exercise where all these elements come together, seeing, hearing and feeling herself in the meeting. She plays around with it a bit until she is as satisfied as she can be.

Finally, Jill makes an important decision about the method of communication. She could, given this is a one-on-one meeting, simply talk to Jack about the update. Maybe just have one or two slides showing the analysis. This would keep the meeting relaxed and informal, arguably. Jill does not believe Jack is strongly Auditory, which might further argue for this approach. So, instead, Jill opts to make the whole presentation visual, using paper copies of the slides she plans to use later with the project team. She feels there are two benefits to this approach which will support what she wants out of the meeting. First, it reduces the chances of her being shot as the messenger of bad news and so get unfairly blamed. Second, it allows her the flexibility to manage the choreography of the presentation in a way that promotes a feeling of supportive collaboration between her and Jack.

We associate people with the feelings they engender in us. People who make us feel good we like, and those who make us feel bad we dislike. Early Kings of Persia were famous for beheading messengers who arrived with bad tidings. The individual becomes associated with the message. Auditory communication (face-to-face speaking) when conveying bad or difficult news yokes the speaker with the content and the negative feelings arising. Also, the recipient tends to breathe higher in their chest (releasing fight or flight chemicals) and finds it harder to think because their eyes, which usually rove around in order to think, are held firmly in place by the speaker's eyes, increasing feelings of tension.

Going visual, or putting the volatile information on a piece of paper, moves the source of the information physically away from the speaker. Although the speaker is still using words to describe the message, the recipient is primarily processing the information visually.[1] Negative feelings are more closely associated with the piece of paper. The recipient, because they can think as they look, being in control of where their eyes move, also breathes more deeply and experiences less anxiety.

ii) Manage yourself emotionally

Jill is nervous. This is a meeting she would rather not have. Not only is Jack a demanding and important client, she does not feel she has had the chance to develop a strong personal relationship with him. Moreover, if he disagrees with her plan to fix things, it puts her in a bind over what to say in the meetings scheduled afterwards. It could all go horribly wrong.

Jill knows she needs to get her head straight. If she walks into the meeting full of anxiety she expects the chances of things going well to be slim.

To address this, Jill plays a couple of quick mind games. She has already pre-visualized the whole meeting, running a version of Predictive Anticipation. This gives her confidence that she has anticipated all the likely outcomes. She is worried that she will come across as a bit of a lightweight, especially compared to her senior partner with whom Jack gets on well. She imagines how she would look, sound and feel if she were a (female Jill) version of her senior partner. It takes a bit of a jump of imagination but she feels how, if she does this, she could come across with more gravitas. She vows to act like him as far as she can, at least for the beginning of the meeting. Finally, she jumps to the future, imagining what it will feel like when the meeting is over, looking back on what happened and recalling Jack's supportive words to her. That makes her feel a lot better (although she realizes she has still to get there!).

Just before she walks in, Jill checks she is breathing low, releasing calming, happy chemicals. She holds her hand below her belly button and feels her imaginary yellow tennis ball reassuringly in place.

iii) Achieve rapport quickly

Normally, when Jill goes into a meeting with a client she is all smiles, her normal charming, chatty self. In fact, this is one of the reasons why clients like working with her.

Going into this meeting with Jack is not a normal situation. Jill recognizes that Jack does not really know her well and so she needs to establish personal Respect as quickly as possible. Without Respect her chances of achieving rapport are limited. She could be her usual friendly self upfront and hope that Respect emerges during the course of the discussion. However, in this case, because of the troublesome subject matter, she has previously decided to reinforce the impression of her having Expertise from the outset, so she adopts the physiology of the Credibility voice pattern as she walks in.

"Good morning, Jill," says Jack looking up from his desk. "How are you?" he says, standing up and reaching out to offer her his hand.

"I'm good thanks, Jack," says Jill, with an unexpressive face, intoning down at the end of the sentence and not blinking. She matches the firmness of Jack's handshake exactly and stands in a posture approximating his. (Jack was expecting a capable but keen-to-please doormat – his sense of Jill from previous group meetings – so he is subconsciously taken aback; the unconscious equivalent of 'Mm, not what I expected. Let's see what happens.')

In the first few seconds Jill establishes a greater degree of Respect than Jack had previously endowed her with from previous first impressions, and pulled off a Pattern Interrupt. With pre-conceptions confounded, Jack is now much more open to what Jill says and does next.

Switching to the Approachable voice pattern, Jill warmly asks, "How are you?", as she takes a seat opposite Jack at his desk.

In fact, Jill had thought carefully about where to sit. If the meeting had been in a conference room or if Jack had invited her to join him at his nearby meeting table she would have chosen to sit at ninety degrees to him. In doing so she could have helped create the unconscious sense that she was on his side (literally and metaphorically), that the two were collaboratively working on the issue. Sitting opposite Jack when the subject matter is contentious increases the chances for confrontation. Unfortunately, Jill has no choice in this situation, so she will have to think of something else.

Re-enforcing her businesslike demeanor, Jill gets straight down to it by opening with her script. She cannot recall whether Jack has a strong leaning to one of the Representational language systems, so she incorporates all three in to her opening lines, as she continues in the Approachable voice pattern:

"It's nice (K) to see you again. You asked (A) us to report on the progress of the MG project. I have looked (V) at in detail and want to share (K) with you the results."

Jack's sensory neurons fire off as he listens to Jill and he feels a bit more emotionally engaged. Though he would be hard put to articulate it, his level of trust just went up a notch.

As it is difficult for Jill to match Jack very closely with the rest of her body language (she cannot see his legs below the desk and her hands are full orchestrating pieces of paper), she models his broad posture by matching how he holds his spine and the angle of his head. If he was sitting back, sloped in the chair, she would likely choose not to match that since it could come across as inappropriate in the circumstances. As the discussion progresses, however, and opportunities to comfortably match him in other areas might appear, Jill will do so if it continues to feel natural to her.

Finally, because Jill is breathing low and as a result speaking more slowly than she otherwise would, Jack is also breathing low. They share a sense of relative calmness between them. As Jill continues, she and Jack should start talking at the same pace, promoting further rapport. If they don't, Jill will adjust her pace of speaking slightly to match his.

So far, it is about as good as it could be.

iv) Identify and aim to manage potential problems

Jill has thought carefully how best to present the update to Jack. First, she knows that there is a danger that Jack is going to blame her, as the project leader and as the source of the unhappy communication update.

She needs to subconsciously distance herself from the bad part of the message. Going visual will help. However, given the 'confrontational' seating arrangements, she needs to move the information off to the side. The simple fact that Jack will then have to look away from Jill to view the material will help distance her from it in his eyes. This is a superior position than having both the negative message and Jill within the same line of sight, which would happen if she presented it directly in front of her, with Jack sitting opposite. Jill will accomplish this by shifting her whole body sideways slightly and putting the 'problem message' slides at the apex of an imaginary triangle formed with her and Jack at the base.

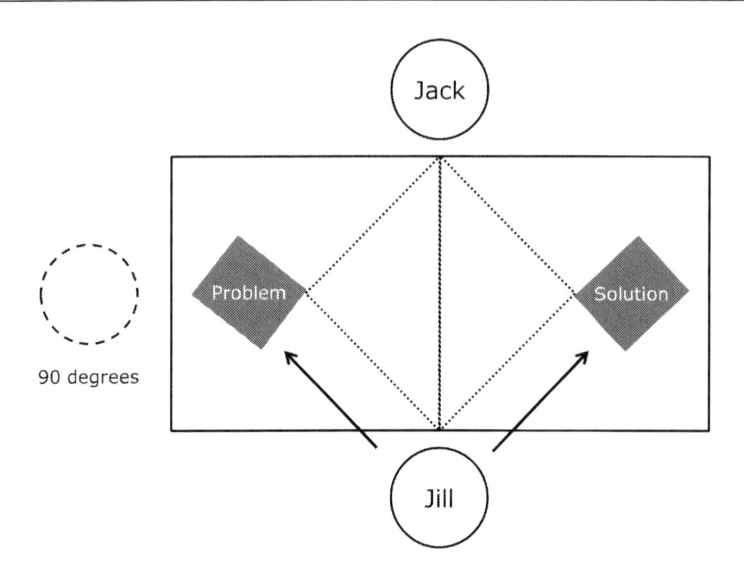

She looks Jack in the eyes and says, "We have a new plan." Jack raises his eyebrows. Then, placing her set of 'problem message' slides down on the table, Jill looks down at the slides and says, pointing with her hand, "The results show that progress is way behind." She then continues with her explanation of why this is, while revealing the explanatory slides as she does so. Only when she has finished (assuming Jack has not interrupted her with any questions) does she then look back at Jack and ask him, "So, what can we do about that?" At no time does Jill look at Jack while talking about the problems.

In their 1981 book, 'Getting to Yes: Negotiating Agreement Without Giving In', the authors Roger Fisher and William Ury of the Harvard Negotiation Project, described their four principles for successful conflict management. The first of these is the requirement to separate the problem from the person, and then be tough on the issue but soft on the relationship.[1] *Achieving this in emotionally charged situations, where the people are associated with the problem, can be challenging, especially if the non-verbals are inadvertently supporting the conscious associations. Breaking these negative associations can be assisted by placing the 'problem' in a different physical location from the person. Unconsciously, Jack is feeling the equivalent of 'Over there, nasty issue. Over here, nice person wanting to help me'.*

Jill now needs to separate the problem from the solution. She shifts her position so she is facing toward the other end of the table and places the good 'solution slides' down at the apex of the original triangle, flipped over.

Keeping her eyes on the slides she continues, "We have a plan to fix it which involves doing X, Y and Z," as she goes on to describe the plan outlined on the slides. Jill then continues with the benefits of her plan, in the same location.

Locations have memories. Our minds create associations with a particular locale and when we return to that place the feelings and sometimes the memories return. A simple example is when you get up from a chair having just thought of something you need to do. Yet, once out of the room you can no longer remember what it was. So, you return to the room and sometimes may have to sit back in the chair again, and the thought returns to you. Similarly, a bad message or event in one locale can contaminate the good message or event which follows in the same place. Keeping the problem and the solution locationally discrete avoids contamination. Jack can then evaluate the solution with a different set of feelings from those communicated by the issue.

Keeping the solution separated from the problem and away from Jill has the added advantage that if Jack is unhappy with the solution it reduces the chance that Jill will be associated with it. Instead, she and Jack can discuss his concerns as if the solution was a third person, over there somewhere. Of course, if Jack likes the solution going forward and Jill is quick on her feet, she should pick up the solution slides and hold them close to her as she wraps things up; Jack then subconsciously transfers his good feelings about the plan to her.

If Jill had been sitting at ninety degrees, achieving this emotional separation between person, issue and solution would have been slightly easier because of the respective seating positions. She would, however, still have had to have found two different locations on the table to present her two sets of slides from; in all likelihood, the problem slides furthest away and the solution slides closest to her.

v) Use supporting voice patterns systematically

In the presentation, Jill switches smoothly between the Credible and Approachable voice patterns. She does this because each voice pattern communicates something different and elicits a different emotional response from Jack. Jill can use the voice patterns to reinforce her communication while at the same time help to preserve her person, and her relationship with Jack, from the difficult associations of the message she is giving.

As we heard Jill at the beginning of the meeting, she entered with the Credible voice pattern (to help establish Respect) and then shifted to Approachable as she introduced the subject, inviting Jack's agreement to continue.

Jill alters her voice pattern to support her communication

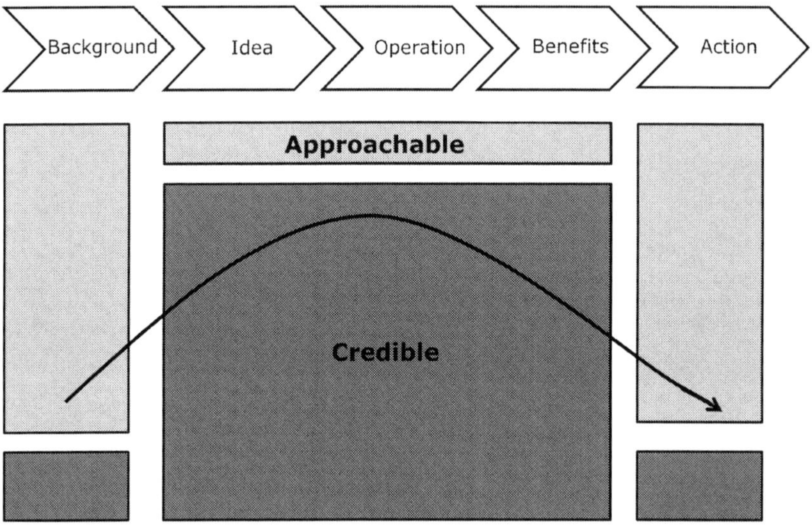

Background
Idea
Operation
Benefits
Action
Approachable
Credible

When she says, "Well, we have a new plan. The results show that progress is way behind. This is because of A, B and C," she speaks in the Credible pattern. This pattern is particularly effective when dealing with the issue level of the conversation. It communicates authoritativeness, especially when combined with low breathing. It says subconsciously to Jack that Jill knows what she is talking about. To help her maintain this speaking pattern she holds her palm down with the fingers together.[3]

Having described the issue to Jack's satisfaction, Jill looks up from the slides on the table and at him, asking in the Approachable voice pattern with her palm face up, "So, what can we do about that?" The Approachable voice pattern is particularly effective when dealing with the relationship element of the conversation. It seeks input and information and communicates affability.

It says to Jack that Jill is interested in what he has to say and is easy to work with. To switch into the Approachable pattern, Jill merely has to turn her palm up, with her fingers splayed loosely. If Jack had felt cold toward the issue, he feels warm toward Jill.

Jill moves on to the solution, switching back to the Credibility pattern as she looks down at the new set of slides she has placed at a different spot on the table. "We have a plan to fix it which involves doing X, Y and Z. Doing this has three benefits..."

After describing the benefits Jill looks up at Jack and asks in the Approachable voice pattern, "How do you feel about that?" If Jack asks any questions that refer to the content of the issue or the solution then Jill will refer back to the material, switching to Credible as she looks at it and answers him. Finally, she closes her presentation with a Credible outline of what she has arranged, followed by a fluid switch back to Approachable as she asks, "... and with your approval I can update everyone?"

Presenting over the telephone

Jill now needs to update the site manager, Bob. Much of the preparation, she has already done.

i) Plan the content and style

The obvious difference between the successful meeting with Jack and this is that the meeting here will take place over the telephone, not face-to-face. That gives Jill a lot less control, raising three challenges.

First, she will be limited to the Auditory and Kinesthetic senses so any type of body matching to build rapport is impossible. She will be reliant on breathing, matching Bob's voice and sticking to his Representational language preference to get and keep rapport. Second, she cannot read Bob's reactions visibly and adapt to them. Finally, she will have little or no control over the sequencing of material: for all she knows, Bob may be looking at the last slide as Jill talks through the first. It is all far from ideal. Jill would much prefer to meet with Bob face-to-face but the timing and logistics simply won't allow for it.

Nevertheless, there is much she can do. She does not have time to find an office with three chairs so she runs through the Mind Reading process in her head. She feels, as a result, that Bob will probably be shocked by the news and initially worried, but happy if there is a clear plan which Jack is happy with. He will, however, be worried about the reactions of some of the project heads, since they will have to do most of the work. Jill anticipates having to use her Insightful Listening skills at the end of the call in order to fully appreciate Bob's concerns; hopefully then she can address the specifics with the project heads during their presentation at the end of the day. She doesn't foresee any other major problems.

Jill is locked in to the content and structure, since her assistant will already have sent the presentation over to Bob's office, so she thinks about how she may need to use her soft skills, particularly given the restricted flexibility of a telephone meeting. Bob is quite strongly Kinesthetic, Jill recalls from their past meetings, so he lives in his feelings, reflected in his use of kinesthetic words. She thinks how she wants to come across, empathetic to Bob's worries but positive and can-do following the meeting with Jack. She feels that Bob will respond best to this approach because he needs to feel understood. Finally, she visualizes (or, more correctly, imagines) how the call should go, listening in her head to what she says and Bob's likely responses.

ii) Manage yourself emotionally

At this point, Jill is feeling a lot more confident than she had been before the meeting with Jack. The issue with Bob, she believes, is not where he will come out (ultimately he will be fine if Jack is fine, although worried about how the project heads might react) but how he feels during the message and as a result the confidence he feels in her.

So, Jill needs to be at her empathetic best with Bob. To help her get into that emotional state she thinks about past situations when people have told her that she demonstrated a great sense of affinity and appreciation for someone's position. She recalls one of those events and remembers what she saw, heard and felt. She then amplifies those sensual memories, making the pictures larger, the sounds noisier and the feelings more intense until she feels awash with empathetic feelings.

Jill makes sure she is breathing low, picks up the phone and dials.

iii) Achieve rapport quickly

"Good morning, Bob," Jill says. She 'puts a smile into her voice' to give it some warmth (which is not difficult to do because she likes him). She knows that Bob will be anxious about how the meeting with Jack went, so she puts that worry to bed straight away. "I had a good session with Jack earlier. He is not happy with where we are but he gets it and is on board with the plan, which I want to share with you." In talking, Jill makes sure she uses kinesthetic words wherever she can.

The other rapport tool that Jill has available is matching Bob's voice. In a face-to-face meeting where Jill could rely on body matching to build a rapport, she would probably match the other person's voice only to the extent that the pace of speaking is broadly similar. With Bob, however, she is heavily reliant on the voice as the primary means with which to build a rapport because they cannot see each other, so she concentrates on getting three things right:

- Getting closer to the pitch of his voice. If Bob spoke in a deep bass and Jill a high soprano, it would probably be impossible to shift her voice the required number of octaves. Furthermore, it would sound a little odd coming from her, so she shifts her voice pitch toward his, to the extent it stills feel comfortable and reasonably natural.
- Speaking at a similar volume. Again, if the difference is large, Jill will take a step closer to Bob without trying to match him exactly.
- Matching the rhythm of his voice. Whether Bob spoke in a musical sing-song voice or more of a monotone, Jill would attempt to echo him as closely as she comfortably could.

Because Jill is breathing low, her voice speed will be slower than if she was breathing high. But if Bob was anxious he might be breathing high, which would accelerate the pace of his speech and its pitch. Jill wants him to breathe low so he is calm and relaxed, and with her doing the same their sense of rapport would increase. So, if she matches his higher speed of speaking and pitch, it is only to help achieve a rapport initially; she will, thereafter, slow down, breathing more deeply, and trust that she can lead him to do the same.

In fact, it is difficult to continue breathing high alongside someone else if they are breathing low. Their calmer demeanor, slower pace of speaking, more resonant voice and sense of being centered is physiologically hard to resist.

iv) Identify and aim to manage potential problems

Jill is unfortunately in much less control here. She cannot ensure that Bob will place the issue slides in a separate location on his desk from the solution slides. She can try by asking him to do so but the outcome is very uncertain. If she had time, she might use slightly different graphics for one set of slides compared to the other. Finally, she might mark out the two elements of the message with her voice, speaking slower to describe the problem, slightly faster and more upbeat to describe the solution.

The best she can do, and where she is in some control, is to reinforce the separation of the person, or her relationship with Bob, from the problem. She does this by speaking in the third person and avoiding personal pronouns. So, she is careful to leave out personal or possessive pronouns, such as 'I', 'My', 'You', 'Your', 'We', 'Our', and so on.

Instead, when referring to the issue and the solution she does so in the third person. So, instead of saying, "Well, we have a new plan...", she would say something like, "There is a new plan..." Similarly, instead of saying, "What can we do about that?", she will say, "What can be done about that?" This way, she verbally avoids contamination between the relationship and the problem. If things with Bob go well, toward the end she could revert back to personal pronouns and associate the good solution with herself or the team: "So, how can you give us a lift to help move this forward as a team?", for example.

v) Use supporting voice patterns systematically

Jill will follow the Approachable/Credible voice pattern strategy she used successfully with Jack earlier. Because Bob can only hear and not see the rest of her associated physiology, she will have to slightly accentuate the verbal component of the patterns.

APPROACHABLE	"Good morning, Bob. I had a good session with Jack earlier. He is not happy with where we are but gets it and is on board with the plan, which I want to share with you.
CREDIBLE	Well, there is a new plan. (Please grab the first set of slides.)
SPEAK MORE SLOWLY	From the results, progress has been struggling. This is because of A, B and C.

APPROACHABLE	So, what can be done about that? (Please get the second set.)
CREDIBLE	There is a plan to fix it which involves doing X,Y and Z. Doing this has three benefits: First... Second... Third...
APPROACHABLE	How do you feel about that?
CREDIBLE/APPROACHBLE	I am sitting with the project team later this afternoon... and with your approval I can update everyone when we are together?"

The one important variation Jill will incorporate is to speak much more slowly as she reveals to Bob just how bad progress has been. Jill thinks that Bob will be shocked by the results and, despite Jack's overall support for the plan, will be deeply worried by the implications. Jill doesn't want Bob to get stuck in the quagmire of what has gone wrong and get sidetracked from hearing the solution she has prepared.

If she'd had time, Jill could have reversed the order of the presentation and delivered it all as 'Answer first' but she could not have done that with Jack, whom she knew, correctly, would want to know the 'Why' first before going on to the 'What' and the 'How'. Anyway, there was no time to change the slides.

When people are shocked by something unexpected they breathe high. Often they will hold their breath. In doing so they stop hearing. You can test this yourself. When you are watching the news on television, take a deep breath and hold it for five or so seconds. Breathe out and then try to remember what was said while you were holding your breath. You will be astonished at how difficult it is to remember anything at all.

So, while breathing low, Jill speaks noticeably slower as she tells Bob about the poor progress and the reasons for that. By speaking more slowly, she lowers Bob's rate of breathing as well as her own. It allows him to hear the whole message and remain calmer than he would otherwise be.

When Jill moves on to describe the plan to fix things, she accelerates the pace of her voice, making it slightly more upbeat, reflecting her own feelings of optimism. The different verbal speed helps to segregate the solution from the problem in Bob's subconscious. Finally, because the two are in a rapport, Jill's positive emotional state will be conveyed to Bob who will as a result feel a little better about things.

Two down. The toughest is next to come. Jill grabs some lunch.

Stand-up group presentation

After lunch, Jill has the meeting scheduled with the project team heads. The purpose is to give them the same news and, having got Jack's support, describe the plan to fix things. Ideally, Jill would like them to feel fired up. Because there will be a number of them at the meeting, a room has been booked with audio-visual facilities so she can link her PC up to a screen.

i) Plan the content and your style

Jill is pretty confident with the content and structure of her message, having delivered it twice now. What worries her about this presentation are three things. First, that the group is diverse with different interests. Second, some of them will not be coming to the meeting in a supportive frame of mind (the project requires extra work, they had not wanted Jill's involvement in the first place and there is a fair bit of blame flying around which they don't want coming in their direction). Third, Jill has met some of the project heads only once or twice, so she has no real idea where they are coming from, and little if any rapport.

Ideally, Jill would have 'pre-wired' each of the project heads before the presentation. Pre-wiring is the process of sharing the planned presentation content in advance with each of the meeting attendees, individually. This ensures there is nothing in the content that will surprise them. Further, it allows them to add previously unknown facts or perspectives that might need to be incorporated. Or it can raise issues that must be addressed in advance. This process of getting individual buy-in helps ensure that there are no surprises at the presentation and promotes support for the content. It avoids landmines. Normally, Jill would not dream of making an important presentation without pre-wiring. Unfortunately, today, there simply isn't time in the schedule.

Over lunch, Jill has thought about where each of the project heads is coming from. Some she knows, some she can only guess. She puts herself in their imaginary seats as they listen to her planned presentation and thinks about how she would react if she were them. What will they feel? Given the baggage she thinks some of them will be coming with (like not wanting her and her firm there in the first place), she concludes that trying to get them all fired up might be an ask too far.

Perhaps she should just aim for the group's resolution to make the plan work, reluctant or otherwise. She can then follow up individually. She decides to focus on the future; success of the project will diminish any questions about earlier blame, she believes. Finally, Jill concludes that trying to win their hearts in this meeting could backfire; she needs Status with them before attempting any such appeals, which she knows she does not yet have with the group as a whole. So, she will have to concentrate on winning (or re-winning) Respect and Credibility. Probably not a lot of smiling, then.

Jill then thinks about ways of using her soft skills to help manage the likely crunch points in the presentation. She suspects that distancing the past from the plan will be important. That leads her to quickly grab a photocopier. As she stands over the machine she thinks about what will happen if any of the project heads decide to vent their frustration at her expense, and what to do in that unpleasant event?

ii) Manage yourself emotionally

Jill is nervous. On the one hand, she knows she has Jack and Bob's support so, at the end of the day, the project heads will just have to get on with it. That is some reassurance. But the meeting itself might be challenging. Like most people, Jill does not like confrontation. She feels as if she could be Daniel in the lion's den.

Jill thinks back to other times when she has given successful presentations in difficult circumstances. What did that look, sound and feel like? She relives those moments in her imagination. It gives her a way of being, a model of herself to adopt in the meeting.

She then decides to leave her ego at the door. This is not about her, she tells herself. It is about the group and the project. She does not have to be anything. It is not about her being or appearing impressive. She just has to share the information. It might be formally structured as a presentation but it is really just a conversation, one which she is merely leading. That mental shift of expectations allows her almost to look forward to the meeting, rather than dreading it. Almost.

Finally, before she goes into the room she makes sure she is breathing low. It takes a couple of goes. When she does, she enjoys the physiological change it brings over her. She feels calmer, more relaxed and strongly centered (although her mind is still buzzing).

iii) Achieve rapport quickly

As Jill walks in, she greets with a handshake those already there. Where she knows someone with whom she feels some rapport she smiles warmly. She also smiles back if any of the others she knows less well smile at her. Otherwise she is at her Credible best, friendly but formal, unblinking and businesslike. She builds rapport where she can, Respect where she needs it.

She gets a cup of tea from the sideboard, noticing that it is laden with the upmarket cookies she had requested, rather than the utilitarian fare normally provided at such meetings. At least the project team will feel that someone cares and has gone to some effort for them.[4]

> *Jill has to kick off the meeting herself, which with a group she is not on especially good terms with, and a difficult subject matter, will be challenging. Ideally, she had wanted John, one of the project team heads whom she gets on with and who is widely respected within the group, to make some introductory remarks. If he had done so, when it came time for Jill to speak, she would have stood where John had stood and matched his body language as closely as she could have without looking unnatural. The generally positive feelings the group had toward John would then have been subconsciously transferred to her, at least for the important beginning. Unfortunately, John didn't want to. Jill is very much on her own today.*

Jill gets on with preparing her materials and ensuring the PC-AV link works. She then stands to one side facing the room once everyone has arrived, getting a sense of the atmosphere. She starts mood-matching, tuning her energy level to the energy in the room. As it is post-lunch the energy level is quite low, though there is an air of tension in the room. She drops her own energy level to something approximating her audience's.

An audience's mood is reflected in its energy level, which can usually be sensed. The energy level may be due to their feelings or expectations, or simply due to how tired they are. If Jill began her presentation with an energy level badly out of synch with her audience, she would make it very difficult to get any rapport. If she did, it would be a very bad start.

"Good afternoon, everyone," she says in the Credible voice pattern, keeping her tone low-key but raising her voice to attract attention. She pauses until she has everyone looking at her, then continues in a quieter voice, "Can I check everyone is here?" There are some nods around the room. "And I'm told everyone is okay for an hour or so?" More nods of agreement and a few 'Yeses'. "Okay, can we look to see we have our phones on mute?" she says, visibly taking her own phone out and flicking the switch. Some of the audience follows her. Jill makes sure she uses all three representational language systems in her three opening questions, K/K/A/V/A.

Getting everyone in a group to agree to something, anything, at the same time starts to promote a climate of agreement. Two 'Yeses' at the beginning of a meeting don't make an agreed conclusion but they start building a positive frame of mind. It is the same principle as the 'Yes-set'. Separately, doing something together promotes rapport – it is similar to body matching. Nodding together, checking phones together, looking at something together all build rapport. When motivational speakers, like Tony Robbins, stand up in front of thousands of people, raise their hand and shout, "Raise your hand if you are happy to be here!", he is not just plunging into some trite warm-up routine, he is very consciously building rapport with his audience to facilitate acceptance of what he says or does next.

iv) Identify and aim to manage potential problems

So far so good. Jill next has to deal with the one issue which is for many people there an obstacle to them feeling good about her or what she is going to say – the elephant in the room. Whose fault was it and who is going to get blamed?

Moving to a new location a couple of steps away and taking a deep, low breath, she says, slightly slower than she normally would, "I've seen Jack this morning and spoken to Bob. They have both gone through the material we are about to discuss. Bottom line, Jack would rather we were not where we are but agrees with the plan going forward and, basically, expects it to get done. It is about what happens now, not what has gone before. Bob, likewise, especially as it most impacts his area. He is prepared to help but is worried whether everyone on this team is sufficiently up for it. So, unless anyone has got any questions at this stage? (Jill walks back to where she will be presenting from and then continues.) I'll share with you the material I went through with them."

If there is known resistance in the room Jill is better off acknowledging it upfront. When resistors know that she knows, even if it is not resolved, the simple acknowledgement reduces their feelings of tension. It makes it easier for them to breathe low, which also promotes the chances of getting rapport since Jill is endeavoring to breathe low too. It makes discussion of the issue, then or later, a more comfortable affair. Jill ensures that the communication of her acknowledgement is from a different location to her place of presentation, avoiding contamination. In this case, Jill hopes to have also resolved the issue by sharing Jack's expectations, while setting a challenge with Bob's feedback (which she had his permission to share). She will find out. At least the elephant is gone.

The project leaders are now feeling a little more relaxed. Most if not all are breathing low, matching Jill. There is a degree of rapport in the group and all are now looking at her. She doesn't have them with her completely because they are yet to see the material, which might hold surprises for some of them. It might not be plain sailing from here on but at least she is not sailing into the wind.

Jill starts, "Well, there is a new plan. I have some paper copies here which show that progress has been struggling." Jill hands out the copies she ran off on the photocopier over lunch. She sits down at the head of the table. Making sure her elbows are off the table (which would increase the pitch of her voice) and speaking slowly she says, "If you turn over the first page you will see that this is due to A... and if you turn over the next page, B... and if you turn over the next page, C."

Having all the group doing the same thing together, turning over the pages, is further building a rapport. Speaking slowly is helping everyone to breathe low, taking it all in. With everyone looking at the slides in front of them the problem is located on the slides, not with Jill, or with them. This is reinforced by her use of the third person.

Standing up and moving to where she wants to present from, Jill turns on her PC screen and says, "So, what can be done about that?"

Jill stands with her hands at her waist, lower arms parallel to the floor. She uses the hand nearest the screen to gesture to the slide; her other hand remains at her waist except when she wants to gesture to the audience. This simple conformation is comfortable to maintain, allows her to transition easily between subject and audience, and avoids her making any inadvertent non-verbal gestures which might send misleading signals.

Turning to look at the screen and pointing with her nearest hand, palm sideways, Jill says, "There is a plan to fix it which involves doing X, Y, and Z." She describes the plan. Then, continuing, "Doing this has three benefits..."

By using paper copies to describe the issues and the AV screen to run through the plan and its benefits, Jill niftily separates the problem from the solution, avoiding possible contamination. If she hadn't, she would have been hard put to create a strong physical separation while just using the AV screen for the whole presentation. She might have tried different graphic styles or used two flip charts at either side of the room, but she didn't think either alternative would work as well in these circumstances.

Very importantly, Jill makes sure she stops talking while moving from her sitting to her standing position. If she continued talking as she transitioned she would have inadvertently linked, auditorily, the bad news part of the presentation with the good news part, diminishing the separation significantly.

At one point in her description of the benefits, one of the project team heads, Dave, interrupts and asks aggressively, "How can you possibly know that?" Everyone takes a breath, high in their chest, looking at Dave, then expectantly at Jill. They have all been anticipating something like this. Jill takes a step to the side, turns to look at him and asks, "Can you please explain what you mean, Dave?" Dave then amplifies on his question. If Jill has an obvious explanation, she first, if she can, refers Dave to a slide on-screen. As Jill looks at the slide, so does everyone else. As they look at the slide, rather than the person, they breathe lower again. If she does not have an answer, or Dave is still unsatisfied, she reverts back to the simple strategy to save herself and the presentation, which her boss had taught her: 'Divert or Defer'. "Okay. What do you think is the answer here, Dave?" If Dave remains unhelpful and the ensuing conversation within the group (another 'diversion') does not resolve it, Jill suggests, "That's helpful. Let me look at it further and I will call you. Okay?"

A number of things are going on here. In the face of an attack, Jill needs to protect herself, then her presentation, then her relationship with Dave:

- *By moving to a new location, Jill eliminates the chance of any negative associations from the attack contaminating the rest of her presentation. Again, locations have memories. Some presenters are so well attuned to this that they mark out in the audience's minds different locations for different activities: so, when the presenter moves to a particular spot, everyone subconsciously knows, for example, the moment has come to ask questions.*
- *By asking Dave to repeat or explain his question, Jill gives herself a moment to get her breathing back down and wins time to think. The questioner finds himself with the opportunity to reflect on the appropriateness of his initial manner and will often rephrase his intervention in a less inflammatory tone.*
- *Referring to the answer on the slide, if she can, Jill achieves the equivalent of 'going visual'. She lowers the tension that accompanies eye-to-eye contact, especially if the material is volatile, and moves the issue away from the relationship level of the communication.*
- *Most times, most people will look where you look. Their eyes follow your eyes. If Jill looks at the audience or at Dave, everyone else looks at Jill or at Dave. If Jill looks at the slide, so does her audience. Jill can raise or lower the tension in the room depending on where she looks. If Jill looked at her audience while talking through the slide, most people would still look at Jill, not the slide. When people look at the visual 'third person', the slide, the relationship is separated from the issue and the chance of everyone continuing to breathe low is increased.*
- *Jill's 'Divert or Defer' strategy acknowledges that sometimes she does not have the answer, or not one that would satisfy in the circumstances, even if correct. The goal is not to be right at the expense of the relationship. The goal is to preserve the relationship so that the bigger goal can be achieved. 'Diverting' allows Dave the chance to provide the answer, or the group to do so. 'Deferring' is the final safety clause which moves the issue out of the room, to be addressed at another, safer time, while allowing the presentation to continue with all relationships largely intact.*

Another difficult situation for Jill would have been if one of the audience had been a *mismatcher* or a *polarity responder*. This simply describes those people who are hardwired to find differences in what they are presented with. They respond with apparent objections which simply reflect their thinking process – they need to consider all the 'what-ifs'. So, they look for the reason that what you have said or shown can be wrong. If they are also strongly auditory, needing to talk in order to think, they blurt out their challenges with annoying frequency. Happily, auditory mismatchers are rare in senior management. However, other types of mismatchers can be challenging enough. Unless the mismatcher is the most senior person in the room (in which case, the question probably needs to be answered there and then, every time), the best strategy is to Defer: "Thanks for that. I know you will have a lot of points to make during this. Can I ask you to make a note of them as we go through and we can deal with them all at the end?" Invariably, most of the points have vanished by the time you come back to consider them.

Polarity responders mismatch by taking the opposite position. If you say 'good', they will say 'bad'. If the interventions are not too frequent, you can manage them pro-actively by saying, "I know you will probably disagree with this..." The polarity responder will often be compelled to take the opposite position and find themselves actually agreeing.

v) Use supporting voice patterns systematically

Jill is by now well practiced in her voice pattern strategy.

The only change she makes is at the beginning and the end. In the group presentation, she has a number of people who doubt her, for a variety of reasons, so she makes all her introductory remarks, including her questions, in the Credible voice pattern. This helps promote the sense that she is in control. At the end, by which point she has achieved a degree of rapport, and agreement to the plan, she closes entirely in the Approachable voice pattern. This draws the group to her and reinforces the feeling that they can and want to work with her. At both times she ensures she uses a mix of V/A/K words.

Because of the tension in the room, Jill had to work very hard to ensure her breathing was low throughout. If she had been breathing high, her Credible voice pattern would have communicated anger instead of definitiveness, and her Approachable voice pattern would have communicated desperation instead of affability.

Jill had an option to use her voice patterns to help lead the group into a positive state. They had started the session as a slightly nervous audience, apprehensive about what would be said and its implications, without a high level of confidence in her. Jill would have liked them to feel, by the end, reassured and positive, ideally excited and energized about what they would now do. To help facilitate this, Jill would first have ensured she herself felt excited and energized toward the latter part of the presentation, and accelerated the pace of her communication slightly, whether in Credible or Approachable. In this way she could lead them into the new emotional state.

For this to work, Jill knew she had to have a strong, continuing rapport with the group, as well as the absence of substantive issues. While there are clues she could look for to tell her whether she still had rapport – did the attendees look at her instead of casting glances at each other?; how quickly did they respond when she asked them to do something?; how coalesced was their response? – ultimately she had to rely on her *intuition*, her feelings. Unfortunately, because of Dave's intervention, she was unsure of the degree of rapport by the time she approached the end. If she had tried to lead them into a new emotional state without rapport she risked losing what she had. Given she had achieved a lot already, they were after all now reassured and willing, she felt that that was a risk not worth taking.

After all, she had got her minimum objective. She had a plan, and a team ready to execute it.

Presenting with Soft Skills and The Personal Impact Plan

With her client, Jack, Jill quickly established Respect so that she could convince him, using her Skill in presenting arguments and building conviction in him that she was Reliable, that she had a good plan. His agreement to the plan and subsequent next steps demonstrated she was a Persuader.

With the rather anxious project leader, Bob, Jill had only to get him on board. She convinced him she knew what she was talking about (her Expertise was solid), and with her soft Communication skills, made him feel comfortable with it. She reinforced the Respect he felt for her while demonstrating her ability to be a good Influencer.

The members of the project team were the ones who had to do something different: they had to believe that there was a goal that was in all their interests to achieve, while overcoming residual bad feelings and reluctance to take on new work. They needed to be sold. In doing so, Jill had moved through the gears from Respect, through Credibility to a Solution with value and sufficient Liking (except perhaps in the case of Dave), in the short-term at least. In very difficult circumstances she showed she could be a Seller.

Summary

Jill demonstrated a range of behavioral flexibility to support the communication of her message and to get buy-in. Without this, it is easy to see how each of the meetings could have gone quite badly. Instead, her plan is in place, relationships are preserved, and in all likelihood her status with the various members of her client's company has increased.

Achieving this was due to Jill being thorough in following her five-step Soft Skills Meeting Plan. She also had to execute well, drawing on all the soft and hard skills she had learned, while thinking on her feet. It was quite a masterclass. Jill should go far.

Chapter 12 Takeaways

- Soft skills support the achievement of your desired outcomes.
- They can be employed individually or together.
- Jill successfully employed most of the soft skills within her five-step Soft Skills Meeting Plan, adapting them to each of the three presentation environments she encountered (one-on-one, telephone, group stand-up):
    i) Plan content and your style;
    ii) Manage yourself emotionally;
    iii) Determine the best way to achieve rapport quickly;
    iv) Identify and aim to manage potential problems; and
    v) Use supporting voice patterns systematically.

Chapter notes

1 Visual cues override auditory information. Astonishingly, this is true even when evaluating something so obviously auditory as music. See, for example, Tsay, Chia-Jung's 'Sight over sound in the judgement of music performance'. *Proceedings of*

the National Academy of Sciences of the United States of America (PNAS). Vol.110 (2012). (Available online.)

2 Fisher, Roger and Ury, William. *Getting to Yes – Negotiating an Agreement Without Giving In.* 3rd Ed. London: Random House Business, 2012.

The three other principles described in the book are: i) focus on interests not positions; ii) create options for mutual gain; and iii) insist on objective measurement criteria.

3 In fact, like many women, Jill finds this hand position a little uncomfortable to maintain. So, when she does, she holds her palm sideways (with her fingers together). This has the added benefit of making affirmative, reinforcing gestures more natural-looking and easier to employ. Most men, by contrast, have little difficulty with the palm down, fingers together posture.

4 There is an unverifiable correlation between how well meetings go and the quality of refreshments provided. People feel better if their comfort has been taken care of. If something extra has been done for them, especially if it is not commented upon, they feel a little special. If it is commented on, they can feel manipulated. Those feelings are then transferred to the person they hold responsible.

Conclusion

Mastering Soft Skills *presents you with a suite of skills to help you influence, persuade, sell and, for those building senior client relationships, achieve Trusted Advisor status should you want it.*

Hopefully this book has also helped you to understand why soft skills are so important. For those readers selling tangible products with little demonstrable advantage, or people-based services against comparably equipped competition, as in professional services, they can be the difference that makes the difference.

Some might see this book as a toolbox, one to visit as required and take out what is needed. As you explore the skills, you can certainly pick and mix. But over the long term, soft skills are more than an occasional tool to pick up and put down again. Practiced with integrity they become part of the way you naturally do things: who you are.

If you were to focus your initial effort somewhere, where should that be? I would suggest you might concentrate on rapport skills and the BIOBA plan, to start. The first is behavioral, the second more analytical; together they represent a powerful combination.

Current understanding suggests that geniuses are made, not born. If you have innate ability, willingness to focus and a commitment to improving your skills, after around ten thousand hours of application you should be among the best in your field.

Would putting the time and effort in to become that good at all these soft skills guarantee you became a paragon in the fields of influence, persuasion and selling? Possibly, but nothing is a panacea. Life, happily, can be unpredictable.

However, it is my experience that you can almost immediately reap important benefits, building and sustaining connected relationships. And, by practicing the skills set out in this book over time, you will have happier, more productive business relationships and, possibly, be very successful.

These connected relationships require you to combine the behavioral flexibility I talk about in these pages with your relevant expertise. The path to achieving it will benefit from a disposition to see your occasional setbacks as learning opportunities and a strong desire to be of assistance, if not having a good heart.

I hope this book has helped.

Good luck!

You can let me know how you get on, or proffer ideas and thoughtful suggestions for improvement, by writing to me at julian@softskillsadvantage.co.

Appendix: List of Takeaways

This appendix duplicates the lists of takeaways at the end of each chapter

You can use this compilation of lists to:

- Quickly review the key points of each chapter; and
- Remind yourself where an area of interest can be found prior to re-reading.

1 – UNDERSTANDING THE HARD FACTS ABOUT SOFT SKILLS

- Buyers screen rationally, choose emotionally.
- 'Rational' evaluations are themselves subject to strong, sometimes controlling, emotional inputs.
- In professional services, when choosing to appoint a service provider, Liking is a critical emotional criterion.
- Hard skills alone are not enough; soft skills make the difference:
  - » by promoting feelings which positively inform the rational evaluation;
  - » by encouraging perceptions of your likeability.
- Because soft skills are part of who you are, you are the difference.

2 – THE PERSONAL IMPACT MODEL

- To Influence, Persuade or Sell, soft skills are as important as hard skills.
- The skills are nested:
  - » To be a Seller requires a Solution with value and Likeability, as well as the Credibility that comes from having the skills of a Persuader and an Influencer.

  - » To be a Persuader requires skill Presenting arguments and Perceived reliability as well as the Respect that comes from having the skills of an Influencer.
  - » To be an Influencer requires Expertise and Communication skills.
- Sequentially, you need to demonstrate you have the earlier skills before the latter ones, hence always go for Respect before Liking in early meetings.
- To win a competitive tender in professional services requires you to have demonstrated sufficient Credibility as well as superior performance in one or both of:
  - » a Solution with value;
  - » Likeability.
- The requirements of a successful Trusted Advisor are an evolution of the skills required to be a successful Seller, as well as, critically, a perceived commitment to always put the client's interests first.

3 – CONNECTING EMOTIONALLY

- Rapport is essential to quickly building connected relationships.
- Having rapport opens up the possibility of influencing, persuading or selling.
- You achieve rapport by gently engaging in the artful dance of body matching.
- With practice, the process of getting rapport becomes unconscious.

4 – TALKING WITH YOUR SENSES

- Using the right sensory language makes you more appealing to the other person – the listener finds it easier to talk with you, senses you get what they are saying and is much less likely to mistrust what you say.
- Where you can use an engaging mix of sensory language the listener will feel enriched and drawn in to you.
- Where you can, match the other person's Representation system in your language; where you cannot, ensure you employ

a mix of all three language systems at the beginning and end of the conversation.

5 – MAKING A GREAT IMPRESSION

- First impressions matter:
  - » they can form within a few seconds and evolve during the meeting;
  - » they can be difficult to change
- You take control of the first impressions you make by Confounding expectations, Showing genuine warmth, Revealing your personal side and using Positive language.

6 – LISTENING WITH BOTH EARS

- To listen when you hear is hard work.
- Use the Insightful Listening Model to improve the content and quality of what you hear by:
  - » Adopting an attitude of acceptance;
  - » Being in a rapport;
  - » Asking good questions; and
  - » Reflecting understanding.

7 – DEVELOPING A POWERFUL VOICE

- Your voice pattern determines how people respond to you and what you say.
- Controlling your voice pattern strongly influences the interaction.
- The two most notable voice patterns are Credible and Approachable: they convey different impressions and ask for different responses from the listener.
- You can comfortably switch from one pattern to another by simply altering the position of your palm.

8 – MASTERING THE ART OF EMPATHY

- To Influence someone, you need to *know where they want to go*, then show them how you can help them get there.

- To Persuade someone, you need to *know what their concerns are*, then show how they can be overcome.
- To Sell to someone, you need to *know what they want*, then offer it to them.
- Mind Reading forces you to delve into these questions; the feelings of empathy arising will generate insights and potential answers which can radically change your thinking

9 – TELLING A COMPELLING STORY

- **B** You need a way of organizing what you want to say when you seek agreement.
- **I** BIOBA is the best framework with which to do this.
- **O** It involves five simple, easy to remember steps: Background, Idea, Operation, Benefits and Action.
- **B** There are three principle benefits:
  - » It works;
  - » It is flexible; and
  - » It makes you think.
- **A** You can easily put it into practice the next time you have to persuade someone.

10 – CONTROLLING YOUR EMOTIONS

- You are how you feel, so control how you feel.
- Think, see, hear and feel the way you want to be and, with practice, you will feel that way.
- This applies to Eliminating Nerves as well as Equipping yourself with the Necessary Skills and Behaviors to be successful.

11 – ENGAGING CONVERSATIONS

- Asking good questions makes the listener think and feel differently.
- You will add more value by asking good questions in a positive framework than by sharing everything you know.
- The SPINE framework provides the most effective structure within which to ask good questions in a business environment:

  - » Situation
  - » Problem
  - » Implications
  - » Need
  - » Empower
- Asking good questions which lead the other person to a sense of being empowered can create a profound and lasting debt of gratitude.
- It enables you to add significant value in areas outside your traditional expertise.

12 – PRESENTING WITH SOFT SKILLS

- Soft skills support the achievement of your desired outcomes.
- They can be employed individually or together.
- Jill successfully employed most of the soft skills within her five-step Soft Skills Meeting Plan, adapting them to each of the three presentation environments she encountered (one-on-one, telephone, group stand-up):

  i) Plan content and your style;
  ii) Manage yourself emotionally;
  iii) Determine the best way to achieve rapport quickly;
  iv) Identify and aim to manage potential problems; and
  v) Use supporting voice patterns systematically.

Glossary

Definitions in italics are courtesy of the Oxford English Dictionary (OED).

BIOBA: Background, Idea, Operation, Benefits, Action.

Communication skills: The ability to convey Expertise with a degree of affability and empathy.

Connected relationship: A feeling of goodwill based on a shared sense of personal regard and confidence in each other's professional abilities.

Credible: *Able to be believed; convincing, capable of persuading people that something will happen or be successful.* A consequence of being a Persuader in PIM.

Expertise: Base knowledge, expertise, experience and value-added ways of thinking.

Hard skills: Skills which are knowledge-, content- or process-based.

Influencer: Someone with *the capacity to have an effect on the character, development or behavior of someone or something.* A consequence of having Expertise and Communication skills in PIM.

Liking: Having sufficient affinity with someone to feel comfortable at the prospect of working productively together to achieve the desired goal.

PIM: The Personal Impact Model.

Persuader: A person able to *induce [someone] to do something through reasoning or argument [or] cause [someone] to believe something.* A consequence of having Respect, Skill in presenting arguments and being seen as Reliable in PIM.

Rapport: A close and harmonious relationship in which the people or groups concerned understand each other's feelings and communicate well.

Reliable: That someone can rely on what you say (or that you believe what you are saying to be true) and that you will do whatever you commit to doing.

Respect: A *feeling of deep admiration for someone or something elicited by their abilities, qualities or achievements.* A consequence of being an Influencer in PIM.

Seller: Someone able to persuade another to enter into a transaction, to give up something of value in return for what the Seller is promising. A consequence of having Credibility, a Solution with value and Liking in PIM.

Skill in presenting arguments: The ability to marshal arguments which elicit agreement and motivation.

Soft skills: *Personal attributes that enable someone to interact effectively and harmoniously with other people.*

Solution with value: A proposed plan or process which offers the prospect of creating benefit. Generally a hard skill, except at the level of Trusted Advisor where it can be a soft skill.

SPINE: Situation, Problem, Implications, Need, Empower.

Status: One's personal and professional standing with another. With a client, Status follows the successful completion of work-stream(s) in PIM.

Trusted Advisor: That person whose track record of work, personal qualities and strong relationship with the client leads to them frequently being the first person the client calls, on a range of subjects. A consequence of having Status, Sustained credibility, Adding value continuously, Intimacy and confidence in their willingness to always put the client's interests first.